Table of Contents

FAPA welcomes all reader comments regarding the information in *Flying Through Time*.
For more aviation industry information, contact FAPA at 1-800-JET-JOBS, Ext. 190.

Flying Through Time

A Financial and Historical Overview of the Global & Major Airlines

Written & Compiled by
Information Florida, David Jones,
David Massey, Andrea White

A FAPA publication

Published by FAPA
4959 Massachusetts Blvd.
Atlanta, GA 30337
1-800-JET-JOBS

Directors: Louis Smith, Molly Smith
Editors: Brian Golden, Teresa Greer, David Jones, Andrea White
Design: Kellie Frissell
Production: Teresa Brolley
Separations: NuVision
Printing: BookCrafters

Library of Congress Cataloging-in-Publication Data
93-072698

FAPA, 1974-
Flying through time.

"A FAPA Book"
Includes bibliographical reference and index.
ISBN 1-56045-004-5

Printed and bound in the United States of America
First printing, 1990
Second printing and revision, 1993

Foreword

The only thing I knew about the airline that hired me in 1949 was that it was the only one that bore the name of its founder — and even that was not quite right. In fact, there were two founders, Paul Braniff, who conceived the company and his brother, Tom, who bankrolled it.

It took me three years and enough applications to paper a hangar to get a job interview. It lasted 10 minutes. The chief pilot thumbed through my World War II Army logs and asked about licenses and college credits. Report next week, he said, and that was that. During the next 33 years I watched Braniff Airways grow from a modest midwestern carrier with South American routes into Braniff International which flew B-747s to Europe and the Far East.

"The more things change, the more they stay the same." Today's airline applicant certainly won't be hired in the first 10 minutes, but he or she may have to wait as long as I did to get an interview. In the meantime, writer's cramp from completing and updating resumes is probable. And, today's new hire will probably see industry changes every bit as electrifying as what I witnessed during my DC-3 to B-747 career. No one can say what the future holds for the world's airlines.

Airline flying remains a tough job to beat and a tough job to get. An interviewer today looks at much more than licenses and hours logged. Among the characteristics sure to impress him or her favorably is some knowledge of airline history, particularly the record of the interviewer's company.

Therein lies the value of this book. Were I looking for a job now I would read and reread these chapters. Then, when United or Fed Ex or USAir called, I'd just about memorize its story. It might provide the edge, but I do not suggest learning a little history simply as a clever way to make points at a job interview. An airline pilot should be as interested in the record of his industry as in day-to-day developments.

Knowing where this industry came from provides the best hint of where it is going, for history does repeat itself. The present upheaval brought on by deregulation is an uncanny replay of the utter turmoil experienced during the airlines' first decade.

As a lifelong aviation history buff with special interest in the airline story, I recommend this reference to anyone wanting to enter our fabulous industry and to the layman who wants to learn more about it.

Len Morgan

Introduction

Airlines in the early days flew mostly airmail. The predecessors of many of today's global and major carriers began when the post office opened airmail contracts to private enterprise. Among the first private operators flying contract mail routes between various cities were Colonial Airlines, the predecessor of American; Western Air Express, a part of TWA; Dickenson/Northwest Airlines; and Varney Speed Lines and Pacific Air Transport, ancestors of United.

The industry saw its first consolidation in 1932. Smaller lines were forced out of business or absorbed when the postmaster general gave all transcontinental airmail rights to just three carriers: United flew the northern route, AVCO (a holding company that later became American Airlines) got the southern tier and the central route went to the merged Western Air Express and Transcontinental Air Transport (TAT).

World War II brought with it many changes for the nation's air carriers. The government mandated that airlines appropriate more than half their fleets to the war effort, and the military enlisted most of the airlines' pilots. Later, an abundance of pilots and planes marked the post-war years. Aircraft produced in record numbers during the war were available to the airlines for expansion.

A wave of mergers took place in the late 1940s and early 1950s. New regional lines sprang up after World War II, and then many sold out to established companies. Also appearing during this time were newly established local service carriers such as Allegheny Airlines, Mohawk Airlines, Piedmont Airlines, North Central Airlines, Frontier Airlines, Bonanza Air Lines and Ozark Air Lines.

The advent of the Jet Age in the late 1950s and early 1960s brought rapid expansion to the major airlines as large carriers switched from piston-engine to jet fleets. Jumbo jets were introduced in 1969, and major airlines scurried to keep pace with the increased automation of the new generation aircraft. Then, a national economic recession in the early 1970s forced airline growth to level off. Major carriers canceled or deferred billions of dollars of new aircraft orders, resulting in massive pilot furloughs. The Arab oil embargo in 1974 sent jet fuel prices soaring, adding to the airlines' distress.

Then, on Oct. 24, 1978, the Airline Deregulation Act of 1978 became law. The Act brought to a close the economic regulation of the airline industry. Carriers had to adjust from government regulation to an economic environment governed by market forces. The result was profits plunged in 1979 and 1980 at most of the established carriers. Free-wheeling price competition led to the demise of weak, undercapitalized companies. The deregulated environment affected hundreds of small and large airlines, and many ceased operations or declared bankruptcy.

Deregulation also brought an explosion of new entrants onto the scene. Former local service carriers, like USAir and Piedmont, and former intrastate airlines, like Southwest, emerged as competitive factors on a nationwide scale. Also with deregulation came the spectacular growth of the hub-and-spoke system. The large airlines received passengers and cargo from small carriers at a hub airport and delivered these to points all over the United States and to many points in other countries. On the other end of the jet flight, the smaller turboprop airline became the destination carrier and delivered the passengers and cargo to small towns from the hub airport.

The early 1980s were a time of great turmoil for the airlines. The recession, coupled with deregulation and skyrocketing oil prices, resulted in one of the worst of the industry's down cycles. Continental became the second major airline after Braniff to file for bankruptcy protection. Eastern Air Lines threatened to do the same. Industry analysts wondered if any carrier would recover from the ravages of the great fare wars of 1982/1983, and there was talk about reregulating the airline industry.

Many major airlines grounded aircraft, furloughed pilots and extracted wage concessions to compete with emerging low-cost, start-up carriers. Then, in November 1983, American shocked the industry when it established a new, two-tier wage scale system for its pilots, one in which the airline paid new pilots on average 50 percent less than current pilot wages. Other airlines followed suit, cementing the existence of the major airline "B" scale wage system.

Industry analysts predicted a great deal of merger activity through the 1980s. Some expected five or six major airlines with numerous commuter carriers as the end result. The analysts were right. The mid to late '80s, dubbed the "consolidation phase," was a period of frenzied merger and acquisition activity. United Airlines received tentative approval to acquire Pan Am's Pacific division. People Express acquired Frontier Airlines; Southwest acquired rival Transtar, formerly Muse Air. Piedmont Aviation and Empire announced a merger agreement.

Folded into their acquiring companies were Republic into Northwest, Western into Delta, AirCal into American, New York Air and People Express into Texas Air's Continental. USAir made plans to merge operations with Pacific Southwest and Piedmont. TWA bought Ozark and holding company Texas Air Corp. acquired Eastern.

The result was the top 10 airlines controlled 95 percent of the traffic and five airlines carried almost three quarters of the business in 1987. The concentration in the industry increased from 10 carriers that held 87 percent of the traffic in 1976 to eight carriers that handled 92 percent of the traffic in 1987. The five holding companies/megacarriers were: Texas Air, UAL, AMR, NWA and Delta Air Lines.

A record number of new pilots were hired in the mid to late 1980s. Airlines prepared for the impending "pilot shortage" by forming ab initio pilot training programs or farm clubs with regional partners. Some major airlines for the first time considered pilot applicants over age 50; most other carriers hired applicants over age 40. Further indication of the increased pilot demand was the considerable reduction in the number of pilots on furlough compared with the early 1980s.

The demand for qualified major airline pilots resulted in continual pilot turnover in the regional airline market. Several regional carriers instituted training agreements to hold their new-hire pilots for at least a year to recoup training costs.

But, the explosive growth of the late 1980s quickly was forgotten as the new decade brought financial chaos to U.S. carriers. The Gulf War hastened a pending recession, fuel prices soared and travel-skittish vacationers stayed home. Fare wars hit the market as several carriers filed or considered filing for Chapter 11 bankruptcy protection. Analysts predicted the downfall of several carriers. Eastern was the first to go; Pan Am followed less than a year later.

On the upside industry experts predict airlines once again will profit by 1995. Meanwhile, airline employees prepare for another round of wage concessions, furloughs and layoffs as managements preach the virtues of cost-cutting as a means of survival in the 1990s.

1

Airborne Express

Airborne's colorful past as flower carrier extraordinaire seems inconsistent with its tough-fisted, disciplined approach to the air cargo business. Solidly positioned as the No. 3 U.S. cargo airline, Airborne maintains its commitment to conservative growth.

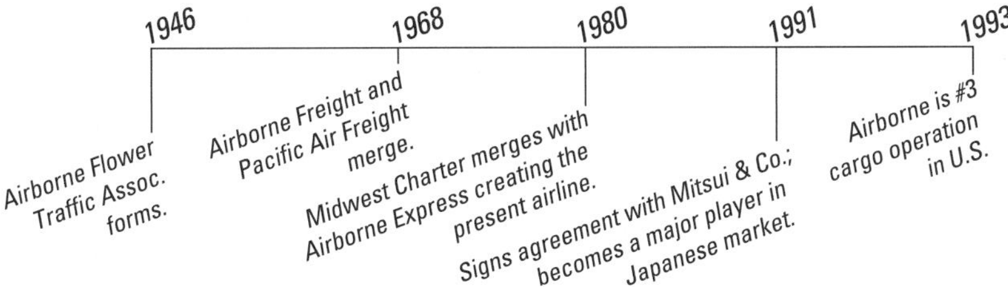

There is something timeless about Airborne Express, though it is less than half a century old. The timeless quality is what this airline, a subsidiary of Airborne Freight Corp., has in common with the battling underdog of any era. It has the "feel" of leadership. It gives the impression that the present moment firmly is in hand.

Airborne had a long, slow development, illustrating a principle of business seldom ignored without disaster: Do what you know how to do now, do it well, and other opportunities will arise. Most of the great airlines were built on this principle and when leadership forgot it and overreached itself, its airlines went into decline and, often, dissolution.

Airborne's history also illustrates a second basic principle of business: Be ready to act when an opportunity presents itself.

The airline's parent company, Airborne Freight, began just after World War II when a rise in consumer spending created a demand for fresh California flowers in Eastern markets. In 1946 the Airborne Flower Traffic Association formed to meet the rapid transport requirements for this perishable cargo, and a year later the association incorporated as Airborne Flower Traffic Inc. It went public in 1953.

Airborne Express
Aircraft fleet and purchase commitments
As of May 1993

Aircraft Type	Current Fleet	Firm Orders	Options
DC-8	25	2	0
DC-9	60	11	0
YS-11	11	0	0
Total	96	13	0

About the same time, Pacific Air Freight Inc., formed in 1949, was capitalizing on the Pacific Northwest's role as the gateway to Alaska. By 1968 it had stations in 36 cities. That was the year when, on Oct. 17, Airborne Freight and Pacific Air Freight merged. The new firm retained the name Airborne Freight Corp. and established headquarters in Seattle, Wash. With its combined resources, the carrier became the nation's second-largest freight forwarder (behind Emery Air Freight).

With the advent of air freight deregulation in 1977, Airborne started chartering aircraft to improve delivery times and this practice led to the April 1980 merger of Midwest Charter Express into Airborne Express Inc., a wholly-owned subsidiary of Airborne Freight Corp. This merger created the present airline.

Through the 1980s, Airborne had key advantages in its campaign to grow while improving profits. It was the lowest-cost operator in the integrated freight industry. It maintained military discipline, went after the large-volume customer with single-minded tenacity and did not overextend its resources. These were the advantages that permitted Airborne to increase shipments 35 percent per year from January 1986 through December 1990 while more than doubling revenues ($542 million in 1986, $1.18 billion in 1990).

The key dates in the preceding paragraphs represent moments of destiny when Airborne management seized the day and acted on an opportunity. All the time between these dates represents daily excellence at what Airborne knows how to do "now." Airborne's handling of its international business illustrates the wisdom of both principles. Seeing the potential for a tremendous expansion of its overseas business, Airborne leaped at the opportunity. But, it leaped without incurring many of the problems associated with international expansion. This made Airborne more agile than its competitors which burdened themselves with the demands of huge overseas operational commitments. Airborne by contrast simply is a freight forwarder for its international business: It uses other carriers to handle all international shipments, both overnight and deferred.

Nor, at this writing, did it plan any basic change in how it conducted international business. Its alliances with overseas express package and heavy freight companies allowed it to avoid tying up financial resources in aircraft and support bases outside the United States. And Airborne's management considered this mode of operating more efficient than establishing international bases, in part because overseas carriers know their local customs and laws. "We don't have to worry about things such as employment regulations," explained John J. Cella, Airborne's executive vice president-international division, in a 1992 interview.

Another reason Airborne considers its method more efficient is the flexibility provided: Airborne can ship to any destination without worrying about filling the cargo holds of specific flights to particular airports.

In short, by sticking with what it knew how to do instead of rushing into the unknown, Airborne sidestepped the aircraft, fuel and ground support expenses and the slow and painful learning process that dogged Federal Express Corp. and United Parcel Service of America Inc. in their international operations. Yet by driving hard to go after international shipments, Airborne orchestrated a tremendous expansion of its Pacific Rim business. The key for Airborne was signing the right types of deals with the right overseas companies, both air freight and ground service.

For example, Airborne, after 25 years of being a middling-sized operation in Japan, finally signed a joint venture agreement with Mitsui & Co. and this deal allowed Airborne in 1991 to penetrate the large Japanese companies for the first time. It also placed Airborne in the "very big market" of Bangkok, Thailand, since Mitsui operated there. To strengthen its Bangkok presence, Airborne signed joint ventures with Thai companies.

In Taiwan, Sydney, Melbourne, Auckland, Singapore and Hong Kong, Airborne used another method to conduct its international business. It established its own offices, but then registered them as local companies run by nationals.

The result of Airborne's strategies in the Pacific Rim as of early 1992 was heady growth, with roughly 52 percent to 55 percent of the company's total international freight the previous year being in the Far East.

Airborne set up its European business in similar ways, with joint venture agreements for some markets and Airborne offices for others.

Another key to Airborne's business was the company's computerized information systems: FIRST (Freight Inventory Release and Shipment Tracking) and FOCUS (Freight On-Line Control and Update System). FOCUS provides real-time tracking service to Airborne on all its shipments worldwide, while FIRST gives customers access to FOCUS data. An additional software package is the Libra II automated shipment processing system provided to Airborne's volume shippers and greatly simplifying their handling of shipments.

By 1993, Airborne, having survived the brutal competition of the early and middle 1980s, stood solidly positioned as the No. 3 U.S. integrated cargo operation, as ready as it could be for the 21st century.

The problem for Airborne was that the difference in size between itself and its two major competitors meant it lacked the resources to withstand a concerted attack on the core of its success, the large-volume corporate market. And the reasons Airborne lacked the size and financial resources for such a defense were the same ones that explained Airborne's particular kind of success: the conservatism of the tried-and-true and the tough-minded pursuit of perceived opportunity.

Sticking with what it knew prevented Airborne from taking the huge entrepreneurial risks that carried Federal Express from zero to the top of the heap in express service. Leaping after perceived opportunity made Airborne a thorn in Federal Express' side. In short, while Airborne's conservatism kept it from growing at Federal Express' pace, its combativeness got Federal Express' attention.

Thus, Airborne Express, a diversified freight operator that targets large business clients, still can provide what fewer carriers than ever seem able to promise: a future.

Exactly what that future will be, its management cannot say. Its heavyweight competitors, Federal Express and UPS, are formidable. Yet this tough, tight-fisted, disciplined airline so far has proven fit for the most cutthroat of competitive environments, and management believes it can grow the company 20 percent per year in the near term without jeopardizing financial stability.

Airborne in early 1993 remained the lowest-cost operator in its industry, but Federal Express was closing the gap. Federal Express, like UPS, had its own tight discipline, and its new emphasis on large-volume contracts posed a threat to Airborne which, as the David opposing two Goliaths, appeared vulnerable. Some industry analysts were predicting a buyout of Airborne by a large trucking firm or an international carrier.

But the most anyone at Airborne would concede was that situations can change with lightning speed in business and that shareholders' interests must be served. Airborne president Robert Brazier conceded that if an offer "made sense from a shareholder's standpoint," the company would have to consider it. The fact is, Airborne Express provides a case study in one kind of business success, but its strength is also its weakness in the business environment of today.

Airborne Express
Aircraft fleet: 1985-1992

Aircraft	1985	1986	1987	1988	1989	1990	1991	1992
YS-11	11	12	12	12	12	12	12	11
DC-8	1	3	9	9	13	21	22	22
DC-9	17	17	19	19	23	30	38	44
Total	29	32	40	40	48	63	72	77

Optimism prevails at Airborne despite its recently experiencing its worst year financially in 23 years. "Ninety-two, from our perspective, was terrible," said Roy J. Liljebeck, Airborne's chief financial officer. "It was the first time in 23 years that we even reported a loss in a quarter."

Price cutting by competitors to offset the drag of a recession led to a second quarter 1992 net loss of $4.185 million (22 cents a share) on revenues of $359.9 million. Airborne managed net earnings for the year of $2,397,000 on revenues of $1,484,316,000. But, although revenues were up 8.6 percent, earnings marked a steep decline from the $27,239,000 of 1991.

The flip side is that many other air carriers did far worse in 1992, and Airborne was rebounding in early 1993. "We think because the economy is growing on its own now, the cutthroat price war has ceased," Liljebeck said in February 1993. More relaxed pricing was expected to increase profits.

What he did not say was the main price cutting was by Federal Express and that this price war was eating into Airborne's large-volume corporate business. Airborne had to seek more low-volume business from smaller shippers to protect market share, but this move left Airborne struggling to maintain its low per-package cost.

What does all this mean?

It means, for one thing, that Airborne is a growing company, not a declining one. It means Airborne is in sound financial condition and could offer employees as secure a future as could be expected in an industry made fragile by the unchecked growth that followed deregulation. But, it also means Airborne is not counting definitely on reaching the 21st century as an independent carrier.

At year's end of 1992, Airborne flew 77 aircraft with a pilot corps of 465 pilots. Its fleet goal for 1993 was to add 10 more aircraft (two DC-8s and eight DC-9s), with pilot hiring to keep up with both schedule increases and attrition. The fleet consisted entirely of DC-8s, DC-9s and YS-11s.

Fleet growth was not projected beyond 1993 because, as Liljebeck said, "that's so much demand-driven in our business." The same held true for the level of pilot hiring, although some hiring was assumed.

Pilots hired by Airborne enter a stable situation, but one involving fairly quick upgrades owing to growth and attrition. Gone for a time was the bitter labor-management atmosphere of 1991 and early 1992, which included formal charges by Airborne officials that the International Brotherhood of Teamsters violated federal law by promoting slowdown tactics. The union also filed charges in federal court stating the company violated The Railroad Labor Act and its status quo provisions. A federal judge ruled both cases were without merit. The tensions between pilots and management subsided when pilots ratified a new labor contract in June 1992. The contract, good through July 1995, covered two years retroactively and three prospectively.

The new contract gave Airborne pilots an average annual increase in base salary of 7.8 percent from September 1989 to August 1994. For the final year of the contract, maximum base pay for a 12th-year captain was set at $130,240.

The contract also provided improvements in per diem and savings. As for the latter, the company agreed to match pilots' contributions to their 401(k) of 35 cents on the dollar up to 6 percent of the pilot's earnings.

Other benefits of flying for Airborne were the company's traditionally top-notch aircraft maintenance and pilot training.

The schedules in and out of Airborne Air Park near Wilmington, Ohio, mostly are nighttime ones, but in 1991 Airborne began flying second-day service to take up capacity slack and this change brought daytime schedules for a few pilots.

Some pilots who have flown for Airborne say it

Airborne Express Financial Statistics

(In millions)	1983	1984	1985	1986	1987	1988	1989	1990	1991	1992
Sales	334.8	417.9	466.0	541.6	632.3	768	949.9	1,182	1,367	1,484
Net Income (loss)	8.93	10.83	8.17	13.22	5.90	7.04	19.08	31.03	27.24	2.4
Assets	127.48	165.73	214.75	271.56	355.72	422.05	470.61	613.53	823.65	964.74
Liabilities	59.02	89.29	133.17	179.81	231.27	294.63	302.48	310.16	536.3	679.1
Net Worth	68.46	76.44	81.58	91.75	124.45	127.42	168.13	236.42	287.34	285.64

has the best training anywhere. "If you can fly for Airborne, you can fly for anybody," a former Airborne DC-9 first officer said.

When pilots do criticize the training, they complain about its inflexibility, not its thoroughness or rigor. Airborne has its own Phase I DC-9 and DC-8 simulators on the grounds at Airborne Air Park, and it requires pilots to use only its standardized callouts during simulator checks as well as in flight. Discipline is militaristic; pilots are expected to perform exactly to specifications. Precise performance is aided by standardized cockpits, with every Airborne DC-8 cockpit identical to every other.

As of early 1993, the median-service-length DC-8 captain had 13 years with Airborne; the most junior DC-8 captain had about two and one-half years. Median for a DC-9 captain was seven and one-half years of service, and for the most junior DC-9 captain, about three years.

A new hire at Airborne must give up any romanticized ideas he or she may have about flying for a jet airline. The company is in the freight business; flying airplanes is a means to an end. The object is to move freight as rapidly as possible from one place to another. Airborne has been excellent at doing what its customers pay it to do, and for this reason it was the most rapidly growing fast-freight company for roughly the last decade. Pilot discipline is only one part of a rigorous discipline that pervades all of Airborne's activities, and to rebel against strict rules in the service of freight transport is to quarrel with Airborne's reason for being.

Airborne was as romantic as it ever is likely to become when it decided in the late 1940s to fly flowers from West Coast to East Coast for profit. The idea was that somebody would pay Airborne if the flowers did not wilt.

The officers responsible for Airborne's decision-making, operations and maintenance at the time of publication are: Robert S. Cline, chairman and chief executive officer; Robert G. Brazier, president and chief operating officer; John J. Cella, executive vice president, international division; Kent W. Freudenberger, executive vice president, marketing division; and Roy C. Liljebeck, executive vice president, chief financial officer.

Airborne Express Statistics

1992 Total Sales
Global/Major Airlines

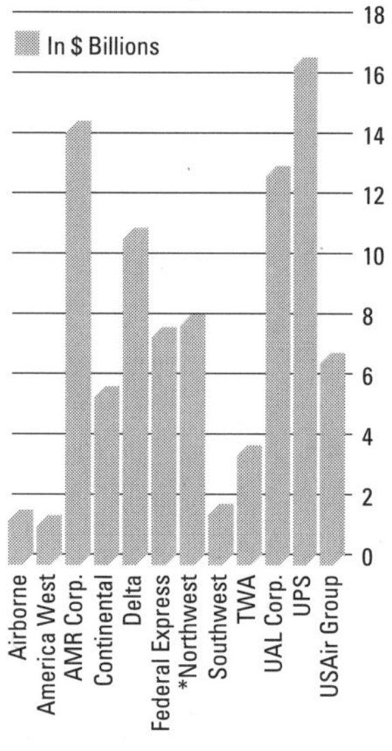

• Information is for Northwest Airlines only and not for parent company NWA Inc.

Airborne Express had total revenues of $1.484 billion in 1992 which was higher than America West's 1992 total revenue.

Airborne's sales increased 343 percent during the period 1983 to 1992. Since 1983, Airborne's total sales increased at least 8.6 percent each year. Its largest one-year sales growth during 1982-1993 was 24.8 percent in 1984, followed by a 24.4-percent sales growth in 1990.

Airborne Express
Total Sales 1983-1992

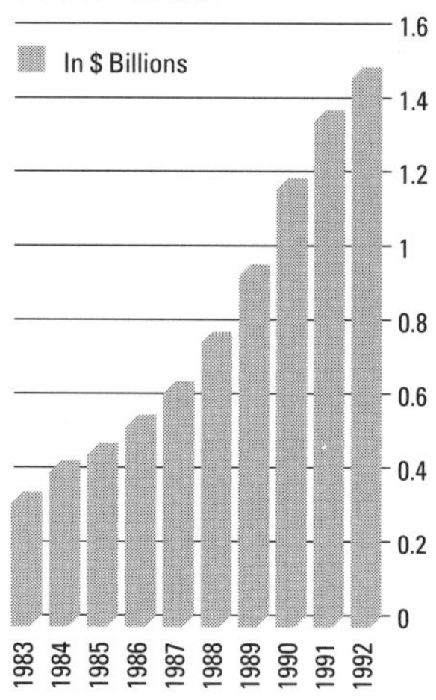

1992 Net Income
Global/Major Airlines

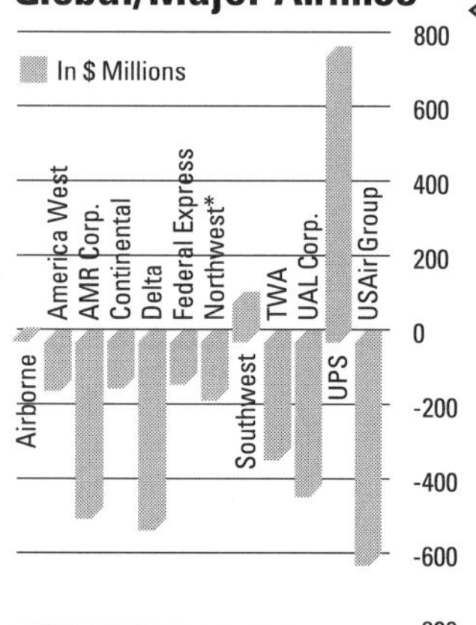

• Information is for Northwest Airlines only and not for parent company NWA Inc.

Airborne joined Southwest and United Parcel Service as the only global/major airlines to post a 1992 net profit.

Airborne posted a profit in each of the last 10 years, although 1992 was its smallest profit over that period. Airborne posted total profits of more than $133.8 million from 1983 to 1992.

Airborne Express
Net Income 1983-1992

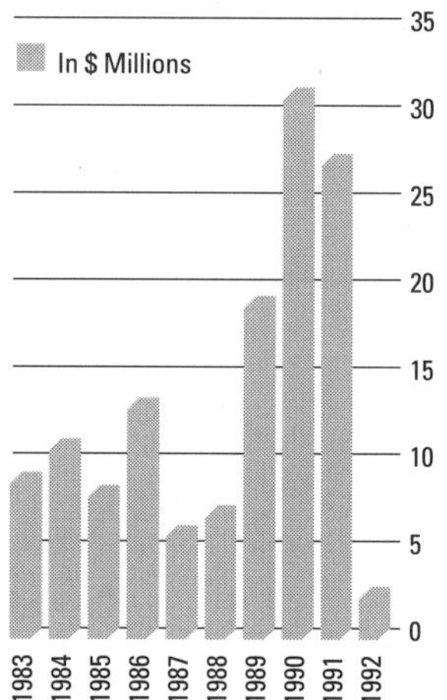

1992 Total Assets & Liabilities
Global/Major Airlines

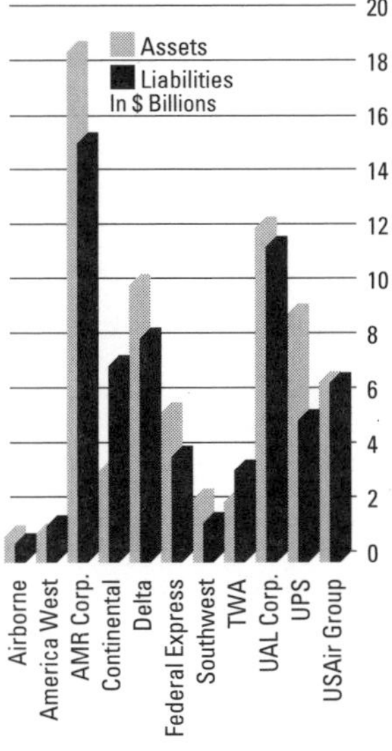

NWA Inc. is a privately held company and would not release 1990-1992 figures.

Airborne finished 1992 with both the lowest assets and liabilities of global and major airlines. Reaching $964.74 million, Airborne's assets grew 17.1 percent in 1992 while its liabilities reached $679.1 million, a 26.6-percent hike. However, Airborne ranked first in percentage growth in both assets and liabilities during 1983 to 1992, partially because of its relative youth at the outset of the 10-year span.

The value of Airborne Express' assets and liabilities grew significantly between 1983 and 1992. Airborne's assets increased in value 657 percent over that period, while its liabilities jumped 1,051 percent between 1983 and 1992.

Airborne Express
Assets & Liabilities 1983-1992

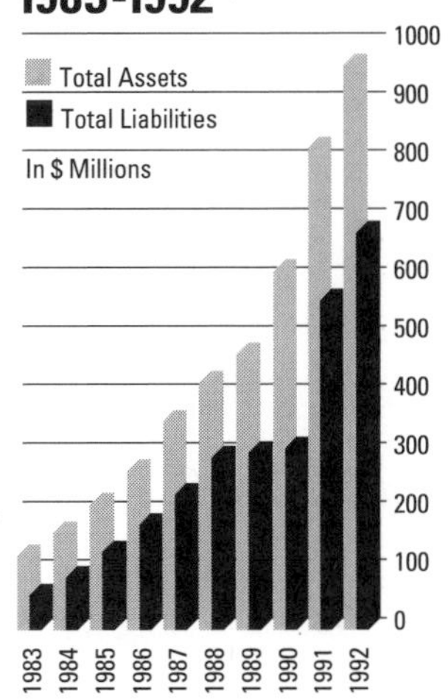

1992 Net Worth
Global/Major Airlines

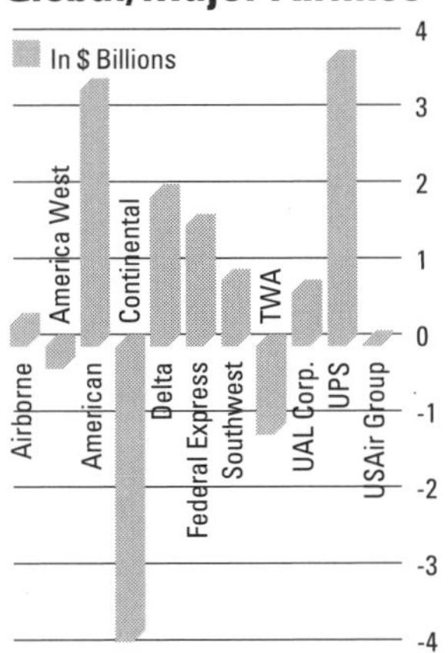

NWA Inc. is a privately held company and would not release 1990-1992 figures.

Airborne Express finished 1992 with a better net worth than America West, Continental, TWA and USAir.

Airborne's net worth increased 317 percent from 1983 to 1992. Its net worth increased every year during that period except from 1991 to 1992, when its net worth decreased six-tenths of one percent.

Airborne Express
Net Worth 1983-1992

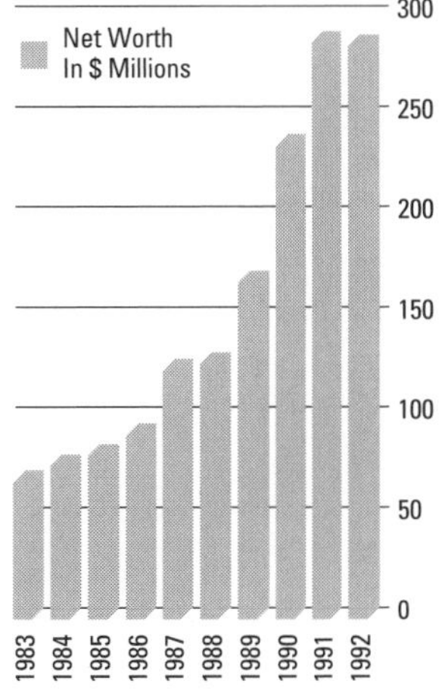

Statistics Related Terms

Assets — A resource having commercial or trade value that is owned (or which the company owns rights to) by a business. Typical examples for an airline include: Cash, securities, property, equipment, capital leases, landing slots and routes.

Financial accounting standard (FAS) 106 — A federally-mandated accounting change made to the way U.S. companies handle post-retirement benefits (other than pensions) to employees. FAS 106, for several U.S. global and major airlines, meant large, one-time, non-cash charges to earnings, further damaging their balance-sheet performance for 1992.

Leveraged buyout (LBO) — Takeover of a company using borrowed funds. Company assets often serve as security for the loans, although investors' assets also may be used.

Liabilities — The total amount the company owes to all creditors.

Net worth or stockholders' equity — The net assets (total assets minus total liabilities) of a company. For companies with more liabilities than assets, the result is a negative net worth or stockholders' deficit.

Yield — The average revenue received for each mile a revenue passenger is carried. Determined by dividing total operating revenue by total revenue passenger miles.

Airborne Express News Abstracts

"Airborne Freight Corp." *Wall Street Journal,* 5 June 1991.

"Airborne Freight Urges U.S. to Revoke Federal Express' $129 Million Contract." *Wall Street Journal,* 16 Jan. 1991.

"Doing Its Own Thing." *Air Transport World,* Feb. 1992, pp. 70-72.

"Federal Express Posts 3rd-period Loss, Cites Charges, Wider Overseas Deficits." *Wall Street Journal,* 19 Mar. 1991, sec. A, p. 6.

"MDC Outlines Twin DC-8 Freighter Plans." *Flight International,"* 25 Sep. 1991, p. 10.

"Night Haulers." *Flying,* Feb. 1990, pp. 46-49.

"Seattle Air-Express Concern to Post Loss for 2nd Quarter." *Wall Street Journal,* 9 July 1992, sec. A, p. 14.

2

America West Airlines

Dubbed the "child of deregulation," America West's rapid departure from niche carrier to major status was a triumph. The carrier, however, met head-on with the unforgiving climate of the 1990s and struggles to maintain its position in the industry.

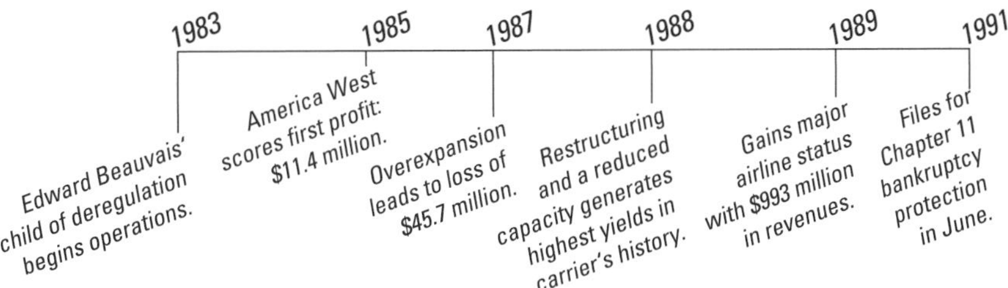

Of the more than 200 airlines to emerge since deregulation, America West is the only one to achieve major airline status. This accomplishment had several causes but predominant among them were the market recognition, marketing strategy and personnel policies of the company's founder, Edward R. Beauvais.

Beauvais was an airline economist who consulted with global and major airlines on rate structures and route systems. He realized early on that Phoenix had the potential to become the "Atlanta of the Southwest." With its near-perfect weather year-round and its proximity to the business centers of the Southwest, Midwest and West Coast, Phoenix met all the requirements of an ideal airline hub. Beauvais consistently recommended to his airline customers that they develop Phoenix as a hub. When all of them failed to accept his advice, he decided to make the plunge himself.

"Again and again," writes Peter F. Drucker in *Innovation and Entrepreneurship: Practice and Principles*, "when market or industry structure changes, the producers or suppliers who are today's industry leaders will be found neglecting the fastest-growing market segments." This proved to be true in the case of Phoenix and airline management.

Armed with $51 million, three B-737s and 280 employees, Beauvais' America West Airlines began service on Aug. 1, 1983. Operating from Phoenix, America West initially offered service to Colorado Springs, Colo.; Kansas City, Mo.; Wichita, Kan.; and Los Angeles. The airline served 13 cities with 10 B-737s by the end of 1983, and America West was well on its way to the successful exploitation of an ignored but very real market.

America West Airlines
Aircraft fleet and purchase commitments
As of May 1993

Aircraft Type	Current Fleet	Firm Orders	Options
A-320	18	0	0
B-737	56	10	10
B-757	11	0	0
Total	85	10	10

The other primary factor in Beauvais' business strategy was participatory management policies. Two lines in John Naisbitt and Patricia Aburdene's *Re-inventing the Corporation* best explain what Beauvais accomplished with personnel: "When you identify with your company's purpose, when you experience ownership in a shared vision, you find yourself doing your life's work instead of just doing time.

"The top-down authoritarian management style is yielding to a networking style of management, where people learn from one another horizontally, where everyone is a resource for everyone else, and where each person gets support and assistance from many different directions."

Beauvais mandated an ownership posture for every employee at America West whereby employees were required to purchase America West stock equivalent to 20 percent of their first year's base pay. Thus, Beauvais removed the psychological barrier between management and labor by defining everyone at the airline as having the same stake in its future. He brought about a shared vision that pointed the way for America West even when times were bad. This vision led pilots to help load baggage, schedule crews or do whatever was needed to meet schedules. It made America West an airline of opportunity, so that, for example, flight attendants could move into the cockpit as they acquired the necessary flight training and experience.

America West grew rapidly from its small beginnings by exploiting a neglected market and motivating its work force. As it began service to nine more cities in 1984, it supported its expansion through the receipt of 11 B-737s and by a stock offering that raised $24.5 million. It earned its first profits in November and December of 1984 although the carrier reported a $15.4-million loss for the year.

The airline's marketing strategy to this point focused on achieving the necessary size to compete effectively. The airline slowed its growth rate as 1985 began, but took another decisive step toward securing a place in the air transport industry. When Republic Airlines closed its Phoenix hub, America West took advantage of the chance to fortify its Phoenix operations. It expanded its Phoenix terminal from nine to 18 gates and increased daily departures significantly. It served 26 cities with a fleet of 32 B-737s by the end of 1985. This also was the first year of profitability as the carrier earned a net income of $11.4 million from operating revenues of $241.3 million.

With its operations in Phoenix secure, America West expanded aggressively in 1986. The carrier launched its "Nite Flite" service to serve cities from its recently developed Las Vegas hub. By the end of the year, America West serviced 35 cities, employed 4,596 people and operated 46 B-737s. However, the company's capacity grew faster than it could fill its seats. As a result, its profits began to decline. The company reported a $3-million profit for 1986.

Rapid expansion continued through 1987.

Boosted by a $31-million investment by Ansett Airlines of Australia which now owns a percentage of the airline, America West began service to destinations on the East Coast. It added service to Chicago, New York and Washington, D.C. The company now had transcontinental routes stretching from Los Angeles to New York through its two "superhubs," Phoenix and Las Vegas. Yet, as 1987 drew to a close, it appeared America West fell prey to the deregulated era's most common demon: overexpansion. Following its devastating 1987 loss of $45.7 million, Wall Street analysts predicted the early demise of America West.

Beauvais and the rest of management had other ideas. As the company entered 1988, it took aggressive steps to return to profitability. The first step involved reducing total capacity. Rather than eliminate cities from its route structure or planes from its fleet, the company achieved its reduction through a 10 percent cutback in the frequency of flights. Additionally, the company's Technical Support Facility became fully operational in 1988. The company now could perform its own maintenance and handle contract maintenance for other airlines.

Management continued to reap benefits from America West's enhanced revenue management system which in 1988 generated the highest yields in the airline's brief history. America West also began putting in place a fleet of de Havilland Dash 8 (DHC-8) turboprop aircraft to feed the Phoenix hub—not a profit-producing feed operation in itself, but another measure to secure the hub through market saturation. These factors, together with the industry's stability that year, enabled America West to produce a profit of $9.4 million for calendar 1988.

America West, having recovered from the 1987 financial storm, began 1989 with an aggressive search for new routes. The company gained more slots at New York's La Guardia Airport and Washington's National Airport. It sought route authority to Australia and Japan before its successful inauguration of B-747 service to Hawaii. And, to support expansion on several fronts, it increased its fleet by 19 aircraft through the addition of two B-747s, three B-757s, nine B-737s and five DHC-8s. The company even bid for the Eastern Shuttle, but delays in raising the necessary financing allowed these assets to go to Donald Trump.

The benefits of the airline's massive growth in 1989 included record profits and reclassification by the Department of Transportation as a "major" airline. From total sales of $993.4 million—revenues that permitted DOT to reclassify America West—the company earned 1989 profits of $20 million.

Far from its small beginnings in 1983, America West began 1990 as a major airline. How did America West succeed thus far when so many other new-entrant carriers failed? No doubt there were several factors, including a previously unfilled market need for a major Phoenix hub. Others say Beauvais' participatory management philosophy was the primary success factor. Determined to build an airline that provided quality service at competitive fares, Beauvais made America West an employee-owned company from the start in the belief that a substantial stake in the airline was the only carrot that could motivate employees to produce as if they owned the company. Beauvais believed an "ownership attitude" built in employees the necessary commitment to quality service and encouraged them to keep operating costs at a minimum.

The management strategy seemed to work. The company's motivated, non-union work force of 11,000 people attracted the ridership necessary to build load factors, and America West's 1989 cost per available seat mile (ASM) was 6.89 cents. Only Southwest Airlines' 6.2 cents per ASM was lower. By contrast, USAir functioned at 10.47 cents per ASM, and Eastern, crippled by a strike, a Chapter 11 filing, ongoing union conflict and an image problem, incurred costs of 23.17 cents per ASM.

America West received *Air Transport World* magazine's Labor/Management Relations Award in 1989, in part because of such progressive items as its child care program, which got America West included in *Working Mother* magazine's list of the nation's top 60 corporations for working mothers.

The year 1990, however, wore two faces for America West: on one side, aggressive expansion to $1.31 billion in revenue and a 39-percent increase in

America West Airlines
Aircraft fleet: 1983-1992

Aircraft	1983	1984	1985	1986	1987	1988	1989	1990	1991	1992
A-320	—	—	—	—	—	—	—	16	16	18
B-747	—	—	—	—	—	—	2	4	2	—
B-757	—	—	—	—	7	7	10	11	10	11
B-737	10	21	31	46	59	60	69	76	66	57
DHC-8	—	—	—	—	3	3	8	12	6	—
Total	10	21	31	46	69	70	89	119	100	86

revenue passenger miles (RPMs); on the other, a loss of \$74.7 million and a worsening cash crunch that ultimately lowered America West's cash and "cash equivalents" to about \$90 million by the end of the first quarter of 1991. Phoenix-based America West, one of the two U.S. airlines to emerge as new majors in 1989-90, had to curtail expansion plans after defaulting on certain loan covenants.

The primary worry concerning America West as a business entity was its debt load. An October 1990 *Business Week* article stated that "America West's breakneck growth has piled up \$624 million in debt," or 85 percent of total capital. In the same month, America West announced an agreement to buy or lease up to 118 Airbus A-320s, with deliveries spread over 15 years. Some analysts were concerned that with rising fuel costs and the 1990 economic downturn, America West might be spreading itself too thin. To the extent that the airline faced a first-half 1991 cash crisis and eventually filed for Chapter 11 protection, the prophets proved correct.

In April 1991, America West cut in half its plans for 1991 capacity growth, eliminated service to five cities and pared its daily service between Honolulu and Nagoya, Japan, to three times a week. It froze hiring and reduced pay for officers and some managers by 10 percent to 25 percent. It also dropped plans to buy assets from distressed airlines.

The carrier filed for Chapter 11 bankruptcy protection in June 1991, and thus had to tone down its ambitions in the face of a cash crunch caused by, according to management, high fuel prices, recession, war and fear of terrorism. Many analysts, however, disagreed with management's assessment and felt the bulk of America West's problems were of its own making. "Overcommitment and overexpansion helped drain the carrier of cash at a time when the industry was suffering record losses," stated an article in *Commercial Aviation Report*, an industry newsletter. An ill-timed, half-off coupon sale also was said to have contributed to the airline's cash problems. Others believed the airline strayed too far from the path that made it a success as a niche carrier, pointing to its Nagoya, Japan, route as an example. An ongoing, expensive, head-to-head clash with Southwest added to America West's problems.

The carrier in August 1991 announced several cost-cutting measures, including a 10-percent work force reduction, discontinued or reduced operations to several cities and pay cuts for employees who did not take cuts earlier. With cost-cutting under way, America West focused on raising much needed cash. Northwest Airlines and GPA Group Ltd. of Shannon, Ireland, came forward with a combined \$55 million in debtor-in-possession financing—\$35 million from GPA Group, the company that leased America West most of its A-320s, and \$20 million from Northwest.

In a separate but related agreement, Northwest and America West agreed to code share on some flights, to reciprocate frequent flyer benefits and to coordinate reservations systems and schedules. Northwest also negotiated a two-year option to purchase for \$15 million America West's Honolulu-Nagoya route.

As often happens in times of financial crisis, a shift in management occurs and in August 1991, Beauvais recommended that then president Michael J. Conway replace him as chief executive officer. Citing Conway's financial expertise as necessary for the carrier to work through Chapter 11, Beauvais said he would continue as chairman. The carrier received an additional \$23 million in debtor-in-possession financing—this time from Kawasaki Leasing International—in December. Also close at hand: another \$15 million from Pacific Rim powerhouse Northwest, coming forth to claim rights to America West's Honolulu-Nagoya route authority.

The Kawasaki financing brought to \$200 million the capital America West raised since entering Chapter 11. The airline expected another financial boost from its new service east through Columbus, Ohio. Red ink, however, continued to flow: America West closed 1991 with a \$222-million net loss, a 191-percent increase over the previous year's \$74.7-million loss.

America West continued to revamp its route network in 1992 by shifting additional flights from Las Vegas to its new Columbus operation. Some analysts labeled the shift "risky" because America West was unknown in that market. Others, however, reported signs of new life at the carrier. In fact, Conway attributed improved 1992 first quarter results to the growing hub operations in Columbus. Yet, just around the corner was another beast to contend with: American Airlines' new simplified fare plan. Initially, Conway claimed fare changes had little effect on the carrier's improved financial status. However, America West filed suit against American alleging unfair pricing less than three months later.

Drastic measures again seemed inevitable. Conway in July 1992 announced cuts of 15 aircraft from its fleet of just more than 100, and the loss of 1,500 jobs to save $7 million a month. America West's remaining two B-747s were among those cut, replaced with wet-leased L-1011s from American Trans Air for the carrier's Phoenix-Honolulu flights. America West also trimmed costs by code sharing with regional carrier Mesa Airlines. America West eliminated its fleet of DHC-8s and Mesa flew as America West Express from Phoenix to small cities in Colorado, California and Arizona.

America West received tentative approval in August on another $53-million loan package: $10 million from Ansett Worldwide Aviation Services, an Australian company leasing 11 planes to America West; $35 million from GPA Group; $1 million from the state of Arizona; and $7 million from a local investment group.

Local investors required that America West increase its eight-member board to nine members, including seven new directors, before they would invest in the company. William A. Franke, a Phoenix-area businessman who helped coordinate the local financing, became chairman, joining the board with six new directors. Beauvais was out; Conway, however, retained his positions of president and chief executive officer.

With Franke at the helm, America West canceled plans for a quick emergence from Chapter 11. Franke focused instead on whether America West should continue as a full-service airline or return to its roots as a niche carrier. Franke cited the success of competitor and chief nemesis, Herb Kelleher at Southwest, as an example. "You're darn right we're going to look at what Herb does," Franke said. "You have to look at Herb as one of the success stories."

Also on the agenda: raising $150 million to $200 million in new equity to pull the airline out of bankruptcy and to ensure continued operations; deciding the future of the poorly performing Columbus hub; and motivating a work force already among the lowest paid in the industry.

America West reported significant improvement in its fourth quarter 1992 results: a net loss of $17.6 million vs. $70.8 million in the third quarter, and for the year, a 1992 net loss of $131.8 million compared to 1991's loss of $222 million.

The officers responsible for America West's decision-making, operations and maintenance at the time of publication are Michael J. Conway, president and chief executive officer; Alphonse E. Frei, senior vice president of finance and chief financial officer; and Don Monteath, senior vice president of operations.

America West Airlines Financial Statistics

(In millions)	1984	1985	1986	1987	1988	1989	1990	1991	1992
Sales	122.6	241.3	328.9	575.4	775.7	993.4	1,315.8	1,413.9	1,294.1
Net Income (loss)	(15.4)	11.4	3.02	(45.7)	9.36	20	(74.7)	(222.0)	(131.8)
Assets	157.5	237.7	385.4	572.3	639.5	835.9	1,165.3	1,111.1	1,036.4
Liabilities	129.4	172.7	327.5	526.4	581.5	748.7	1,144.1	1,277.6	1,331
Net Worth	28.1	65	57.9	45.9	58	87.2	21.1	(166.5)	(294.6)
ASMs	2,374	3,658	5,296	10,318	12,200	13,725	18,286	20,627	19,271
RPMs	1,247	2,284	3,233	5,786	7,120	7,934	11,114	13,030	11,781
Load Factors	52.5%	62.4%	61%	56.1%	58.4%	57.8%	60.8%	63.2%	61.1%

America West Airlines Statistics

1992 Total Sales
Global/Major Airlines

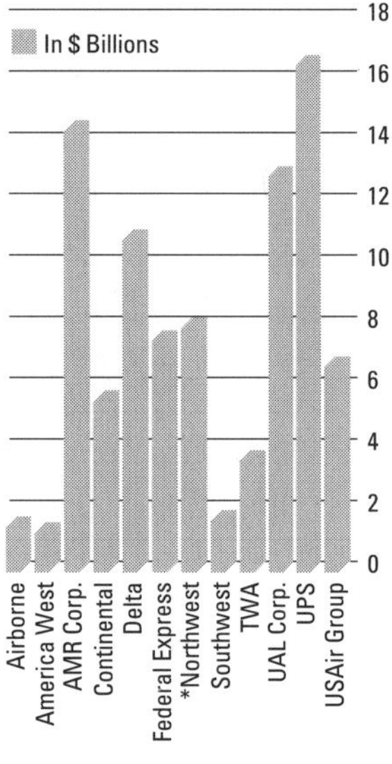

• Information is for Northwest Airlines only and not for parent company NWA Inc.

America West finished 1992 with total sales of $1.29 billion which was the lowest reported revenue for a global/major airline for 1992, $391 million behind Southwest.

Since 1984, its first full year of operations, America West's sales increased 956 percent from $122.6 million in 1984 to $1.29 billion in 1992.

America West
Total Sales 1984-1992

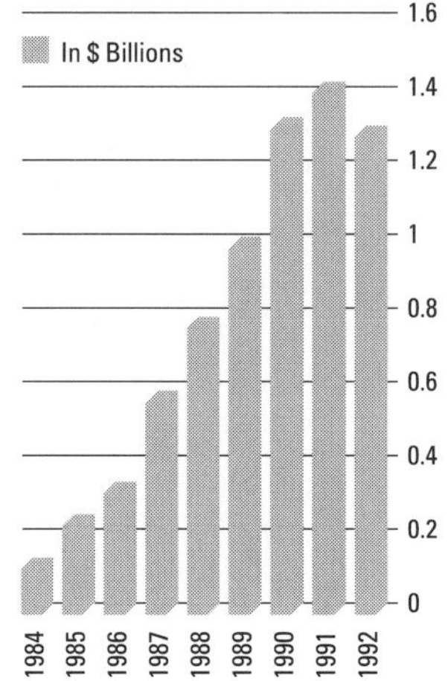

1992 Net Income
Global/Major Airlines

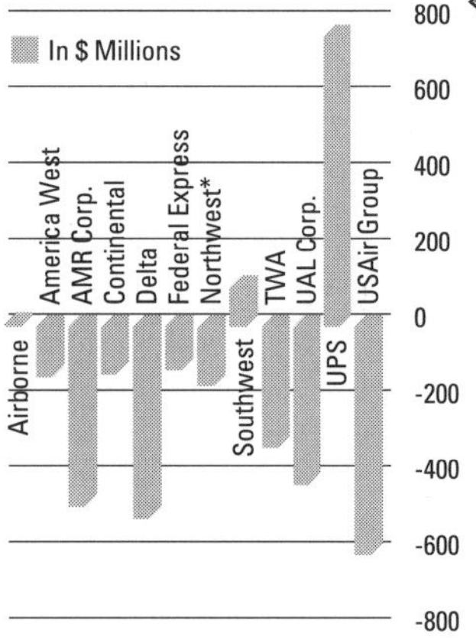

• Information is for Northwest Airlines only and not for parent company NWA Inc.

America West's 1992 net loss of $131.8 million still was better than six other global or major carriers.

America West's financial performance fluctuated between 1984 and 1992 as it struggled to establish its route system. After posting a profit in both 1988 and 1989, the airline lost $428.5 million from 1990-92.

America West
Net Income 1984-1992

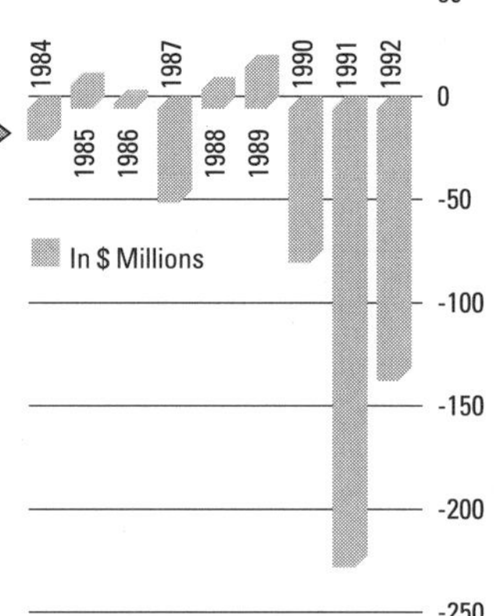

1992 Total Assets & Liabilities
Global/Major Airlines

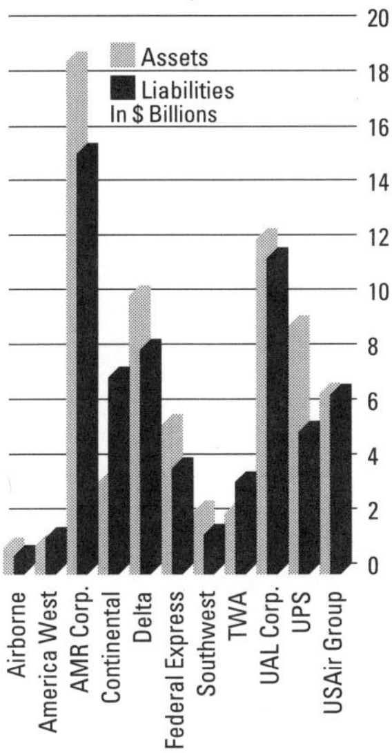

NWA Inc. is a privately held company and would not release 1990-1992 figures.

America West was the second-smallest of the major airlines in 1992 based on its total assets.

America West's assets increased 558 percent between 1984 and 1992, from $157.5 million in 1984 to $1.04 billion in 1992.

Its liabilities increased 929 percent during the same period, from $129.4 million in 1984 to $1.33 billion in 1992.

America West had a net stockholder's deficit of $294.6 million at the end of 1992, and possessed almost $412 million in long-term debt.

America West
Assets & Liabilities 1984-1992

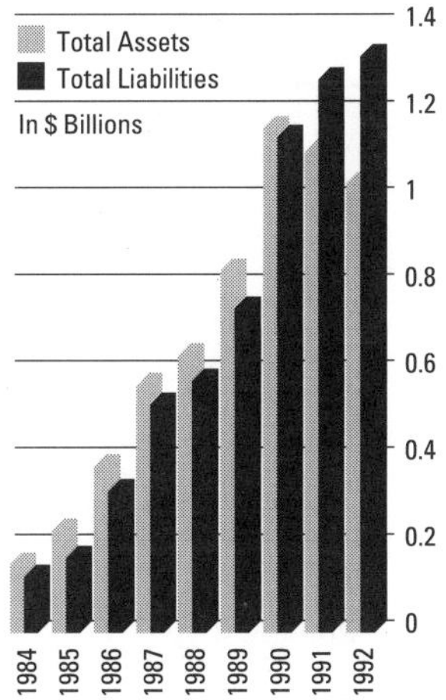

1992 ASMs & RPMs
Global/Major Airlines

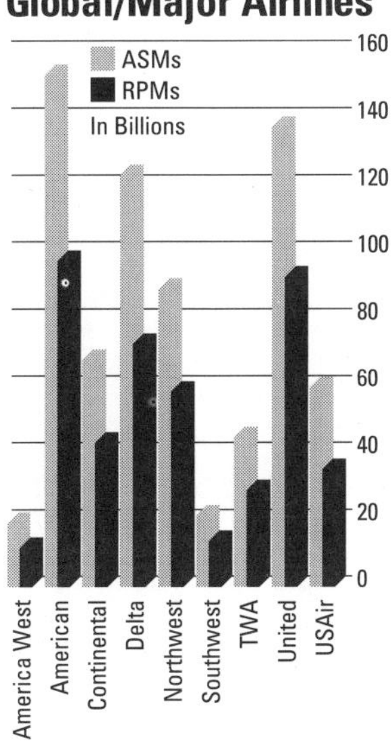

America West was the smallest of the passenger-carrying global or major airlines in 1992 in terms of capacity (as measured in available seat miles), trailing Southwest by 2.1 billion ASMs.

America West's capacity as measured in available seat miles (ASMs) increased 712 percent between 1984 and 1992. However, it cut capacity after filing Chapter 11 in June 1991.

The company's revenue passenger miles (RPMs) increased 845 percent between 1984 and 1992, from 1.2 billion miles in 1984 to nearly 11.8 billion in 1992.

America West
ASMs & RPMs 1984-1992

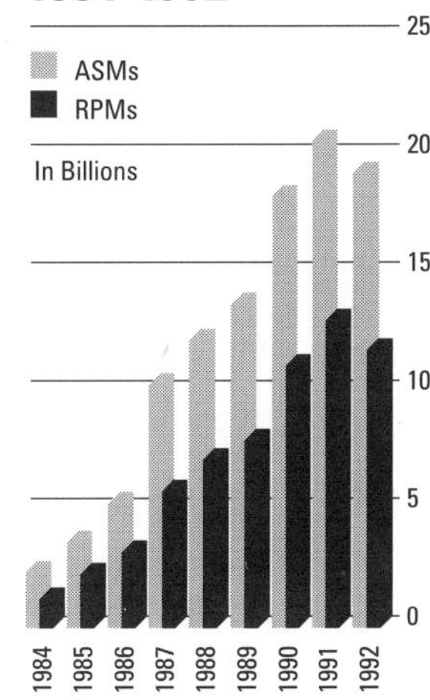

1992 Net Worth
Global/Major Airlines

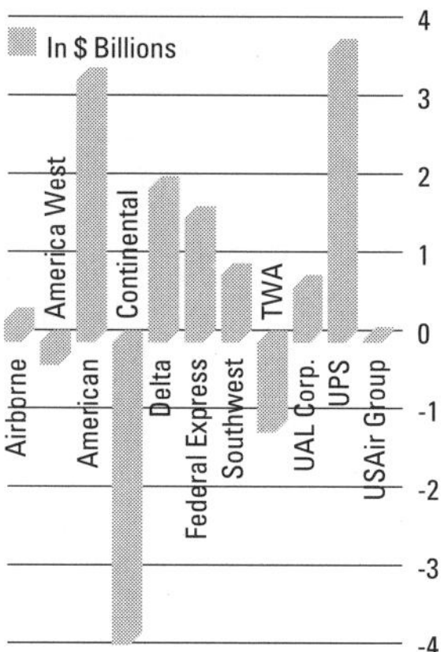

NWA Inc. is a privately held company and would not release 1990-1992 figures.

America West's 1992 stockholders' deficit of $294.6 million was better than that of Continental and TWA. However, in terms of total assets America West was the second-smallest of the global and major airlines (and the smallest passenger-carrying global/major airline) at the end of 1992. Its assets were valued at $1.04 billion while its total liabilities were $1.33 billion.

America West saw a decrease from a $28.1-million net worth in 1984 to a stockholders' deficit of $294.6 million in 1992. In 1984 the company had total assets valued at $157.5 million. At the end of 1992 the company's assets increased to $1.04 billion—a 558-percent jump.

Meanwhile, during the same period, America West's liabilities increased 929 percent, from $129.4 million in 1984 to $1.33 billion in 1992.

America West
Net Worth 1984-1992

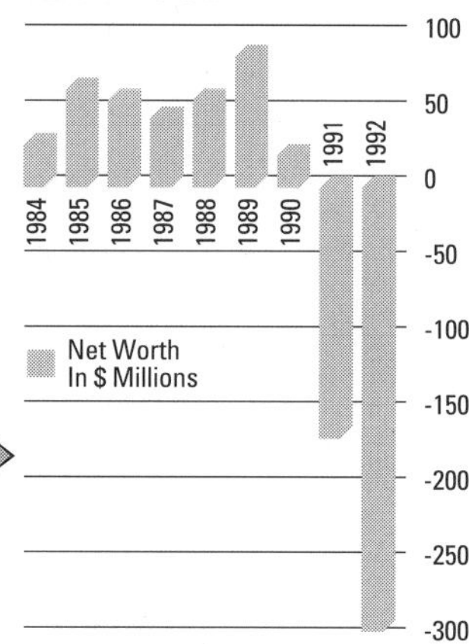

Statistics Related Terms

Assets — A resource having commercial or trade value that is owned (or which the company owns rights to) by a business. Typical examples for an airline include: Cash, securities, property, equipment, capital leases, landing slots and routes.

Available seat miles (ASMs) — Represent the number of seats available for passengers multiplied by the number of scheduled miles those seats are flown.

Cost per available seat mile — Represents operating and interest expense divided by available seat miles.

Financial accounting standard (FAS) 106 — A federally-mandated accounting change made to the way U.S. companies handle post-retirement benefits (other than pensions) to employees. FAS 106, for several U.S. global and major airlines, meant large, one-time, non-cash charges to earnings, further damaging their balance-sheet performance for 1992.

Leveraged buyout (LBO) — Takeover of a company using borrowed funds. Company assets often serve as security for the loans, although investors' assets also may be used.

Liabilities — The total amount the company owes to all creditors.

Net worth or stockholders' equity — The net assets (total assets minus total liabilities) of a company. For companies with more liabilities than assets, the result is a negative net worth or stockholders' deficit.

Passenger load factor — Revenue passenger miles divided by available seat miles over a set period of time.

Revenue passenger miles (RPMs) — The number of miles flown by revenue-producing passengers.

Yield — The average revenue received for each mile a revenue passenger is carried. Determined by dividing total operating revenue by total revenue passenger miles.

America West Airlines News Abstracts

"America West Adding Atlanta Flights." *The Atlanta Journal-Constitution,* 2 April 1992.

"America West Declares 50%-Off Sale a Success." *Aviation Week & Space Technology,* 18 Feb. 1991, p. 24.

"America West Declares Bankruptcy, Begins Route Restructuring." *Aviation Week & Space Technology,* 8 July 1991, p. 30.

"America West Gets Help From Group of Arizona Firms." *Wall Street Journal,* 19 Aug. 1992.

"America West Leasing L-1011." *Aviation Week & Space Technology,* 3 Aug. 1992, p. 16.

"America West President Named CEO." *The Atlanta Journal-Constitution,* 27 Aug. 1991.

"America West Slates Schwarzkopf Parody." *Wall Street Journal,* 8 May 1991, sec. B, p. 6, col. 1.

"America West Still Bullish." *Flight International,* 15-21 July 1992, p. 17.

"America West to Offer Atlanta Flights." *The Atlanta Journal-Constitution,* 29 May 1991.

"America West to Sell Commuter Operation." *Air Transport World,* Aug. 1991, p. 102.

"America West's Beauvais Resigns; Conway Fills Post." *Wall Street Journal,* 20 July 1992, sec. C, p. 11.

"America West." *The Atlanta Journal-Constitution,* 1 Aug. 1991.

"America West: Where Did All the Money Go?" *Commercial Aviation Report,* 1 Aug. 1991, p. 4.

"Chapter 11 Won't Change Plans for Atlanta, America West Says." *The Atlanta Journal-Constitution,* 29 June 1991.

"Financial Worries Force America West to Cut Back." *Wall Street Journal,* 29 April 1991, sec. A, p. 6.

3

American Airlines

American prides itself on a history that includes many firsts in aviation. An industry leader in market share as early as 1937, the largest of the "Big Three" carriers continues in the 1990s to set the trends in a changing industry.

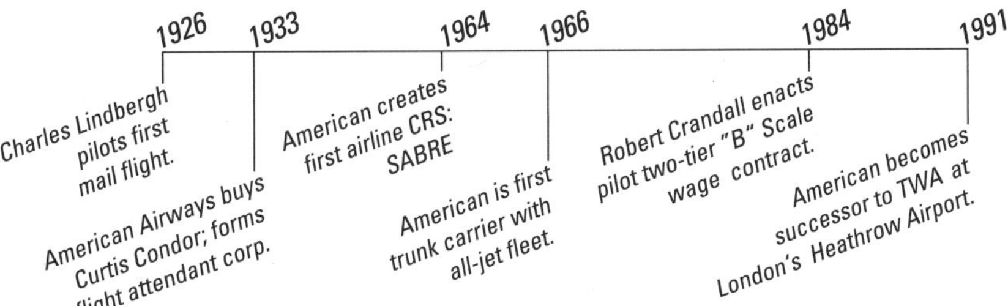

The birth year was 1926; the pilot, Charles Lindbergh; the occasion, the first flight for Robertson Aircraft Corp.'s St. Louis-Chicago airmail contract.

That flight by Robertson Aircraft, a small taxi service, flying school and airplane sales firm, is as good as any other "beginning" one could choose for American Airlines. Another predecessor was Colonial Air Transport which flew the Boston-New York airmail route. Colonial began business as The Bee Line, a small charter service formed in Connecticut in 1923. Colonial incorporated in 1924, received Airmail Contract #1 on Nov. 7, 1925, and began its first passenger service in April 1927 between Newark, N.J., and Boston.

A third major predecessor of American Airlines was Embry Riddle Co., which started in 1927 as an airplane sales and service, flight instruction, taxi and charter service company. Embry Riddle's financial needs were the catalyst that pulled together the elements of American. Embry Riddle had a close association with Fairchild Aviation Corp., namely, the franchise to sell Fairchild Aircraft. When Embry Riddle needed capital to expand its service, Fairchild invested money in the corporation and helped form Aviation Corp. (AVCO) to finance other operators of airmail routes. When AVCO incorporated on March 1, 1929, its holdings included Colonial Airways, Robertson Aircraft and Embry Riddle.

AVCO acquired 85 companies flying more than a dozen types of aircraft in the years 1929-1930. Realizing its financial structure was weak, AVCO reorganized in February 1930 as American Airways Inc. A chaotic route structure and continued financial problems brought another reorganization in 1934.

American Airlines
Aircraft fleet and purchase commitments
As of May 1993

Aircraft Type	Current Fleet	Firm Orders	Options
A-300-600R	35	0	0
B-727	137	0	0
B-757	70	21	31
B-767	59	12	14
DC-10	58	0	0
F-100	43	32	75
MD-11	17	2	20
MD-80	260	0	10
Total	679	67	150

The route links of American Airways, which acted as a holding company for the airlines, were not well-developed, and each carrier in American Airways flew its own equipment. In 1931, after much study, American Airways ordered the first aircraft ever built to airline company specifications, the Pilgrim 10-A. It bought the Curtiss Condor in 1933, the first aircraft equipped with sleeping facilities for passengers. The Condor brought the need for flight attendants—then called stewardesses. American disputes with United the distinction of developing the first flight attendant corps.

Behind the reorganization of American Airways as American Airlines Inc. in 1934 lay one of the most well-publicized confrontations in early aviation history: Dave Behncke and the Air Line Pilots Association (ALPA) vs. E. L. Cord and Century Air Lines. Cord wanted to establish a nationwide network of low-cost airlines to fly airmail contracts, beginning with Century, where he demanded of his pilots a steep pay cut. Behncke wanted to stop Cord and use the confrontation to establish ALPA as a national industry force. Behncke succeeded with the aid of U.S. Rep. Fiorello La Guardia and the crash of a Century plane. Cord closed Century Air Lines in April 1932. But, Cord then parlayed the sale of his other airline, Century Pacific, into control of AVCO.

Thus, in 1934 American Airways incorporated as American Airlines Inc. The Roosevelt Administration awarded American new airmail contracts and American got a more efficient route structure and a new company president, Cyrus Rowlett Smith, one of Cord's lieutenants. Cord was the force behind the scenes though Smith proved to be an able leader. Known throughout the company as "C. R.," Smith led American Airlines into the Jet Age.

Smith set out to mold the struggling regional carriers of American into a cohesive national airline. Making passenger revenues paramount instead of the airmail contracts that were supreme for Cord, Smith introduced the air travel industry's first major sales promotion. American's "Air Travel Plan" of 1934 proved so successful the airline soon needed more aircraft. Since no existing airplane met American's needs, company engineers worked with Donald Douglas to develop a new aircraft. The result: the 21-passenger DC-3 which American received in the late 1930s. American was the world's largest airline by the end of the decade.

American inaugurated its first international service (to Toronto), assembled a fleet of 80 aircraft and flew more than 27 million miles in a single year by the time the United States entered World War II. But U.S. entry into war brought the Army Air Corps' creation of the Air Transport Command (ATC) and the appropriation of half of American's fleet. C. R. Smith became deputy commander of ATC. The American Airlines fleet shrank to 55 aircraft in 1942 and to 44 aircraft in 1943.

Aircraft production soared during the war, however, and more demand was placed on the airlines for priority travel. The result: aircraft were allocated to the airlines. American Airlines flew more than 45 million miles by the end of the war, increased its international routes to include flights into Mexico and ordered Convair 240s and DC-6s. The end of the war brought Smith back to the helm of the airline.

Smith, keenly aware of the excellent training given to aviators in the armed forces, stressed the hiring of military pilots to ensure a well-qualified pilot corps and to decrease the cost of training. He also added cargo service to American's offerings.

The next 20 years of Smith's reign at American saw the inauguration of transcontinental flight and jet flight; the company's creation of its Sabre computer reservation system; the withdrawal in 1963 of American's pilots from ALPA and the creation of the Allied Pilots Association (APA) as their bargaining agent.

American was the first airline to put jets into widespread domestic service (the late 1950s) and the first of the Big Four domestic trunk carriers—TWA, United, Eastern and American—to have an all-jet fleet (it sold its last piston-engine plane in December 1966). APA became the first in-house pilot union that survived. When American created Sabre in 1964, Sabre was the world's largest business computer system and the first of the airline CRSs.

Smith left American in the late 1960s to become Secretary of Commerce in the Johnson administration. He walked away from an airline that was stumbling into trouble. Part of the trouble was with the new pilot union, the APA; part was with ill-advised rapid expansion; and part was with the federal government which launched an investigation of illegal kickbacks and political campaign contributions.

The entire 1970s was a decade of tribulation. American's expansion of fleet and route system included, on one hand, investment in such widebody aircraft as the B-747 and the McDonnell Douglas DC-10 and, on the other, the addition of Pacific and Australian routes in 1970 and of Caribbean routes in 1971 when American acquired Trans Caribbean Airlines. The Pacific and Australian routes proved too costly. American suspended service on its trans-Pacific routes as well as some service to Hawaii in 1974, and then exchanged them with Pan Am for routes from the northeastern United States to Bermuda, Barbados and Santo Domingo.

American, a business executives' airline that stressed on-time performance, lost its competitive edge in 1972 during a pilot slowdown called when contract negotiations bogged down. The cost of the slowdown, which did not end until April 1973, is estimated at $10 million to $20 million. Over the same period, George Spater, the company president, refused to trim the widebody fleet to cut costs. Federal investigations of kickbacks culminated in two indictments of company officials in 1972 and in probes of illegal donations by American to the Nixon re-election committee.

These threats to the esprit de corps and financial well-being of the company forced Spater to resign. Smith replaced him temporarily.

The Arab oil embargo in 1974 staggered American with increased fuel costs. Smith took a wide range of cost-cutting steps. He placed about 350 pilots on half-duty in hopes of retaining pilot proficiency while reducing the payroll. He canceled orders for 25 DC-10s, changed route schedules and laid off 3,000 field and staff employees.

Albert Casey replaced Smith as president in February 1974. During the late 1970s the airline restructured substantially.

Robert L. Crandall became president of American Airlines in 1980, and in 1982 the company took on the structure it retains today. AMR Corp., a holding company, incorporated to place such non-airline activities as AA Energy Co., Flagship International and American Airlines Training Corp. out of the airline's organizational structure. Crandall became

American Airlines
Aircraft fleet: 1983-1992

Aircraft	1983	1984	1985	1986	1987	1988	1989	1990	1991	1992
A-300	—	—	—	—	—	—	25	25	29	35
BAe-146	—	—	—	—	6	6	6	6	—	—
B-727	166	164	164	164	164	164	164	164	168	143
B-737	—	—	—	—	31	24	11	18	—	—
B-747	13	—	—	—	2	2	2	2	2	—
B-757	—	—	—	—	—	—	8	26	46	58
B-767	8	10	15	22	29	45	45	45	47	58
DC-10	37	53	56	56	60	61	59	59	59	59
MD-80	20	33	56	88	118	153	180	213	248	260
MD-11	—	—	—	—	—	—	—	—	5	11
F-100	—	—	—	—	—	—	—	—	9	39
Total	244	260	291	330	410	455	500	558	613	663

chairman, president and CEO of AMR Corp. and president of American Airlines. Today, AMR Corp. includes several companies, among them Sabre Travel Information Network Division, Sabre Computer Services Division, AMR Services Corp., AA Decision Technologies Inc., AMR Eagle Inc., AMR Information Services Inc., AMR Investment Services Inc. and AA Direct Marketing Corp.

Crandall unveiled a "Growth Plan" in 1984 that employees came to view as holy writ. The plan called for American to grow from within instead of through merger. Crandall pursued this growth by seeking—and getting—from American's unions (the APA, the Transport Workers Union and the Association of Flight Attendants) the first of the industry's two-tier or B-scale labor contracts. The company plowed the money saved back into new planes, new facilities and expanded operations.

And a lot of money was saved: American continued an astonishing, unrelenting, year-in and year-out hiring binge at the new B-scale or "market" pay rates. From June 1984 when American began hiring pilots to meet "Growth Plan" needs through the end of 1989, the airline interviewed 22,287 pilot job applicants. Of those, 4,426, or 19.86 percent, were on the payroll on Dec. 31, 1989. American was the nation's largest, fastest growing and most profitable air carrier. Its fleet of more than 500 aircraft was the largest commercial fleet in the world except for that of Aeroflot, the Soviet carrier.

The only airline acquisitions by the AMR group during that six-year growth period were AirCal in 1987; Simmons Airlines, Wings West Airlines and Command Airways in 1988; and Executive Air in 1989. It acquired AirCal for its strategic north-south air markets along the West Coast. The other four airlines are regional/commuter carriers bought by AMR's commuter subsidiary, AMR Eagle Inc., to solidify hub feed.

AMR Corp.'s profits in the 1980s totaled $2.26 billion. Delta, the second most profitable U.S. airline in the 1980s, earned $1.69 billion. AMR had assets worth $10.9 billion as of Dec. 31, 1989, and 1989 revenues were $10.48 billion.

In early 1990 when American made a big push to overtake everybody except Northwest and United in international service, company officials predicted $15 billion a year in revenues by 1995. AMR's revenues in 1990 rose to $11.72 billion, up $1.24 billion from 1989. American also finished 1990 with 16.6 percent of U.S. airlines' worldwide traffic, vs. 16.5 percent for United, reaffirming its position over United as the U.S.' biggest airline. It had roughly $700 million more revenue than United and $900 million more than Delta. But 1990 also brought AMR a loss of $39.6 million—its first in eight years. At fault were recession, labor tensions and high fuel costs escalated by the Persian Gulf War.

Red ink could only slow, not stop, the execution of AMR's $17-billion, five-year expansion strategy for American Airlines. American signed an agreement in August 1990 to buy Eastern's Latin and South American routes for more than $600 million. In December it responded to United's deal to acquire Pan Am's London routes by attempting to buy TWA's six London routes, but the DOT blocked part of the TWA sale. Also in 1990, American agreed to merge its Sabre CRS with Europe's largest CRS, Amadeus (a joint venture of Air France, Iberia Air Lines, Deutsche Lufthansa and Scandinavian Airlines System).

The year 1991 began with retrenchment: an 11-percent cutback in flight schedules overall. American, which was in contract negotiations with its pilots' union, blamed cutbacks at Nashville and Raleigh-Durham, together with discontinued service in the Los Angeles-San Francisco shuttle market, on the union, the Allied Pilots Association. American placed national ads that named the wrong union (ALPA) and accused its pilots of conducting a sick-out campaign that helped to blight fourth-quarter 1990 results (a $215.1-million loss on sales of $3 billion). The APA countered in a *Wall Street Journal* article that American's overly ambitious expansion plans caused the cutbacks.

The smoke cleared in February when American and its pilots agreed to a new contract giving the pilots an 8-percent pay hike retroactive to January 1990. Included in the contract were pay increases and parity for B-scale pilots in the sixth year instead of nine. The airline and its pilots left a few issues for settlement by binding arbitration including four work rule- and 14 health care-related issues.

American, with pilot friction behind it, canceled the cutbacks and pushed ahead with expansion plans, announcing increased flights out of its San

Jose hub by the end of May and hourly service between San Jose and Los Angeles. The U.S. and Britain signed an agreement in mid-March allowing American to be considered "successor" to TWA's landing rights at London's Heathrow Airport. The DOT soon after approved American's purchase of the three TWA routes it most wanted (New York-London, Los Angeles-London and Boston-London) for $445 million, the price it originally agreed to pay for all six TWA routes into Heathrow.

American continued its quest to acquire assets from weak or failing carriers and, in conjunction with TWA, in July bid $310 million to buy Pan Am assets including North Atlantic routes, the Pan Am shuttle and some aircraft. The carrier eventually lost its bid to Atlanta-based Delta Air Lines.

American in 1991 was the largest carrier to Latin America and across the North Atlantic based on available passenger seat miles (ASMs). The year also saw American take delivery of its first MD-11 aircraft, initially used to link Pacific Rim cities. International business will account for one-third of American's total revenues by the end of the 1990s, according to Crandall.

American changed course when second-quarter 1991 earnings showed a 92-percent decrease from the previous year. The company in September announced capital spending cuts of more than $8 billion through 1995, including aircraft option deferrals for 93 aircraft and rescheduled deliveries for ordered aircraft. Four months later, the carrier posted record year-end losses of $239.9 million. American at the start of 1992 maintained its commitment to lower costs and announced layoffs of more than 1,200 workers, the largest since the early 1980s.

Frustrated by competition from Chapter 11 airlines operating under what Crandall termed "an unfair economic advantage," American altered its air fare structure and in April 1992 introduced its "value pricing plan." The simplified fare structure lowered by up to 50 percent the price of American's top fares and eliminated 85 percent of the fares the airline offered. The revamped structure established four basic fare categories: first class, a new coach category and two discount categories. American also eliminated its corporate, meeting and convention discounts.

Reaction to American's value plan was mixed, though three carriers—America West, Continental and Northwest—filed suit against American alleging the carrier engaged in predatory pricing intending to drive them out of business. Other carriers reacted by cutting prices even further, causing American to reduce summer fares by as much as 50 percent. In any event, AMR reported second-quarter losses of $166 million and third-quarter losses—traditionally the industry's strongest quarter—of $85 million. Amidst the turmoil, American emerged as the victor in a bidding contest with United over TWA assets at Chicago O'Hare; and American purchased 40 take-off and landing slots and three gates from TWA for $221 million.

Mounting financial losses and the continued operation of Chapter 11 carriers signaled the end of value pricing. Crandall then focused attention on more global matters, specifically, foreign airline

American Airlines Financial Statistics

(In millions)	1983	1984	1985	1986	1987	1988	1989	1990	1991	1992
Sales	4,763	5,354	6,131	6,018	7,198	8,824	10,480	11,720	12,887	14,396
Net Income (loss)	227.9	233.9	345.8	279.1	198.4	476.8	454.8	(40)	(240)	(475)
Assets	4,728	5,261	6,421	7,528	8,423	9,792	10,877	13,354	16,208	18,706
Liabilities	3,429	3,748	4,240	5,019	5,592	6,424	7,112	9,627	12,414	15,357
Net Worth	1,300	1,513	2,181	2,501	2,831	3,368	3,766	3,727	3,794	3,349
ASMs	52,447	58,667	68,336	75,087	88,743	102,045	15,222	123,773	133,472	152,996
RPMs	34,099	36,702	44,138	48,792	56,794	64,770	73,503	77,085	82,335	97,425
Load Factors	65%	62.6%	64.6%	65%	64%	63.5%	63.8%	62.3%	61.7%	63.7%

access to U.S. markets via their increased investment in U.S. carriers. Crandall, joined by other airlines' top brass, namely United's Stephen Wolf, Delta's Ronald Allen and Frederick Smith of Federal Express, vocally opposed British Airways' 44-percent bid for USAir. "If the United States government simply wants to turn international aviation over to foreign carriers, fine. We're on our way," Crandall told USA *Today*. British Airways eventually dropped its bid for USAir, though a modified version of the initial proposal surfaced some months later.

Meanwhile, American finalized its own plans to acquire a one-third stake in Canadian Airlines International. Under the proposal, subject to American and Canadian government approval, American would gain a one-third equity stake in Canadian, a 25-percent voting stake and two of eight seats on CAI's board of directors in exchange for a cash infusion of $195 million. AMR also would provide to Canadian administrative services, such as accounting and data processing estimated to generate $115 million for AMR its first year.

American in late October announced plans to lay off between 500 and 1,000 managers as part of a plan to cut expenses by $300 million in 1993. By year's end, 286 managers received pink slips while another 290 resigned. Prompted by fourth-quarter losses of $200 million and year-end losses totaling $935 million after FAS 106 (year-end losses totaled $475 million before FAS 106), Crandall called 1992 "one of the most difficult and challenging years in the history of commercial aviation." He refuted others' claims of an industry turnaround and labeled 1993 the year of "retrenchment and austerity," according to the *Wall Street Journal*. AMR management is considering several options to help ensure a quick return to profitability, including reducing its fleet, replacing jet service with flights by its regional airlines, abandoning markets where it competes with low-cost competitors and adding service in areas where it is strong, such as Dallas, Chicago, Miami and San Juan.

The officers responsible for the decision-making, operations and maintenance of American Airlines at the time of publication are Robert L. Crandall, chairman, president and chief executive officer; Robert W. Baker, executive vice president of operations; Donald J. Carty, executive vice president of finance and planning; David L. Kruse, senior vice president of maintenance and engineering; and Cecil D. Ewell, vice president of flight and chief pilot.

American Airlines Statistics

1992 Total Sales
Global/Major Airlines

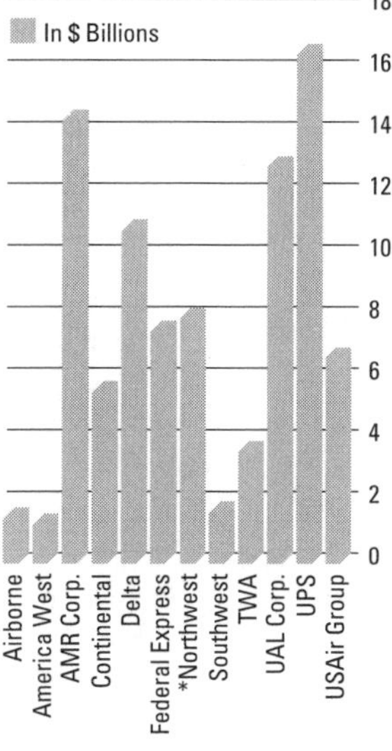

• Information is for Northwest Airlines only and not for parent company NWA Inc.

AMR Corp., the parent of American Airlines, was second in the industry in 1992 with total sales of nearly $14.4 billion. AMR trailed only United Parcel Service (UPS) in total revenue for 1992.

American Airlines contributed $13.58 billion to AMR's total 1992 sales.

During the period 1983 to 1992, AMR's sales increased 202 percent primarily due to the company's rapid expansion.

American's capacity, as measured in available seat miles (ASMs), increased 192 percent between 1983 and 1992.

Another factor contributing to AMR's sales growth is the increase in American's yield per revenue passenger mile (RPM). Between 1983 and 1992, American's yield increased 7.2 percent from 11.39 cents per RPM in 1983 to 12.21 cents per RPM in 1992, although yield per RPM declined in 1992 for the first time since 1986.

AMR Corp.
Total Sales 1983-1992

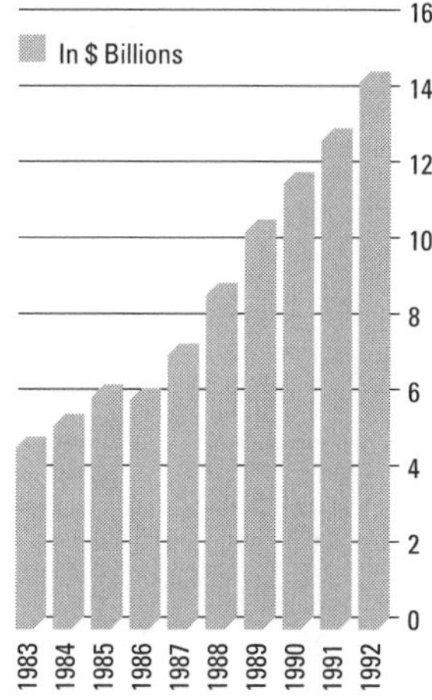

1992 Net Income
Global/Major Airlines

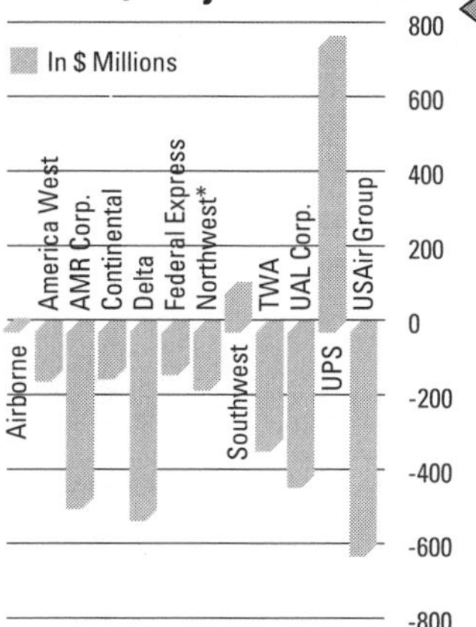

• Information is for Northwest Airlines only and not for parent company NWA Inc.

AMR's 1992 net loss was the third-largest of the U.S. carriers (without FAS 106 charges applied).

Finishing 1992 with larger losses were Delta (for its fiscal year ended June 30) and USAir Group Inc.

AMR recorded a profit every year from 1983-89. The 1990s started off poorly and got worse, culminating in a 1992 net loss (before FAS 106) of $475 million. American Airlines wasn't the only airline to post a large 1992 net loss, however.

AMR Corp.
Net Income 1983-1992

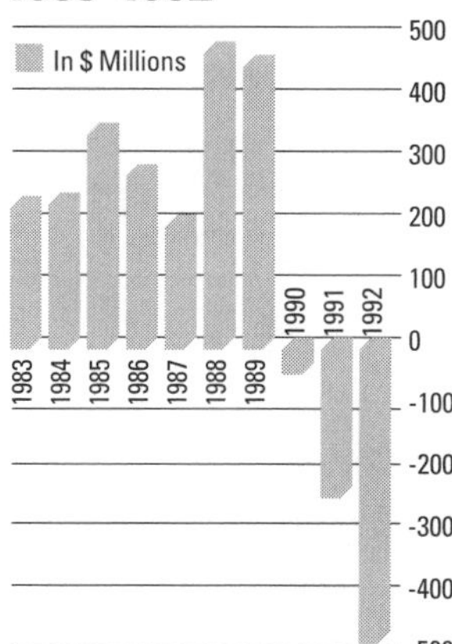

1992 Total Assets & Liabilities

Global/Major Airlines

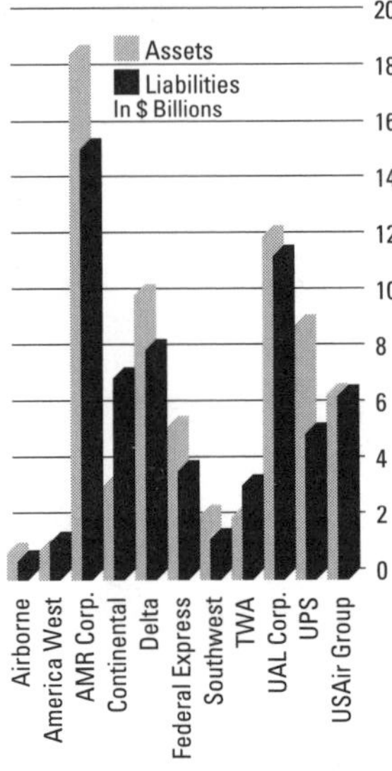

NWA Inc. is a privately held company and would not release 1990-1992 figures.

AMR led the industry in 1992 with assets valued at $18.7 billion. The next largest company in 1992 was UAL with total assets of nearly $12.3 billion.

AMR finished 1992 with total liabilities of $15.36 billion and a net worth of $3.35 billion. Additionally, the company had $5.6 billion in long-term debt at the end of 1992.

AMR's total assets grew from $4.7 billion in 1983 to $18.7 billion in 1992. This represents a 297-percent increase in assets.

Total liabilities grew during this same period from $3.4 billion to $15.36 billion, an increase of 352 percent.

AMR Corp.

Assets & Liabilities 1983-1992

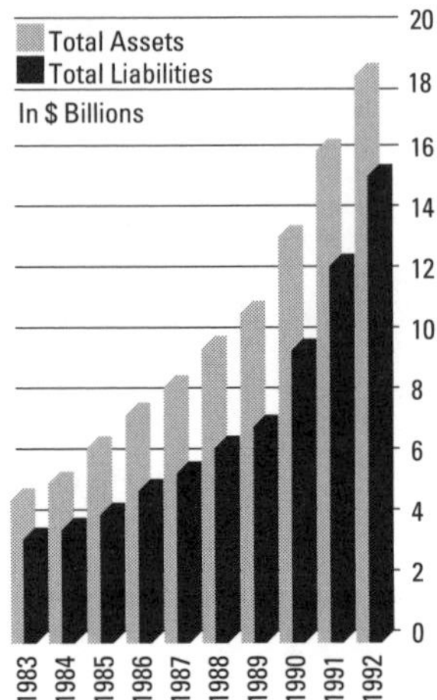

1992 ASMs & RPMs

Global/Major Airlines

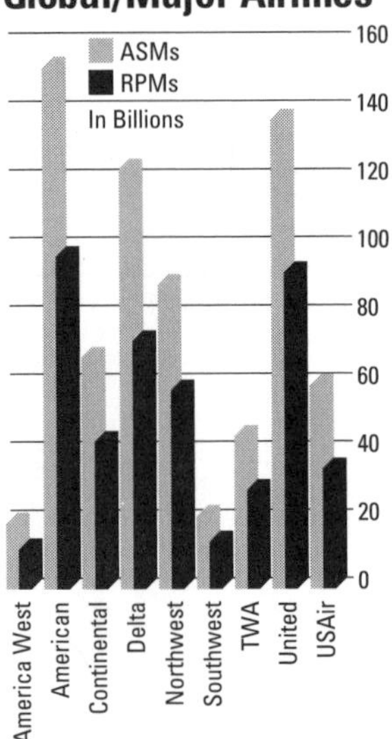

American finished 1992 as the largest airline in the industry as measured by available seat miles (ASMs).

American had less than 153 billion ASMs in 1992 while its closest competitor, United, had 137.5 billion.

American flew 97.4 billion revenue passenger miles in 1992, resulting in a 63.7 percent load factor.

American enjoyed tremendous growth between 1983 and 1992. The airline's capacity, as measured by ASMs, increased 192 percent from 52.4 billion in 1983 to just under 153 billion in 1992.

During the same period, the number of revenue passenger miles (RPMs) flown increased 186 percent.

American

ASMs & RPMs 1983-1992

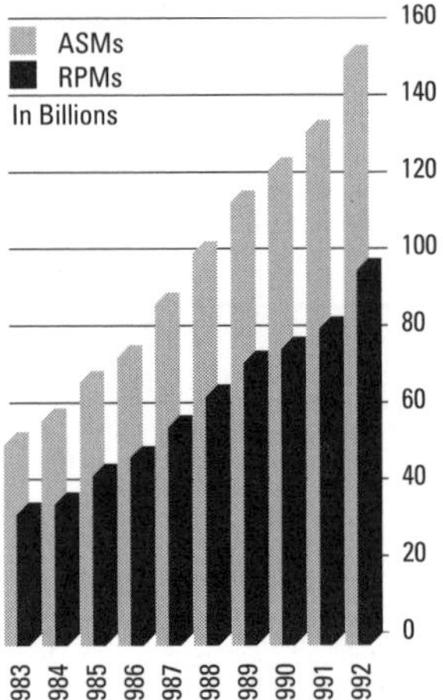

1992 Net Worth
Global/Major Airlines

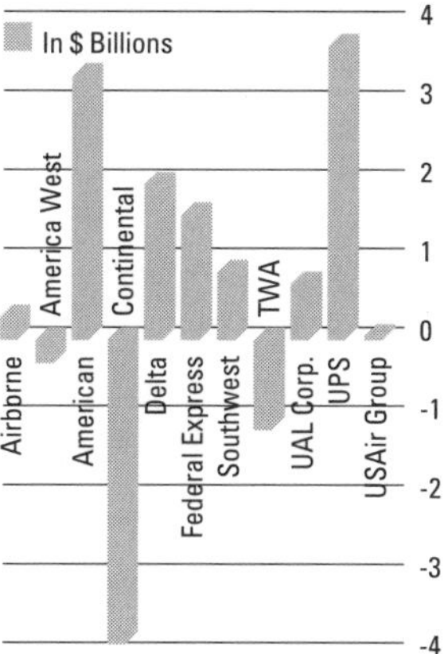

NWA Inc. is a privately held company and would not release 1990-1992 figures.

AMR Corp. finished 1992 with the second-highest net worth in the industry. With total assets valued at $18.7 billion and total liabilities of $15.36 billion, AMR's net worth at the end of 1992 was $3.35 billion, falling short only to United Parcel Service (UPS).

AMR's net worth increased 158 percent between 1983 and 1992, from $1.3 billion in 1983 to $3.35 billion in 1992, although it experienced an 11.7-percent decline in net worth from the year previous. From 1983-92, AMR's assets increased 296 percent while its liabilities increased 348 percent. The company reported 1992 assets valued at $18.7 billion compared to 1983 total assets valued at $4.7 billion. Similarly, AMR's reported liabilities at the end of 1992 totaled $15.36 billion while its 1983 liabilities were valued at $3.4 billion. AMR finished 1992 with the healthiest net worth among passenger-carrying airlines, although it placed second in the industry behind UPS.

AMR Corp. Net Worth 1983-1992

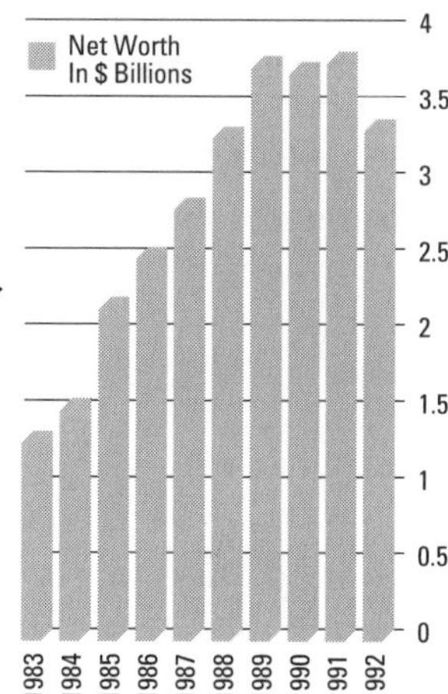

Statistics Related Terms

Assets — A resource having commercial or trade value that is owned (or which the company owns rights to) by a business. Typical examples for an airline include: Cash, securities, property, equipment, capital leases, landing slots and routes.

Available seat miles (ASMs) — Represent the number of seats available for passengers multiplied by the number of scheduled miles those seats are flown.

Cost per available seat mile — Represents operating and interest expense divided by available seat miles.

Financial accounting standard (FAS) 106 — A federally-mandated accounting change made to the way U.S. companies handle post-retirement benefits (other than pensions) to employees. FAS 106, for several U.S. global and major airlines, meant large, one-time, non-cash charges to earnings, further damaging their balance-sheet performance for 1992.

Leveraged buyout (LBO) — Takeover of a company using borrowed funds. Company assets often serve as security for the loans, although investors' assets also may be used.

Liabilities — The total amount the company owes to all creditors.

Net worth or stockholders' equity — The net assets (total assets minus total liabilities) of a company. For companies with more liabilities than assets, the result is a negative net worth or stockholders' deficit.

Passenger load factor — Revenue passenger miles divided by available seat miles over a set period of time.

Revenue passenger miles (RPMs) — The number of miles flown by revenue-producing passengers.

Yield — The average revenue received for each mile a revenue passenger is carried. Determined by dividing total operating revenue by total revenue passenger miles.

American Airlines News Abstracts

"3 Airlines Criticize USAir-British Airways Deal." *The Atlanta Journal-Constitution,* 2 Oct. 1992, sec. G, p. 1.

"AAnd We'll AAim to AApologize For AAll AAberrant AApologies." *Wall Street Journal,* 3 Jan. 1991, sec. B, p. 1, col. 1.

"Action on the North Atlantic." *Air Transport World,* June 1991, pp. 23-28.

"Airline Blasts Pilots for Delays; Contract Talks Climate Sours." *Aviation Week & Space Technology,* 7 Jan. 1991, p. 37.

"Airline Stocks Nosedive as Wall Street Responds Negatively to New Fare Cuts." *Wall Street Journal,* 29 May 1992.

"Airlines Expect $2B Loss in '90." *USA Today,* 17 Jan. 1991.

"Airlines Face Weaker Control of Reservations." *Wall Street Journal,* 13 Aug. 1992.

"American After TWA London Routes/Assets." *Airport Journal,* Jan. 1991, p. 11.

"American Agrees to Buy TWA Routes." *The Atlanta Journal-Constitution,* 3 May 1991.

"American Air Criticizes Its McDonnell Douglas Jet." *Wall Street Journal,* 21 Feb. 1991, sec. B, p. 6, col. 6.

"American Air Places Jet Order." *Wall Street Journal,* 12 Feb. 1991, sec. C, p. 17, col. 6.

"American Air to Ground 11% of Its Flights." *Wall Street Journal,* 7 Jan. 1991, sec. A, p. 3, col. 4.

"American Airlines Chief Delivers Grim Message." *The Atlanta Journal-Constitution,* 19 Nov. 1992, sec. E, p. 8.

"American Airlines Posts Record '91 Loss." *The Atlanta Journal-Constitution,* 16 Jan. 1992, sec. C, p. 3.

"American Airlines' Contract Proposals Rejected by Union." *Wall Street Journal,* 31 Jan. 1991, sec. A, p. 4, col. 2.

"American Alters Its Fleet Upgrade Plans." *Flight International,* 3-9 June 1992, p. 10.

"American Best Airline Says Quality Study." *USA Today,* 5 March 1992, sec. B, p. 1.

"American to Boost Flights." *Wall Street Journal,* 15 Feb. 1991, sec. A, p. 4, col. 1.

"American to Curb West Coast Shuttle." *Wall Street Journal,* 4 Jan. 1991, sec. B, p. 1, col. 3.

"American to Simplify Fares, Shrink Price Range." *Wall Street Journal,* 9 April 1992, sec. B, p. 1.

"American's Less-Than-Exploding Hubs." *Air Transport World,* Sep. 1992, pp. 101-106.

"American's Pilots Want Carrier to Invest in Another Airline to Boost Code-sharing." *Aviation Week & Space Technology,* 3 Feb. 1992, p. 31.

"American, TWA Bid for Pan Am." *The Atlanta Journal-Constitution,* 22 July 1991.

"American, Union Settle Key Contract Issues; Pilots to Pay Some Health Care Costs." *Aviation Week & Space Technology,* 18 Feb. 1991, p. 32.

"American, United Nearly Tied for Biggest U.S. Airline." *The Atlanta Journal-Constitution,* 8 Jan. 1992.

"AMR 1st-Period Profit Was $20 Million; Bleak 2nd Quarter is Seen for Industry." *Wall Street Journal,* 16 April 1992.

"AMR Buys Most Metro Airlines Assets." *The Atlanta Journal-Constitution,* 23 Dec. 1992.

"AMR Had Loss of $85 Million in 3rd Quarter." *Wall Street Journal,* 22 Oct. 1992, sec. A, p. 3.

"AMR is Fighting Many Foes as it Seeks to Finish Buying TWA London Routes." *Wall Street Journal,* 2 April 1991, sec. A, p. 2, col. 3.

"AMR Posts Loss of $195.6 Million for First Quarter." *Wall Street Journal,* 18 April 1991, sec. A, p. 5, col. 4.

"AMR Posts Loss of $200 Million for 4th Quarter." *Wall Street Journal,* 21 Jan. 1993, sec. A, p. 3.

"AMR Reaches Tentative Pact With Its Pilots." *Wall Street Journal,* 11 Feb. 1991, sec. A, p. 4, col. 4.

"AMR Reports $215.1 Million 4th-Period Loss." *Wall Street Journal,* 17 Jan. 1991, sec. B, p. 8, col. 1.

"AMR Won't Take Delivery of MD-11 Due to Problems." *Wall Street Journal,* 27 Feb. 1991, sec. A, p. 6, col. 5.

"Bid Likely to Escalate Price of Pan Am." *The Atlanta Journal-Constitution,* 23 July 1991, sec. C, p. 1.

"Can American and Its Pilots Avert a Collision?" *Business Week,* 21 Jan. 1991, p. 62.

"Clear Skies for American, United, Delta." *USA Today,* 5 Aug. 1991, sec. B, p. 2.

"Continental Sale of Route to AMR Gets U.S. Approval." *Wall Street Journal,* 10 Jan. 1991, sec. B, p. 6, col. 6.

"Crandall: Let Market Work." *The Atlanta Journal-Constitution,* 1 July 1992.

"Dogfight; United and American Battle for Global Supremacy." *Business Week,* 21 Jan. 1991, pp. 56-62.

"Earnings: AMR Stock Rises Despite Huge Loss." *USA Today,* 17 Jan. 1991.

"Expert: Being on Time Isn't Everything for Airlines." *USA Today,* 5 March 1992, sec. B, p. 6.

"Flight Plans: How the Airlines Stack Up." *Wall Street Journal,* 17 June 1991, sec. B, p. 1.

"High Flying American Runs Into Turbulence." *The Atlanta Journal-Constitution,* 17 Jan. 1991, sec. D, p. 1.

"McDonnell Disputes Talk of Problems With MD-11." *Wall Street Journal,* 22 Feb. 1991, sec. B, p. 4, col. 4.

"New Transatlantic Battle Looms as Airline Balance of Power Shifts to Surging Big 3 American Carriers." *Aviation Week & Space Technology,* 22 July 1991, pp. 29-30.

"Open Skies for BA and KLM Only if for U.S. Airlines Too." *Wall Street Journal,* 23 Sep. 1992.

"The American Dream." *Flight International,* 26 Aug.-1 Sep. 1992, pp. 33-35.

"The Battle of O'Hare." *Forbes,* 22 June 1992, p. 40.

"Tokyo, London Routes Buy Approved." *Aviation Week & Space Technology,* 14 Jan. 1991, p. 28.

"TWA Cleared to Sell 3 London Routes to AMR." *Wall Street Journal,* 15 March 1991, sec. A, p. 3.

"United, American Cleared for Landing at London's Heathrow as New Era Dawns." *Wall Street Journal,* 12 March 1991, sec. B, p. 1, col. 3.

4

Continental Airlines

Aviation pioneer Robert Six piloted Continental as it flew mail, survived the war, lasted the Jet Age and thrashed its way through the turbulent '70s. A survivor of two bankruptcies, Continental hopes investment capital and a new image will change its fortune in the 1990s.

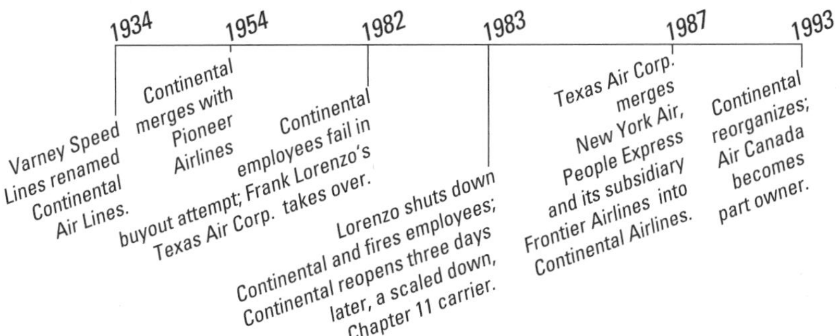

Continental's history goes back to a tiny carrier with a comic book name, Varney Speed Lines, which began airmail service under government contract on July 15, 1934, from Denver to El Paso, Texas. The little airmail carrier was one of four airlines started by Walter Varney. Two of the airlines failed and one figured into United Airlines' past. Soon after starting Varney Speed Lines, Varney left to become a test pilot for Lockheed, giving control of the airline to Louis Mueller.

Mueller remained with Varney and its successors until 1965. Mueller moved the airline's operations from Denver to El Paso and adopted the marketing slogan "Trail of the Conquistadors." He sold a minority interest in Varney in 1936 to Robert Six, another aviation pioneer. Six soon became president and remained in that position for the next 46 years.

Varney Speed Lines operated Lockheed Vega aircraft which seated a maximum of six passengers. Four of the five Vega aircraft in Varney's fleet crashed by mid-1937. Mueller and Six then mortgaged their homes, bought three Lockheed 12s, renamed their airline Continental and moved headquarters back to Denver.

Hardly, so far, the stuff of legends. But Mueller and Six had staying power and government contracts.

Continental Airlines
Aircraft fleet and purchase commitments
As of May 1993

Aircraft Type	Current Fleet	Firm Orders	Options
A-330	21	0	0
B-727	85	0	0
B-737	88	50	50
B-747	7	0	0
B-757	0	25	25
B-767	0	12	18
B-777B	0	5	5
DC-9	34	0	0
DC-10	20	0	0
MD-80	64	0	0
Total	319	92	98

Continental, operating under the slogan "Fly the old Sante Fe Trail," became the first scheduled airline to file a route application with the Civil Aviation Authority (CAA) created in 1938. Yet the CAA was slow to respond to Continental's requests for more routes, and Continental was providing service to only seven cities by the end of 1940. Then World War II brought the airline its first taste of financial stability when the company received a government contract to modify military aircraft. Continental primarily was a mod shop in the years 1942 to 1945, modifying 2,000 B-17s, 400 B-29s and numerous P-51s. The company did establish routes into Kansas, Texas and Oklahoma in 1944 and 1945, but Continental entered the postwar period still a small airline.

Growth remained slow. Stymied in its attempts to generate passenger revenue, Continental entered an agreement with Sears Roebuck & Co. to ship merchandise between Kansas City and Denver.

Continental used the 1950s to mature. Its 1954 merger with Pioneer Airlines helped since this gave Continental access to Dallas/Fort Worth and Austin. It already flew into Houston. Continental received authority in 1955 to fly between Chicago and Los Angeles. To support its service expansion, the company ordered four B-707s, five Viscounts and five DC-7Bs. Arrival of the B-707 in 1959 ushered in the Jet Age for Continental. Arrival of the DC-7Bs brought a marketing campaign called "Gold Carpet Service" which called for white-gloved supervisors to meet flights and roll out a gold carpet for the passengers.

Continental still was a small airline entering the 1960s, albeit a jet airline with some truly "Continental" routes. The 1960s brought more government largesse and a more rapid expansion than Continental had yet achieved.

The Civil Aeronautics Board (CAB) in 1961 granted Continental authority to fly nonstop between Houston and Los Angeles, and Continental moved its corporate headquarters to Los Angeles two years later. In 1964 the company received an Air Force contract to fly from Travis Air Force Base, Calif., via Honolulu or Anchorage, Alaska, to Tokyo, Okinawa, Taipei, Clark Air Base, Saigon, Danang, Cam Ranh Bay and Bangkok. This contract lasted until 1973 when U.S. military involvement in Southeast Asia finally wound down.

Continental established a subsidiary in 1965, Continental Air Services, headquartered in Bangkok, Thailand with flight operations based at Vientiane, Laos. This subsidiary supported U.S. military operations in Indochina during the Vietnam War and lasted until 1975.

Continental, capitalizing on its new Pacific experience and desiring expanded operations, combined with United Micronesia Development Corp. and Aloha Airlines in 1966 to form Air Micronesia. This Continental affiliate originally served nine islands in the Trust Territories of the Pacific using two B-727s. It added service to Guam and Saipan. Air Micronesia supported a new tourist industry with direct links to Japan. The airline also was the only transportation link between these small islands and was important to the Trust Territories government and U.S. military facilities for movement of cargo, mail and passengers. It was not profitable, however, and lost money in 11 of its first 13 years of service.

While Air Micronesia brought red ink to Continental, almost everything was in the red at Texas International. TI experienced serious financial difficulties about the time Continental had its headiest success.

Trans-Texas Airways/Texas International

Trans-Texas Airways, the forerunner of Texas International, began service Oct. 11, 1947, with two DC-3s and 96 employees. The brainchild of R. E. McKaughan, Trans-Texas Airways flew to eight cities in Texas. Trans-Texas extended its service to Arkansas, Louisiana, Tennessee and Mississippi in the early 1950s.

Trans-Texas added routes to New Mexico in 1963 and to Mexico in 1966. Minnesota Enterprises Inc., a Midwestern bus company, bought Trans-Texas in 1968 and changed the name to Texas International Airlines. The airline added service later in 1969 to Denver. Los Angeles and Salt Lake City became TI service points in 1970, and it added Mexico City in 1972.

But, Texas International was bleeding to death by 1971. Chase Manhattan Bank hired Francisco "Frank" A. Lorenzo and Robert J. Carney, principals in a financial consulting partnership begun on just $2,000, to devise a salvage plan for TI. Lorenzo and Carney quickly worked out a deal to take Texas International off Chase Manhattan's hands: a $35-million refinancing that gave Lorenzo and Carney (through Jet Capital Corp., their holding company) 59 percent of the voting rights in TI. The paper trail shows that the $1.3 million ostensibly paid by Jet Capital for TI was a paper-only transaction. The consulting fees paid to Lorenzo and Carney by Chase Manhattan permitted the two young deal-makers to recover the $35,000 they invested in the takeover. Chase Manhattan, TI's major creditor, deferred its claims, and the people at Texas International had a new future: Frank Lorenzo.

Lorenzo and Carney were as decisive at the helm of TI as in conference with Chase Manhattan officials. They eliminated unprofitable routes, raised fares and tried to slash costs. The cost-cutting ran head-on into TI's 80-percent union work force, but Lorenzo bored ahead. The Air Line Employees Association (ALEA) called a strike that had the potential to destroy the company, yet, fueled by $8 million in mutual-aid contributions from other airlines, Texas International sailed through 1975 with only a $4.2-million loss.

TI, to regain market share lost during the strike, started an aggressive low-fares marketing campaign to lure cost-sensitive passengers. Backed by considerable government subsidies on several routes, the strategy worked and TI showed a 1976 profit of $3.5 million. Profits continued to grow over the next three years, peaking in 1979 at $41.4 million.

The year of TI's peak was a watershed year for Continental. The crash of an American Airlines DC-10 at Chicago's O'Hare International that killed 272 people prompted the FAA to ground the nation's entire DC-10 fleet for investigation of flaws and corrective modifications. This move crippled Continental which had a large portion of its capacity tied up in the DC-10. This also was the year of fuel crisis because of an Arab oil embargo that the Carter administration could not break. Continental suffered a 1979 loss of $13 million. The next year, Robert Six retired as president of Continental and Alvin L. Feldman took over.

Continental Airlines
Aircraft fleet: 1983-1992

Aircraft	1983	1984	1985	1986	1987	1988	1989	1990	1991	1992
A-300	—	—	—	6	12	12	12	17	23	23
B-727	60	64	64	106	106	96	94	94	100	89
B-737	—	1	16	86	99	97	94	94	94	91
B-747	—	—	—	8	8	8	8	9	8	7
DC-9	34	41	29	47	46	41	41	41	34	34
DC-10	11	13	15	16	15	15	15	17	17	20
MD-80	—	—	11	45	66	65	65	65	61	64
Total	105	119	135	314	352	334	329	337	337	328

The change of guard looked promising: A mechanical engineer with stints at General Dynamics in San Diego and at Aerojet General Corp., a subsidiary of General Tire, Feldman had one resounding success behind him. General Tire placed Feldman in charge of its aviation subsidiary, Frontier Airlines, and in 1971 Feldman pulled Frontier out of a financial hole and restored its profitability.

Feldman initiated merger talks with Western Air Lines. The CAB began a mandatory administrative review that was expected to lead to approval by the spring of 1981. Then a double hammer stroke of fate changed Continental's future.

The first stroke was the size of Continental's 1980 losses, aggravated by internal frictions that surfaced near the end of the year when the airline's flight attendants struck. Since the pilots and machinists did not join the flight attendants on the picket line, the main effect of the 12-day strike was to call attention to labor unrest, although the December turmoil did contribute to Continental's $21-million loss.

Frank Lorenzo activated the second stroke in early 1981 when he announced that Texas Air Corp. had acquired 9.5 percent of Continental's stock and intended to make an offer for a controlling interest.

The move was well-timed. TI's fortunes had changed radically, but the world did not yet know that 1981 would result in a $34.9-million loss. Causes for the loss: DOT subsidies, the magic carpet for TI, were reduced sharply at the same time that Southwest Airlines, a tough new competitor, cut into the margins. Even TI's famous "peanut fares," cut-to-the-bone interstate ticket prices started in the last months before the airline industry deregulated, could not blunt the onslaught of Southwest.

Lorenzo was convinced that TI had to expand to prosper. Already in the summer of 1978 TI made a bid for National Airlines with Eastern and Pan Am joining the chase shortly thereafter. Although Pan Am eventually acquired National, TI made a capital gain of $34.6 million from the sale of its 9.2 percent share of National stock. Lorenzo then followed the same pattern in an attempt to acquire TWA: Rebuffed, he nonetheless added millions to Texas Air's acquisition fund when TWA bought him off.

Lorenzo began his effort to acquire Continental with two competing theories about the airline industry. On one hand, he held to the "upstart" theory that small, never-regulated airlines like Southwest quickly could outmaneuver older companies configured to respond to a regulated environment. He tested this theory by creating non-union New York Air in 1980. On the other hand, Lorenzo began to feel that TI would need "critical mass" to survive.

Lorenzo created Texas Air Corp. in June 1980 as a holding company for Texas International and New York Air, and in early 1981 he went after Continental. Continental's employees began a crusade to buy the company through an employee stock option plan (ESOP) to thwart the takeover. Simultaneously, Continental's management continued its attempt to merge the airline with Western. As tensions stretched to the breaking point during this period, Feldman, Continental's president, died.

Lorenzo won the takeover war and on Oct. 31, 1982, Texas International Inc. and Continental Airlines Inc. merged. Next, Lorenzo created Continental Airlines Corp. as a holding company for the Houston-based Continental and Texas International.

New ownership was not a magic cure for Continental. The carrier experienced a $41.8-million loss in 1982 and a $218.4-million loss in 1983. Blaming high labor costs for Continental's difficulties, Lorenzo requested $150 million in concessions from his employees by Sept. 19, 1983. Continental pilots already agreed to significant wage and work rule concessions in 1981 and 1982. A dispute continues to this day among pilots involved in that labor-management confrontation over whether Lorenzo's conditions were issued as an ultimatum: ALPA's national leaders say yes; pilots who crossed the subsequent picket lines say no.

In any event, on Sept. 24, 1983, Lorenzo closed Continental's doors on an hour's notice and filed for protection under Chapter 11 federal bankruptcy provisions. Then he fired all 12,000 employees. A scaled-down Continental Airlines was flying again within three days of the filing, offering reduced fares.

Continental rehired 4,000 former employees to staff its operations at 40 percent to 60 percent of their previous wages. It also invoked emergency work rules for its pilots. ALPA responded on Oct. 1 by calling a strike. The flight attendants' union, though spurned by the pilots during its own 12-day strike of December 1980, supported the pilots. Even so, the strike failed when 4,000 employees crossed the picket lines. A majority of pilots who crossed the line signed a petition to remove ALPA as representative, though ALPA maintained the union legally could not be decertified without an official election.

Continental remained in bankruptcy for three years and, shielded from its creditors, expanded. The carrier earned profits of $50.3 million in 1984 and $61.9 million in 1985. Cynics suggested that Lorenzo extolled the virtues of deregulation while using a form of "government subsidy" — protection from creditors and unions — to build Continental back to the competitive strength it enjoyed under the military and other government subsidies of the Vietnam War era.

Continental labored under a severe handicap in its comeback bid: It had no computer reservations system to match those of American and United. And Lorenzo continued to yearn for "critical mass." So, after making a second bid to acquire TWA and failing again (TWA's unions sided with Carl Icahn, a rival bidder for TWA), Lorenzo captured Eastern Airlines in February 1986. Financial circles regarded Texas Air's $640-million deal for Eastern and its 300 aircraft, multitude of routes and System One CRS operation as a steal. The purchase also included $3 billion in debt and a cash fund of $463 million. Texas Air resisted legal and political action by ALPA and the International Association of Machinists and Aerospace Workers to force the merger of Eastern with Continental. The merger would have brought Eastern's unions into Continental where they could have campaigned to represent Continental's non-union employees. Texas Air quickly spirited System One away from Eastern, however, as well as numerous routes it gave to Continental.

Still, Continental was not growing fast enough, so Texas Air acquired non-union People Express on Dec. 30, 1986, a purchase that brought with it the bankrupt Frontier Airlines. Also acquired in this deal: 72 airplanes, about 1,000 non-union pilots and an additional $750 million in long-term debt.

Now Continental's fleet was too diverse and People Express' operations did not meld easily into Continental's. In 1987, Continental lost $258.1 million on revenues of $4.1 billion. The battle against red ink continued in 1988 as Continental lost $315.5 million, but in 1989 the carrier finally reported a profit, $3.1 million.

Continental's executive offices have had a revolving door. After Alvin Feldman's death, George Warde, a former president of American Airlines, served as Continental's president until December 1982. Stephen Wolf, a former vice president at Pan Am, succeeded him. Phil Bakes came next, taking over in April 1984 and staying until October 1986, when he left Continental to become president at Eastern Air Lines. Thomas Plaskett, who came to Continental from American, replaced Bakes. Plaskett stayed only nine months before he decamped for Pan Am to become president. Martin Shugrue replaced Plaskett in October 1987 after being removed from the Pan Am board of directors, but he lasted only until February 1989 when D. Joseph Corr succeeded him. Corr came to Continental from TWA where he was credited with turning TWA's operation around. But Corr left eight months later, replaced by Mickey Foret, previously the executive vice president for finance and planning at Continental.

Fresh air swept through Continental in August 1990. Scandinavian Airline Systems (SAS), renowned

Continental Airlines Financial Statistics

(In millions)	1983	1984	1985	1986	1987	1988	1989	1990	1991	1992
Sales	1,113	1,185	1,705	2,273	4,124	4,698	5,077	5,281	5,551	5,575
Net Income (loss)	(218.4)	50.3	61.9	43	(258.1)	(315.5)	3.1	(2,343.9)[1]	(305.7)	(125.3)
Assets	908	1,080	1,271	2,948	3,831	3,994	3,934	3,415	3,523	3,328
Liabilities	1,017	1,135	1,258	2,676	3,432	3,899	3,847	6,850	7,263	7,194
Net Worth	(109.1)	(54.7)	13.2	271.7	398.4	94.9	86.7	(3,435)	(3,740)	(3,866)
ASMs	15,396	17,414	25,320	36,787	64,176	66,487	62,891	64,844	66,196	67,881
RPMs	9,274	10,923	16,407	22,910	39,637	40,498	38,772	39,174	41,433	43,072
Load Factors	61.3%	62.7%	64.8%	62.3%	61.8%	60.9%	61.7%	60.4%	62.6%	63.5%

[1] Includes impact of Eastern Air Lines' Chapter 11 and liquidation proceedings. Some of the losses (write-offs associated with the Pension Benefit Guaranty Corp.) were renegotiated.

for its fine customer service and esprit de corps, bought the bulk of Lorenzo's stake in Continental Airlines Holdings Inc. for more than $17 million and Lorenzo turned over the helm of Continental to Hollis L. Harris, who retired as president and chief operating officer of Delta Air Lines on Aug. 9, 1990.

Some people felt the changes only could do Continental good. Yet when high fuel prices devoured the cash reserves that normally would service Continental's heavy debt, Harris had no choice but to take Continental into Chapter 11 in December 1990. The move accorded well with the carrier's checkered past.

Continental Airlines seized a high ground in public perception out of proportion to its economic importance when its fate became entangled with that of Texas International, Lorenzo's first airline. Continental until then always was a marginally-successful-to-shaky airline that depended in one way or another on government largesse for its better years. An investor looking at the years from 1982 to the arrival of Harris might conclude that the more things change for this airline, the more they stay the same.

Continental Airlines had an operating profit of $8.8 million in the first quarter of 1990 and a total profit, including one-time gains, of $21.3 million. Continental's situation worsened as fuel prices rose and recession crimped sales, and by year's end the carrier had an operating loss of $427 million. Total 1990 sales came to $5.281 billion, compared to $5.077 billion in 1989.

Continental blamed erosion of load factors, RPMs and revenues on the economy, rising fuel prices, fears related to war and terrorism, and the Frank Lorenzo legacy which left Continental strapped with debt and sent Hollis L. Harris searching for the business flier who abandoned the airline.

Harris also sought a buyer for System One after Electronic Data Systems, a General Motors subsidiary, canceled its agreement to buy Continental's CRS. Atlanta-based Worldspan discussed with Continental Holdings its interest in buying the CRS part of Continental's System One in early 1991. System One formerly belonged to Eastern.

The largest part of Continental's debt load was from off-balance-sheet aircraft leases totaling $4.4 billion. Twelve aircraft companies agreed to defer, reduce or forgive lease payments on 98 airplanes in Continental's fleet in a restructuring package worth nearly $190 million in savings for the airline. The leasing debt agreement, while not solving Continental's debt problems, did shave $2 million a month from the carrier's debt service costs.

Continental already had a wisp of good news in January when the Department of Transportation approved the sale of its Seattle-Tokyo route to AMR Corp. for $150 million. And the airline's pilots agreed to forgo a pay raise and defer an incentive payment tied to fuel savings.

Other achievements of Continental after filing bankruptcy:

The carrier added 44 New York-area departures, replacing many of Eastern's Florida runs.

It bought from Eastern six Airbus A-300 planes and 64 slots and six gates at New York's La Guardia Airport.

It launched a new image campaign with plans to spend up to $50 million to repaint planes, change the corporate logo and put employees in new uniforms.

The bad news is that Continental lost $194.8 million in the first quarter of 1991 — $157.8 million on an operating basis (excluding costs related to bankruptcy-law proceedings). Continental's total first-quarter loss was only $1.2 million less than that of AMR Corp., parent of American Airlines, which is twice Continental's size.

Continental was the subject of much merger interest despite its less-than-attractive balance sheet. Northwest was one known suitor. President Hollis Harris quickly ended further merger speculation by informing employees in a taped message the company stopped any discussions that might lead to an acquisition by another airline. Also, Harris told employees, Continental no longer would consider selling major chunks of assets: it would remain independent, focusing on expansion, and on upgrading and enhancing its image.

Management's plans, however, were short-lived. Continental confirmed in May 1991 it was talking with several groups about buying part of the company. The carrier sought $600 million in capital and wanted to restructure its $4.5-billion secured debt and more than $2.5 billion in unsecured claims. Continental did arrange in June for $120 million in debtor-in-possession financing, principally from Chase Manhattan Bank.

In a sharp reversal from Harris' strategy, the company announced in August it would ground 22 planes, reduce its flight schedule by 6 percent and eliminate 600 jobs. "We are at war with forces within the company and outside the company," Harris told employees in a taped phone message. "I ask all the people of Continental and all the friends of Continental to join those already praying daily....God will show us a way to survive." The day after his plea, Harris resigned, reportedly under pressure from company directors unhappy with the airline's spiraling costs. Robert Ferguson, formerly Continental's executive vice president and a lieutenant of Lorenzo, replaced Harris and became the airline's ninth CEO in nine years. Joining Ferguson at the top were two other Lorenzo allies: Lewis Jordan and Charles Goolsbee.

Ferguson and Co. bid a hasty retreat to Continental's "pre-Harris" days; they quickly set about cutting jobs and wages, and selling assets to reduce costs and raise cash. The first casualty: the bulk of the New York La Guardia operation, bought just eight months earlier from Eastern, sold to USAir for $61 million. Ferguson also eliminated 890 management and clerical positions, instituted a pay cut for company officers and imposed a six-month wage freeze on all non-contract employees.

Continental workers continued to bear the brunt of the ailing economy. Management reduced employee wages by $108 million—an average 10 percent reduction per worker—in response to American Airlines' fare initiative. Speculation that continued wage cuts would fuel union interest was tempered when the International Association of Machinists ratified a new collective bargaining agreement with Continental's 6,500 flight attendants in June, the first such pact in nine years. But, months earlier, a group calling itself the Independent Association of Continental Pilots petitioned the National Mediation Board to represent Continental pilots—among the lowest paid in the industry—and pilots at regional affiliate Continental Express.

Meanwhile, Continental began to attract serious investor interest despite its growing labor unrest. An October 1992 *USA Today* article described the carrier as "the Scarlett O'Hara of airlines" in reference to its "growing bevy of eager suitors...." What made Continental so attractive? Its three key hubs where it enjoyed a 35-percent market share in Denver, a 78-percent share in Houston and a 50-percent market share in Newark. Also enticing were its low labor costs and position as the fifth-largest U.S. airline based on revenue passenger miles (RPMs). Potential buyers included AeroMexico and Houston-based firm Maxxam's Charles Hurwitz who bid $400 million; Alfredo Brener, whose family controls Mexicana Airlines, who bid $385 million; Air Canada, led by former Continental CEO Hollis Harris, and two Fort Worth investors who bid $425 million; Lufthansa German Airlines and billionaire Marvin Davis who bid $400 million; and Florida Air president Jack Robinson, a former Continental executive, who offered $425 million.

Soon the investor field narrowed to just two. Continental accepted the bid from Air Canada and Air Partners in November 1992, and Continental's creditors approved the company's reorganization plan in February 1993. Continental emerged from Chapter 11 bankruptcy in April after Air Canada and Air Partners L.P. invested $450 million for a combined 54 percent of the company. Air Canada, due to U.S. foreign ownership laws, maintains a 24-percent voting interest in Continental while Air Partners retains a 41-percent voting interest.

Continental Airlines Holdings' net loss in the fourth quarter of 1992 was $14 million with year-end net losses totaling $125.3 million.

The senior executives responsible for Continental's decision-making, operations and maintenance at the time of publication are Robert R. Ferguson III, president and chief executive officer; Charles T. Goolsbee, executive vice president of corporate affairs; John E. Luth, senior vice president of restructuring; and Donald Valentine, senior vice president of marketing.

Continental Airlines Statistics

1992 Total Sales
Global/Major Airlines

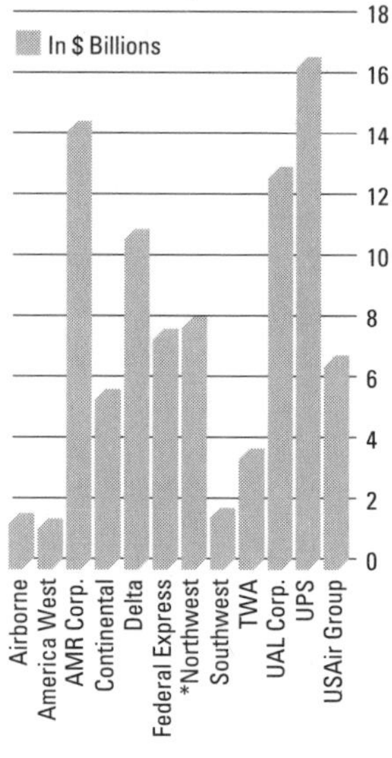

• Information is for Northwest Airlines only and not for parent company NWA Inc.

Continental Airlines Holdings Inc. (CAH) earned $5.58 billion in revenues in 1992.

Continental experienced a 401-percent increase in sales since 1983.

In the 1990s, sales increased 9.8 percent. Continental may experience faster growth now that it emerged a second time from Chapter 11 bankruptcy protection with $450 million in cash to help it expand.

Continental Airlines Holdings Inc.
Total Sales 1983-1992

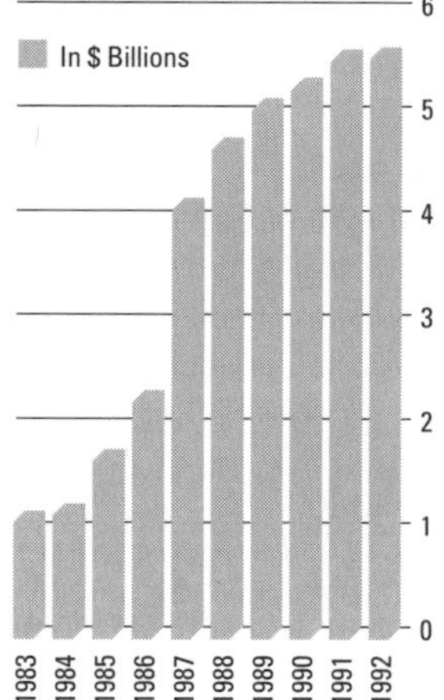

1992 Net Income
Global/Major Airlines

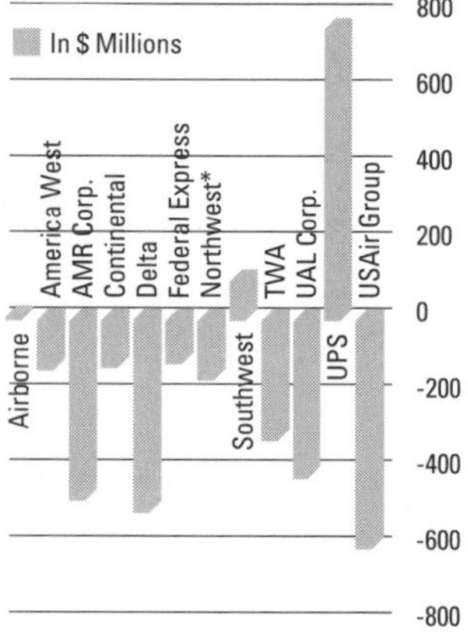

• Information is for Northwest Airlines only and not for parent company NWA Inc.

CAH finished 1992 with a net loss of $125.3 million.

Continental Airlines Holdings lost $431 million in 1991-92, including an improved net loss of $125.3 million in 1992.

Continental Airlines Holdings Inc.
Net Income 1983-1992

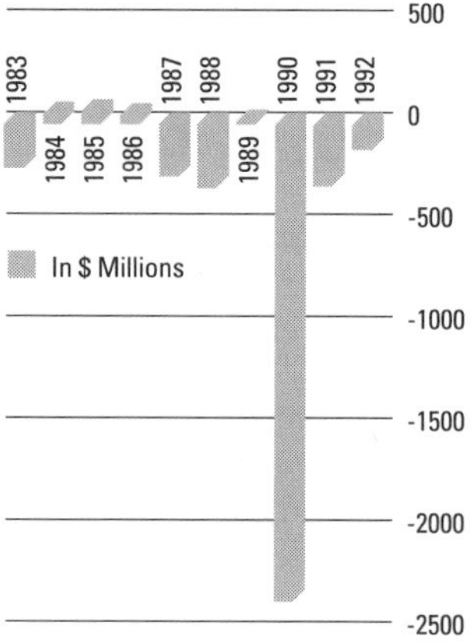

1992 Total Assets & Liabilities

Global/Major Airlines

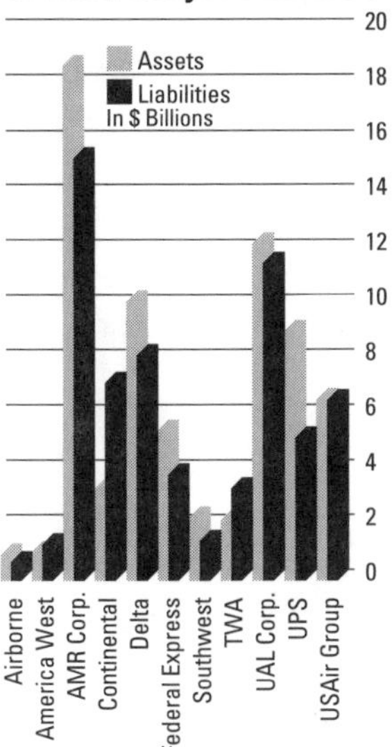

NWA Inc. is a privately held company and would not release 1990-1992 figures.

Continental finished 1992 with total assets valued at $3.33 billion.

This made Continental the eighth largest U.S. airline in the industry in terms of total assets.

Continental's total liabilities at the end of 1992 were $7.19 billion resulting in a net stockholders' deficit of $3.87 billion.

Continental's total assets grew 340 percent from 1983 to 1988, then decreased 16.7 percent between 1988 and 1992.

Total liabilities during this period increased 670 percent from $1 billion in 1983 to $7.19 billion in 1992.

Continental's long-term debt at the end of 1992 was $204.2 million, although its emergence from bankruptcy could have a positive impact on Continental's long-term debt.

Continental Airlines Holdings Inc.

Assets & Liabilities 1983-1992

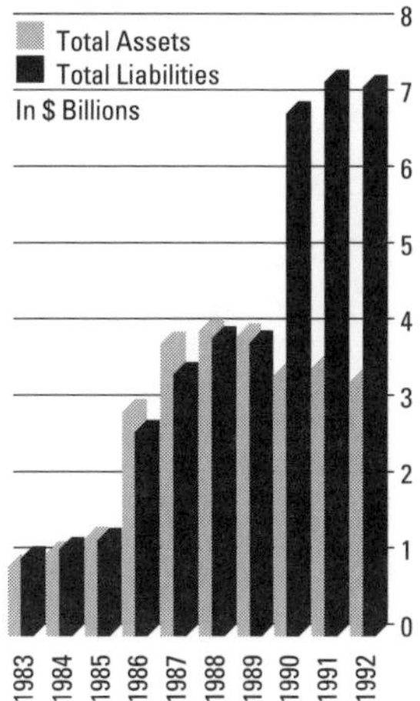

1992 ASMs & RPMs

Global/Major Airlines

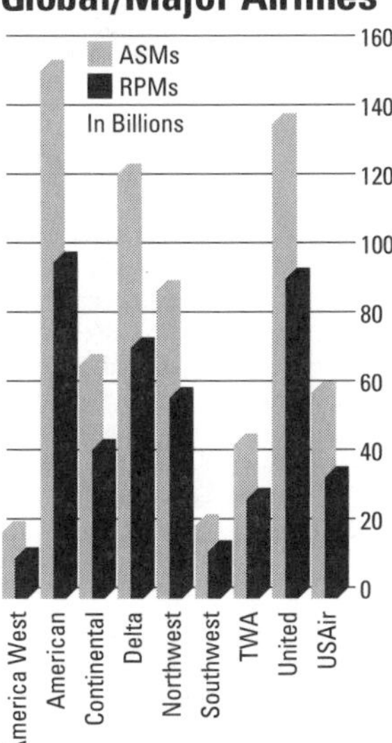

Continental finished 1992 as the fifth-largest airline in terms of both available seat miles (ASMs) and revenue passenger miles (RPMs) flown.

Continental's ASMs grew 332 percent between 1983 and 1988, then grew only 2.1 percent from 1988 to 1992.

RPMs jumped 337 percent from 1983 to 1988, but increased only 6.4 percent from 1988 to 1992.

Continental's capacity in 1992 increased for the third consecutive year.

Continental

ASMs & RPMs 1983-1992

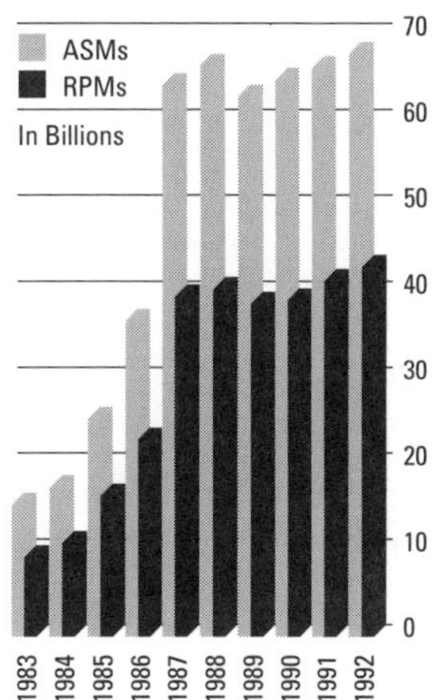

1992 Net Worth
Global/Major Airlines

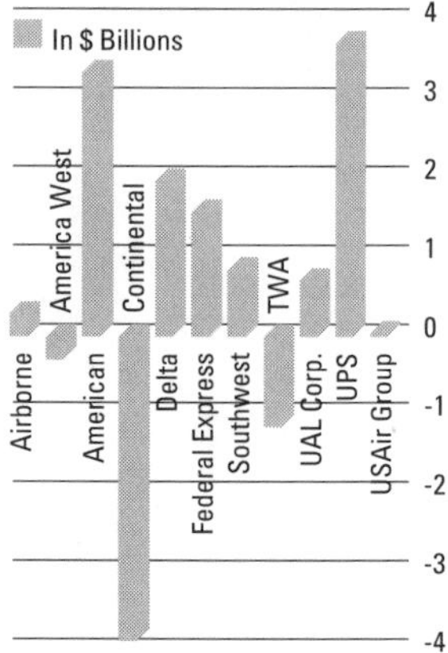

NWA Inc. is a privately held company and would not release 1990-1992 figures.

Continental has the lowest net worth (largest stockholders' deficit) of any U.S. airline. Its liabilities, however, could be reduced significantly by its emergence from bankruptcy and reorganization of debt.

After maintaining positive net worths from 1985-89, the 1990s thus far haven't been kind to Continental in the net worth department because of the demise of Eastern Air Lines and other factors.

Continental Airlines Holdings Inc.
Net Worth 1983-1992

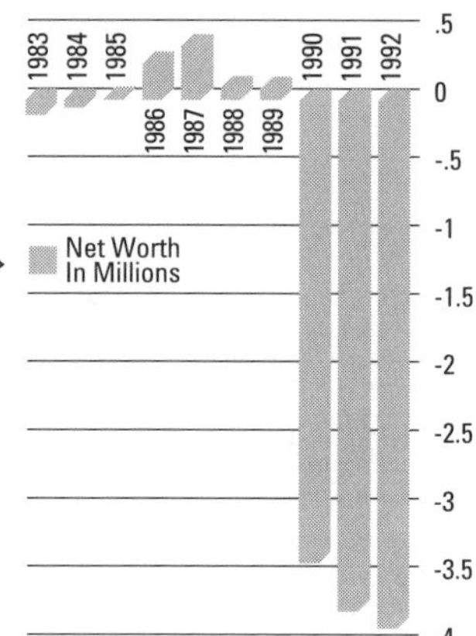

Statistics Related Terms

Assets — A resource having commercial or trade value that is owned (or which the company owns rights to) by a business. Typical examples for an airline include: Cash, securities, property, equipment, capital leases, landing slots and routes.

Available Seat Miles (ASMs) — Represent the number of seats available for passengers multiplied by the number of scheduled miles those seats are flown.

Cost per available seat mile — Represents operating and interest expense divided by available seat miles.

Financial Accounting Standard (FAS) 106 — A federally-mandated accounting change made to the way U.S. companies handle post-retirement benefits (other than pensions) to employees. FAS 106, for several U.S. global and major airlines, meant large, one-time, non-cash charges to earnings, further damaging their balance-sheet performance for 1992.

Leveraged Buyout (LBO) — Takeover of a company using borrowed funds. Company assets often serve as security for the loans, although investors' assets also may be used.

Liabilities — The total amount the company owes to all creditors.

Net worth or stockholders' equity — The net assets (total assets minus total liabilities) of a company. For companies with more liabilities than assets, the result is a negative net worth or stockholders' deficit.

Passenger load factor — Revenue passenger miles divided by available seat miles over a set period of time.

Revenue passenger miles (RPMs) — The number of d miles flown by revenue-producing passengers.

Yield — The average revenue received for each mile a revenue passenger is carried. Determined by dividing total operating revenue by total revenue passenger miles.

Continental Airlines News Abstracts

"Air Canada Gets Time to Study Making Bid for Continental Air." *Wall Street Journal,* 23 July 1992.

"Air Partners Names Two More Investors in Bid With Air Canada for Continental." *Wall Street Journal,* 11 Nov. 1992.

"Continental Air Finally Arranges Bank Financing." *Wall Street Journal,* 14 June 1991.

"Continental Air Gets Fourth Bid in Three Months." *Wall Street Journal,* 17 Sep. 1992, sec. A, p. 3.

"Continental Air Gets Some Relief on Lease Payments." *Wall Street Journal,* 4 Feb. 1991, sec. B, p. 7, col. 1.

"Continental Air May be Target of Perot Group." *Wall Street Journal,* 3 Sep. 1991, sec. A, p. 4.

"Continental Air Posts Loss of $194.8 Million for the First Quarter." *Wall Street Journal,* 1 May 1991.

"Continental Air Reaches Accord on Some Debt." *Wall Street Journal,* 3 April 1991, sec. A, p. 3, col. 4.

"Continental Air to Cut $108 Million in Wages; Northwest to Fire 110 Pilots." *Wall Street Journal,* 25 June 1992, sec. A, p. 6, col. 1.

"Continental Air to Sell Interest in Air Micronesia." *Wall Street Journal,* 29 Oct. 1991, sec. A, p. 4, col. 1.

"Continental Airlines Gets $425 Million Bid." *Wall Street Journal,* 1 Oct. 1992.

"Continental Airlines Holdings' Creditors Seek to Sue Former Chairman Lorenzo." *Wall Street Journal,* 13 Feb. 1992.

"Continental Airlines is Expected to Sell Air Micronesia Interest for $250 Million." *Wall Street Journal,* 11 Oct. 1991.

"Continental Airlines Plans Attempt to Upgrade Image." *Wall Street Journal,* 13 Feb. 1991, sec. A, p. 4, col. 2.

"Continental Airlines, Eastern Air Creditors Reach Tentative Pact." *Wall Street Journal,* 13 July 1992.

"Continental Digs Its Way Out of Trouble." *Flight International,* 15-21 May 1991, p. 11.

"Continental Faces Hurdles in Proving Predatory Pricing by American Airlines." *Wall Street Journal,* 11 June 1992.

"Continental Flying Into More Turbulence." *The Atlanta Journal-Constitution,* 23 Aug. 1991, sec. G, p. 3.

"Continental Sale of Route to AMR Gets U.S. Approval." *Wall Street Journal,* 10 Jan. 1991, sec. B, p. 6, col. 6.

"Continental to Take Over 3 Gates at Hartsfield." *The Atlanta Journal-Constitution,* 5 June 1991.

"Continental: Writing the Book on Chapter 11." *Business Week,* 18 March 1991, p. 35.

"District Court Upholds Continental Lease Pacts." *Aviation Week & Space Technology,* 8 April 1991, p. 32.

"Eastern Slots, Gates are Purchased by Two Carriers." *Wall Street Journal,* 19 Feb. 1991, sec. A, p. 15, col. 1.

"Eastern's Failure May Hurt Other Stragglers." *USA Today,* 22 Jan. 1991.

"Flight of Fantasy: Northwest, Continental Merger." *USA Today,* 23 Aug. 1991, sec. B.

"Lorenzo to Pay Continental's Creditors $5 Million." *The Atlanta Journal-Constitution,* 9 Jan. 1993.

"Officials in Denver, Houston Fear Continental's Fiscal Woes." *Aviation Week & Space Technology,* 9 Sep. 1991, pp. 30-31.

"Parent of Continental Air Posts Loss Totaling $2.25 Billion for 4th Quarter." *Wall Street Journal,* 22 March 1991, sec. A, p. 2, col. 5.

"The Calamities of Continental." *Air Transport World,* Oct. 1991, pp. 48-56.

"TWA, Continental Talk of Merger, Despite Debt." *Wall Street Journal,* 13 Dec. 1991.

5

Delta Air Lines

Unlike other carriers with one vocation, airmail delivery, Delta Air Lines combined its mail service with another specialty: crop-dusting. A hub-and-spoke pioneer, Delta grew from its Southern heritage to global prominence.

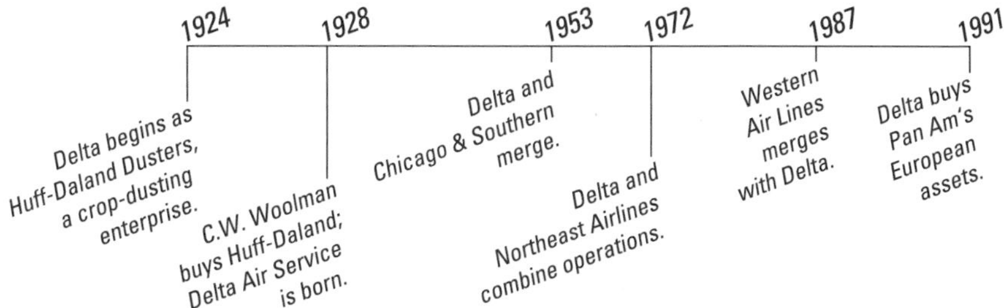

Delta rose to prominence from its origin in 1924 as a public-spirited service to farmers. Delta began as a crop-dusting company and continued that business through 1966. It did not operate its first passenger flight until June 17, 1929 (Dallas to Jackson, Miss.), and even then, passenger transport took a back seat to crop-dusting and, later, airmail and support of World War II military operations.

When cotton was king in the South and tens of thousands of bales of it lined nearly every commercial river wharf and rail freight depot, the boll weevil was a mite-sized Attila the Hun. Against the devastation wreaked by the boll weevil, C. W. Woolman, an agricultural engineer and aeronautical enthusiast, organized Huff-Daland Dusters, a subsidiary of Huff-Daland Manufacturing Co. of New York. Woolman wanted to provide fast, efficient aerial application of lead arsenate, then the only effective insecticide against the boll weevil. After a tentative first year of operations out of Macon, Ga., Huff-Daland Dusters moved its headquarters to Monroe, La., in 1925 to take advantage of Monroe's centrality with respect to the South's larger cotton fields.

The parent company, Huff-Daland Manufacturing, built the first plane designed specifically for crop-dusting, and Huff-Daland Dusters' 1925 fleet of 18 planes then was the largest privately-owned aircraft fleet in the world. Soon the fleet was 25 airplanes strong, in assorted sizes, and was known as "Ton of Dust."

Delta Air Lines
Aircraft fleet and purchase commitments
As of May 1993

Aircraft Type	Current Fleet	Firm Orders	Options
A-310	22	8	0
B-727	152	0	0
B-737	73	33	78
B-757	84	6	38
B-767	51	11	11
L-1011	56	8	29
MD-11	9	8	29
MD-88	115	10	4
MD-90	0	26	134
Total	562	110	323

The five years from 1926 to 1930 saw swift changes in the company. Woolman expanded his crop-dusting operations to Peru, where the seasons were reversed, to give his company year-round revenues. While there, Huff-Daland Dusters became the first North American airline to operate an airmail route in South America, a 1,500-mile journey between points in Peru and Ecuador.

Woolman, with the aid of Monroe businessmen, bought the assets of Huff-Daland Dusters from the parent company in 1928, and in November the company became Delta Air Service. D. Y. Smith, Sr. became the first president while Woolman retained the titles of vice president and general manager. Smith and Woolman then led Delta through the difficult Depression years.

Delta sold its South American airmail route to Pan American Grace in 1928, and sold its crop dusters to a Peruvian firm. Delta changed its name to Delta Air Corp. in 1930. At a time when airmail contracts determined whether an airline would live or die, Smith and Woolman pulled Delta through the critical Depression years of 1930-1933 without such a contract (Delta did not receive its first U.S. airmail contract until July 4, 1934). Crop-dusting and airmail were the core of Delta's business in the years 1934 through 1939, but in 1940 the Civil Aeronautics Board (CAB) worked a revolution in Delta's future by awarding the carrier several air routes radiating from Atlanta. Delta moved its general offices and overhaul base to Atlanta in 1941.

Delta, like other airlines, performed work for the government during World War II. It modified aircraft for the military and maintained a military supply route. This work provided a stable economic base for Delta's gradual buildup of passenger service near the end of the war. Delta, responding to its reorganized revenue base, adopted its present name, Delta Air Lines Inc., on Dec. 18, 1945.

Chicago & Southern Air Lines

Delta found its growth path intersecting those of other airlines after World War II. The first of these was Chicago & Southern Air Lines (C&S) which began in California as Pacific Seaboard Airlines, but changed its name and geographic location after winning the Chicago-New Orleans airmail route. Pacific Seaboard began airmail service on June 3, 1934, and in December 1935 became Chicago & Southern Air Lines with operations in the Mississippi Valley.

Carleton Putnam, founder and president of Chicago & Southern, led the carrier during the 1930s and 1940s to a reputation as a profitable and well-managed airline serving the South Central United States before expanding service into the Caribbean in the early 1950s.

The Caribbean was not enough, Putnam felt: Chicago & Southern needed further expansion to remain competitive. But, given economic and regulatory constraints, Chicago & Southern's only realistic chance of expanding was through merger. Putnam surveyed the scene and concluded that complementary route systems and a shared business philosophy made a merger with Delta Air Lines the best choice. He entered into discussions with Delta, and on May 1, 1953, the CAB approved the merger. The merger worked: Route systems fit hand-in-glove and both airlines had a "family" atmosphere that instilled company-wide esprit de corps.

A beefed-up Delta became a leader in the transition into the Jet Age. Delta was the first airline to bring the DC-8, Convair 880 and DC-9 into service. It also inaugurated the hub-and-spoke system as a response both to the mixed nature of its fleet and to the demands of competing with the giant in its back yard, Eastern. Instead of attacking Eastern head-on, which management decided might be suicidal, Delta initiated guerrilla warfare, sending its smaller propeller aircraft into many little communities and bringing traffic from those points back to its Atlanta hub where jets then took the passengers to their destinations. In this way, Delta began to close the gap on Eastern in passengers carried. More importantly, Delta furthered the loyalty of its customer base by keeping passengers within its system from beginning to end of a journey.

By 1978, the year of deregulation, several other airlines, notably Eastern, Piedmont and American, saw the competitive wisdom of the hub-and-spoke system, and in a deregulated environment Delta, Eastern, Piedmont and American forced the rest of the airline industry to adopt the same strategy or perish. TWA, for one, fell into serious disarray in part because it was slow to accept the hub-and-spoke system.

Delta was large enough by 1978 to rival Eastern head-on. One reason was that in 1972 it underwent another merger.

Northeast Airlines

Northeast Airlines, the merger partner, began in 1933 as Boston-Maine Airways, operating a single route under contract from National Airways. Boston-Maine purchased National in 1937, and in 1940 it changed its name to Northeast Airlines. This airline expanded its service from New England southward along the East Coast to Washington, D.C., and Norfolk, Va., throughout the 1930s and 1940s. It added service to points in Florida in the early 1950s, and in 1959 introduced a B-707 jet leased from TWA on its New York-Miami route.

It experienced financial difficulties by 1960, however, and in 1965 it was sold to Storer Broadcasting Co. It then had a brief period of prosperity, but by 1972 the carrier was devastated financially and began seeking a merger. Following negotiations with Delta, Northwest and TWA, the company agreed to merge with Delta and, on Aug. 1, 1972, the deal was completed. Delta now found itself flying to 98 cities, including six in five other countries.

Delta in the late 1970s received some route awards from the CAB that helped it grow. Delta's first trans-Atlantic service, Atlanta to London, began on April 30, 1978, and a year later Delta began service between Atlanta and Frankfurt.

Delta was in much better position to thrive in a deregulated environment than its chief Southeast rival, Eastern. Delta's debt load was paltry compared to Eastern's ($1.6 billion of which was assumed through a decision in 1978 to buy new aircraft), and while Eastern was torn increasingly by labor-management strife, Delta management won its employees' dedication and loyalty through such policies as never laying off people during a recession; bargaining in good faith with its pilot union; and maintaining a "family feeling" throughout the airline. Therefore, Delta and Eastern exchanged places.

On the West Coast, another pioneering airline, Western, was neither Delta-fortunate nor Eastern-wretched. But it found itself needing a merger.

Delta Air Lines
Aircraft fleet: 1983-1992

Aircraft	1983	1984	1985	1986	1987	1988	1989	1990	1991	1992
A-310	—	—	—	—	—	—	—	—	21	21
B-727	116	107	102	102	132	131	130	129	147	153
B-737	—	20	33	33	86	74	74	72	72	71
B-757	—	—	10	19	28	38	52	61	69	79
B-767	10	10	15	15	22	30	30	40	46	51
DC-8	13	13	13	13	12	7	—	—	—	—
DC-9	36	36	36	36	36	36	36	34	29	—
DC-10	—	—	—	—	9	6	—	—	—	—
L-1011	44	38	36	35	35	39	40	39	48	56
MD-80	—	—	—	—	8	22	46	70	85	108
MD-11	—	—	—	—	—	—	—	2	2	6
Total	219	224	245	253	368	383	408	447	519	545

Western Air Lines

Western Air Lines organized as Western Air Express in 1925 and made its first flight—airmail from Los Angeles to Salt Lake City—in April 1926. In 1930 it became the first airline to introduce the Fokker F-32 — then the largest airliner in the world, a four-engine aircraft that could carry 32 passengers — to commercial airline operations. About the same time, Irving Krick, a Western employee, developed the air mass analysis system of weather forecasting. Krick's highly effective system helped give Western the nickname "the airline with perpetual tailwinds," and by the end of 1930, Western, flying 15,832 route miles, was the largest airline in the world.

This good fortune did not last. The Post Office Department canceled all but one of Western's airmail contracts in 1934, reducing the airline to flying its original Los Angeles-Salt Lake City route plus a spur to San Diego. Western responded by shaping its own good fortune: The carrier rebuilt around the DC-3 and passenger service and became the first airline to complete 10 years of operation without a single passenger fatality.

Western seemed on the way to prominence when war with Germany and its allies broke out. World War II then slashed Western's fleet to five aircraft as the military requisitioned the rest for the war effort. Western's other contributions to the war included pilot training for the military and operations to fly personnel and material to Alaska.

Western, like American and Delta, began reshaping itself as World War II progressed. Western expanded into the Rockies and northern Plains in 1944 by merging with Inland Air Lines. As the airline grew, it became the first carrier to introduce half-fares for children and the first to have in-flight television. Western continued to grow an increment at a time throughout the regulated era; yet when deregulation arrived, it remained a small carrier compared with the giants roaming its markets.

The predictable happened: Free-wheeling price competition drove fares down and Western began losing money in 1980. Red ink poured freely through 1984. The carrier made a comeback in 1985 when it reported profits of $67.1 million, but by then management was convinced Western needed to merge with a giant to protect its stockholders' investment. Delta and Western announced a merger agreement on Sept. 9, 1986. The merger became final on April 1, 1987.

Airline mergers tend to cause tensions, in part because of seniority problems among the pilots and other unionized employees, in part because of clashes in organizational policies and culture. Such problems especially were notable in the Northwest-Republic and Continental-People Express mergers. But even Delta's most difficult merger, Delta-Northeast, was easy compared to most airline mergers because Delta's management worked hard to make newcomers feel wanted. After the most recent one, Delta-Western, Delta preserved Western employees' jobs by moving roughly 1,500 people from Los Angeles to Atlanta.

Delta served 132 domestic cities in 42 states, the District of Columbia and Puerto Rico immediately after the Western merger. It also operated flights to 23 international destinations in 11 foreign countries. From then until mid-1990, Delta added service from Atlanta to Dublin, Ireland; Seoul, Korea; Taipei, Taiwan; and Hamburg, Germany. Service began, too, from Cincinnati to Frankfurt, Germany.

While the airline world crumbled around it, Delta Air Lines kept two of its traditions alive by expanding in the midst of the 1990-1991 recession and preserving labor peace with a contract that reportedly made Delta's pilots the highest-paid in the industry.

Delta also was one of the first competitors on the scene to scoop up assets when Eastern Air Lines quit flying. Delta bought 18 gates on Concourse B at Atlanta's Hartsfield International Airport for $41.4 million; nine landing slots at Washington National Airport for $5.4 million; seven slots at La Guardia Airport for $3.5 million; and 10 Lockheed L-1011-50s for $60 million.

Delta bought six long-range Lockheed L-1011-500s from Air Canada in May 1991 in a transaction valued by industry analysts at about $120 million. Delta made the Air Canada deal, like the Eastern L-1011 purchase, to bolster its expanding international service. The Air Canada purchase brought Delta's total Lockheed L-1011 fleet to 55 aircraft. Delta also expected the delivery of 45 other aircraft in 1991. To aid in taking on so many aircraft, Delta began a $400-million program in March to expand and modernize its maintenance and support operations.

As of late May 1991, Delta flew to 32 cities in 14 other countries and was a leading candidate to absorb the remains of Pan American Airways.

Meanwhile, without buying Pan Am assets, Delta expanded internationally. Already scheduled to begin service to Copenhagen, Berlin and Hong Kong in 1991, Delta also was considering a hub in Taipei and bidding for two of TWA's London routes (Baltimore and Philadelphia).

Delta took these steps despite heavy losses in the first six months of fiscal 1991 (covering fourth quarter 1990 and first quarter 1991). Over that stretch, Delta lost $259.4 million on sales of $4.35 billion. Delta earned a profit of $197.4 million on sales of $4.22 billion in the corresponding period of its fiscal year 1990.

Delta previously sat on the sidelines watching United and American scoop up international assets from financially ailing carriers. Then, in April 1991, Delta issued $476 million in common stock to raise money for international expansion. Three months later the carrier reached a tentative agreement with Pan Am officials to buy about two dozen of Pan Am's trans-Atlantic routes, its hub in Frankfurt, Germany, its Northeast shuttle and 45 jets. The price: a paltry $260 million—low compared to other airline deals, such as United's $290-million purchase of five Pan Am routes to London and American's $445-million buy for routes from Trans World Airlines.

However, when a bankruptcy court judge approved Delta's purchase one month later, the cost had risen to $1.4 billion because of a last minute joint offer from United, TWA and American. The scope of the transaction: $416 million for Pan Am assets including its European operations, Northeast shuttle, 24 leased B-727s and 21 leased A-310s plus spare engines and other parts. Delta also would pay $305 million for 45-percent equity in a newly reorganized Pan Am, provide emergency loans totaling $80 million to keep the carrier operating and assume $669 million in Pan Am liabilities.

Chairman and chief executive officer Ronald Allen, responding to concern in the Delta community over the timing of the transaction made during a miserable financial year for all airlines, said in a 1991 interview he did not believe Delta risked too much financially. The carrier had $700 million in cash on hand at the end of June, including the $476 million raised through the stock issue. Less than half the $1.39-billion cost reportedly would be in cash. Delta's pilot union, ALPA, responded with a 17-month extension of its contract in view of the financial strain the Pan Am buy placed on the airline. Delta did manage a third quarter 1991 net profit of $13.1 million, though the carrier warned the European expansion would depress fourth-quarter results.

The Pan Am deal gave Delta a much coveted international gateway at New York's JFK International where most of Pan Am's trans-Atlantic routes originated; Delta had little presence at JFK before the deal. Delta boosted its trans-Atlantic weekly round trips from 92 to 195 by Nov. 1, 1991. International cities served by Delta jumped from 34 to 57 and nations served rose from 16 to 34. Delta's new destinations from New York included Barcelona,

Delta Air Lines Financial Statistics

(In millions)	1983	1984	1985	1986	1987	1988	1989	1990	1991	1992
Sales	3,616	4,264	4,684	4,460	5,318	6,915	8,090	8,582	9,171	10,837
Net Income (loss)	(86.7)	175.6	259.5	47.3	263.7	306.8	460.9	302.8	(324.4)	(506.3)
Assets	3,247	3,269	3,627	3,786	5,342	5,748	6,484	7,227	8,411	10,162
Liabilities	2,350	2,220	2,340	2,484	3,405	3,540	3,864	4,631	5,905	8,197
Net Worth	897	1,049	1,287	1,302	1,938	2,209	2,620	2,596	2,506	1,965
ASMs	47,916	50,935	51,637	53,336	69,014	85,834	90,741	96,463	104,328	123,102
RPMs	26,097	26,099	29,062	30,123	38,415	49,009	55,904	58,987	62,086	72,693
Load Factors	54.5%	51.2%	56.3%	56.5%	55.7%	57.1%	61.6%	61.2%	59.5%	59.1%

Spain; Brussels; Geneva; Helsinki, Finland; Lisbon, Portugal; Madrid; Milan, Italy; Moscow; Nice, France; Oslo, Norway; Rome; Stockholm; Tel Aviv, Israel (via Paris); and Zurich, Switzerland. From Frankfurt, Germany: Athens, Greece; Bombay, India; Bucharest, Romania; Budapest, Hungary; Delhi, India; Istanbul, Turkey; Moscow; Prague, Czechoslovakia; Vienna, Austria and Warsaw, Poland.

Originally Delta forecast the reorganized Pan Am would post an $83-million profit by 1995. But it was apparent by October 1991 there were flaws in the reorganization plan. Pan Am soon ran out of cash and Delta increased its initial $80 million in loans to $140 million. Pan Am's November traffic was 20 percent below management projections, and it became clear the reorganized carrier's revenues would be substantially lower and costs higher than projected. Delta in December refused Pan Am's request for more funding and the ailing carrier shut down.

Delta's net loss totaled $326.2 million the first nine months of the company's 1992 fiscal year, more than the $324.4 million the carrier lost for the fiscal year ended June 30, 1991, the worst year in its history. Though international traffic was strong, costs associated with operating new routes resulted in a significant increase in operating expenses.

A week after Delta reported fiscal 1992 third-quarter losses of $151.6 million, the carrier announced capital spending cuts of more than $5 billion over nine years and canceled plans to acquire 100 aircraft. Of the $5-billion reduction, $3 billion would occur over the next four years.

Delta in July announced it would lay off most of its 3,500 temporary and part-time workers as part of a program to cut costs by $700 million. The move was made after Delta posted a record fiscal 1992 year-end loss of $506.3 million. Delta's revenue increased 18 percent in 1992 but costs jumped 20 percent. The cuts would save $375 million in 1993 and $700 million annually by fiscal 1995. No permanent employees were laid off though reductions included a pay and hiring freeze, revised medical and dental insurance benefits, and work force cuts through attrition.

The losses were large enough to halt Delta's planned expansion into Latin America. The airline announced it would postpone start-up flights between Orlando, Fla., and Caracas, Venezuela; Guatemala City, Guatemala; and San Jose, Costa Rica. Delta also announced it would slash its California corridor flight schedule by two-thirds.

Ronald Allen in September asked Delta's board to reduce his salary by $100,000—the amount equal to a raise received months earlier. Nine senior officers also took 5-percent pay cuts. However, ALPA refused management's request to postpone a Sept. 1 pay increase, opting instead to conduct an analysis of the company's finances before agreeing to concessions. Delta responded by announcing its first pilot furlough in 35 years—103 pilots on Dec. 1. Senior vice president of operations Harry C. Alger called the furloughs "a necessary and prudent business decision" since cutbacks in aircraft orders "reaffirmed a projected surplus of pilots." ALPA cried foul, claiming the furloughs were a negotiating tactic by management and violated its contract. Delta canceled the furloughs in November when ALPA agreed to reduce pilots' minimum monthly flying hours.

Delta, unaccustomed to such large financial losses, again took steps to stem costs and in December announced a 5-percent wage reduction for all non-contract employees. Delta also postponed $400 million in aircraft orders until sometime after fiscal year 1995—in addition to the $900 million in deferred aircraft orders already announced. Additionally, the carrier began reevaluating its expansion plans and planned to cut any unprofitable flights. "We're going through a period of major restructuring," Allen said in an interview in *USA Today*. "We're powering down to be as lean as we can."

Speculation rose that Allen, who in 1987 became the carrier's youngest CEO at age 46, soon would be replaced. Delta's board of directors quickly quashed the rumors, however, by adding the titles of president and chief operating officer to Allen's portfolio pending president Whitley Hawkins' March 1 retirement. Also on March 1, Harry Alger, formerly senior vice president of operations, became the number two man at Delta as its new executive vice president of operations.

Signs that Delta's cost-cutting efforts began to pay off were evident by the end of the calendar year. Delta's net loss was $126.3 million—less than United's or American's—for the quarter ending Dec. 31, and unlike its competitors, Delta's fiscal second-quarter loss was less than the previous year's loss for the same quarter.

Delta announced in February 1993 another $500 million in delays and/or cuts in jet purchases for 35 aircraft on firm order or option. The 35 aircraft represented approximately 8.5 percent of the 410 airplanes Delta had on order. Delta also announced 601 pilot furloughs, with 136 pilots furloughed June 1, 1993. Allen said in an interview he sees no quick turnaround for the industry. "Overseas, many economies remain distressed, and we here at home see bankrupt carriers continuing to force uneconomic pricing on the non-bankrupt carriers. All this leaves Delta with no choice but to address those areas in which we have control over spending."

Delta did report improved results for its 1993 fiscal fourth quarter ending June 30. The carrier posted a net profit of $7.149 million before FAS 106 charges. Delta's 1993 fiscal year net loss was $414.8 million before one-time accounting charges, an improvement over its 1992 fiscal-year loss of $506.3 million.

The senior executives responsible for Delta's decision-making, operations and maintenance at the time of publication are Ronald W. Allen, chairman, president and chief executive officer; Harry C. Alger, executive vice president of operations; James W. Callison, senior vice president of corporate and external affairs; and Thomas J. Roeck, Jr., senior vice president of finance, chief financial officer.

Delta Air Lines Statistics

1992 Total Sales
Global/Major Airlines

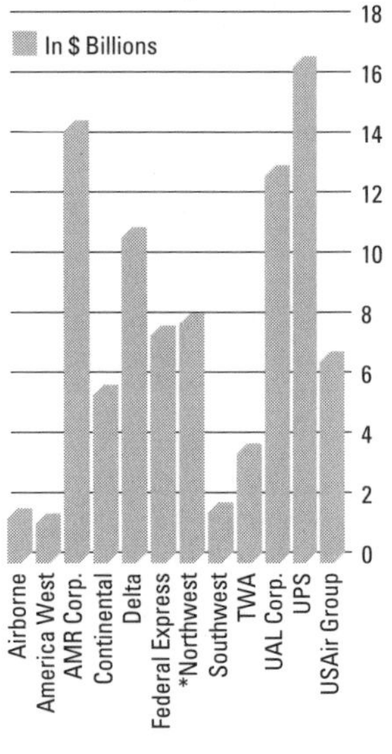

• Information is for Northwest Airlines only and not for parent company NWA Inc.

Delta finished (fiscal) 1992 with the fourth-highest revenue in the industry.

Delta's sales increased 200 percent between 1983 and 1992. The company's 157-percent increase in capacity resulted from its purchase of many Pan American World Airways' assets and general growth. These factors, along with the the demise of Eastern Air Lines in early 1991, contributed to Delta's increase in sales.

Delta
Total Sales 1983-1992

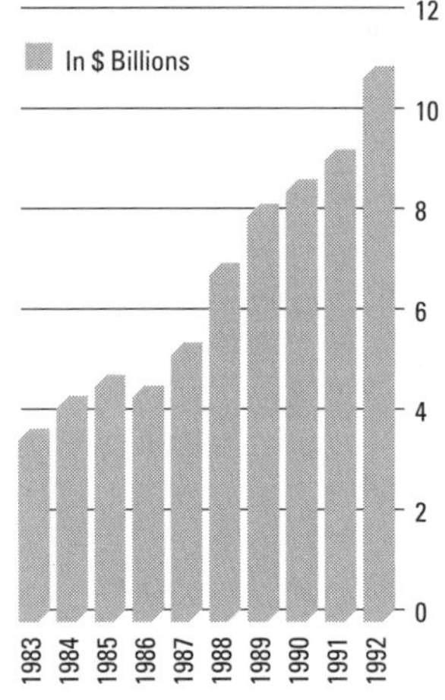

1992 Net Income
Global/Major Airlines

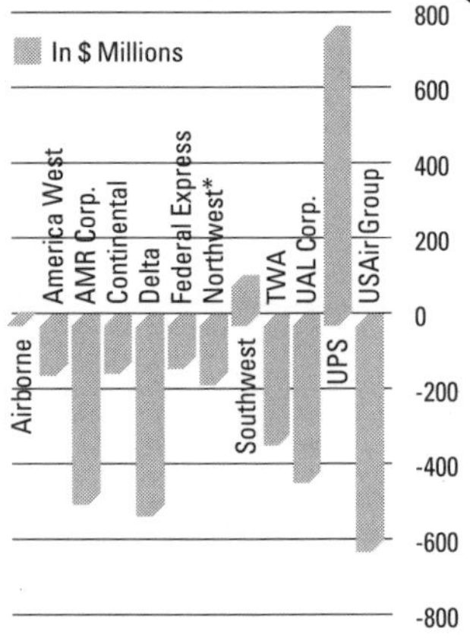

• Information is for Northwest Airlines only and not for parent company NWA Inc.

Delta had the second-worst net loss in the industry for (fiscal) 1992.

Delta's fiscal 1991 and 1992 losses were its second and third, respectively, since 1947. It also expects a net loss for fiscal 1993.

Delta
Net Income 1983-1992

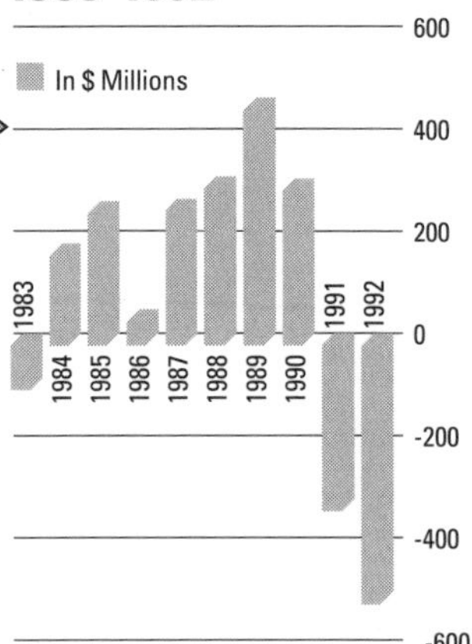

1992 Total Assets & Liabilities
Global/Major Airlines

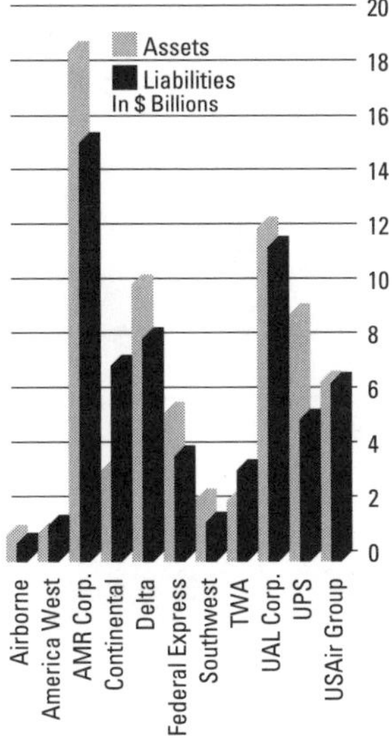

NWA Inc. is a privately held company and would not release 1990-1992 figures.

Delta posted record net losses each of the past two fiscal years (ended June 30, 1991 and 1992, respectively).

Delta's assets were valued at $10.16 billion in 1992 which made it the third-largest airline in the industry based on total assets.

Delta's 1992 liabilities totaled $8.2 billion and it finished the year with a net worth of $1.97 billion.

Delta's assets increased 213 percent between 1983 and 1992, from $3.25 billion in 1983 to $10.16 billion in 1992.

Its liabilities increased 249 percent during the same period, from $2.35 billion in 1983 to $8.2 billion in 1992.

Delta
Assets & Liabilities 1983-1992

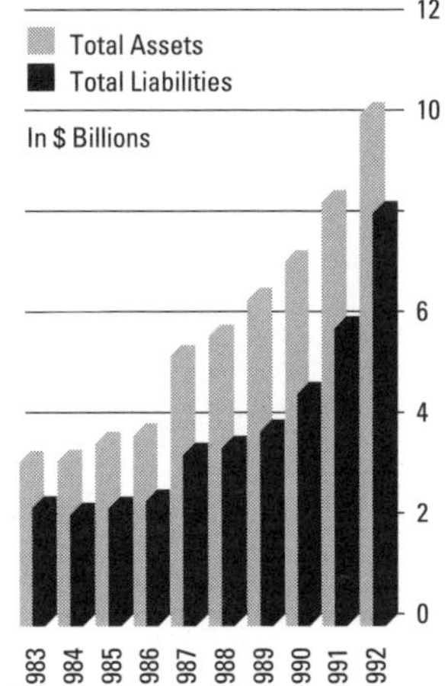

1992 ASMs & RPMs
Global/Major Airlines

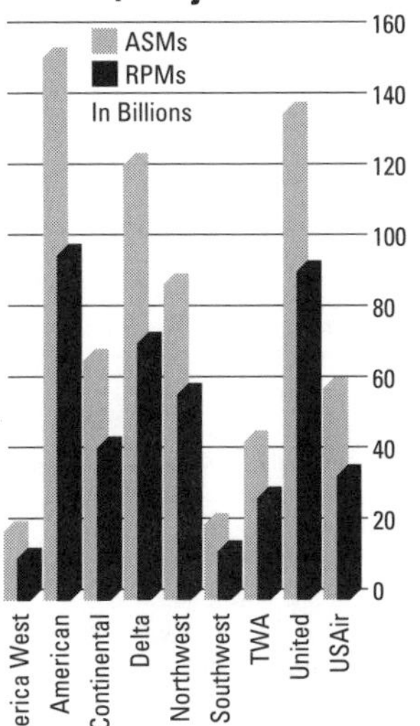

Delta had the industry's third-largest capacity in 1992 (although it actually compares from July 1, 1991 to June 30, 1992 at Delta with calendar years at the other passenger-carrying airlines). Additionally, the company flew 72.69 billion revenue passenger miles (RPMs) which gave it a load factor of 59.1 percent for its fiscal year. Delta's 1992 yield was 13.91 cents per RPM.

Delta enjoyed tremendous growth between 1983 and 1992. The company's capacity increased 157 percent since 1983. Delta also saw a 179-percent increase in the number of revenue passenger miles flown since its fiscal 1983.

Delta
ASMs & RPMs 1983-1992

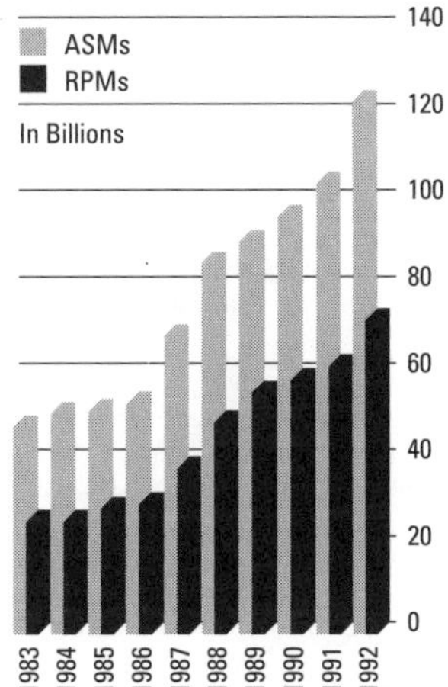

1992 Net Worth
Global/Major Airlines

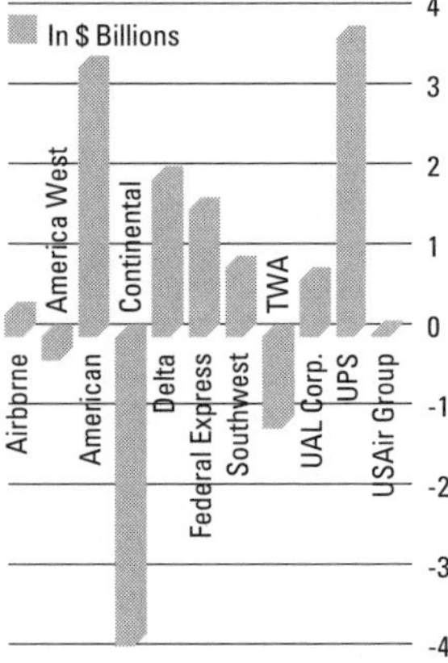

NWA Inc. is a privately held company and would not release 1990-1992 figures.

Delta finished its fiscal 1992 with a net worth of $1.97 billion—the third-best net worth in the industry.

Delta's net worth climbed 192 percent between 1983 and 1989, but declined in fiscal 1990, 1991 and 1992.

Delta Net Worth 1983-1992

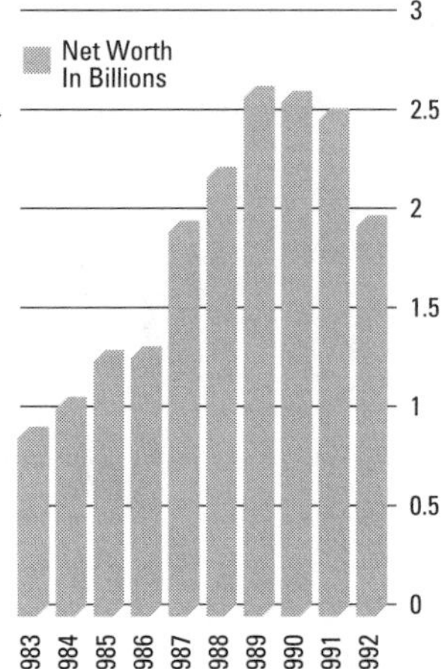

Statistics Related Terms

Assets — A resource having commercial or trade value that is owned (or which the company owns rights to) by a business. Typical examples for an airline include: Cash, securities, property, equipment, capital leases, landing slots and routes.

Available Seat Miles (ASMs) — Represent the number of seats available for passengers multiplied by the number of scheduled miles those seats are flown.

Cost per available seat mile — Represents operating and interest expense divided by available seat miles.

Financial Accounting Standard (FAS) 106 — A federally-mandated accounting change made to the way U.S. companies handle post-retirement benefits (other than pensions) to employees. FAS 106, for several U.S. global and major airlines, meant large, one-time, non-cash charges to earnings, further damaging their balance-sheet performance for 1992.

Leveraged Buyout (LBO) — Takeover of a company using borrowed funds. Company assets often serve as security for the loans, although investors' assets also may be used.

Liabilities — The total amount the company owes to all creditors.

Net worth or stockholders' equity — The net assets (total assets minus total liabilities) of a company. For companies with more liabilities than assets, the result is a negative net worth or stockholders' deficit.

Passenger load factor — Revenue passenger miles divided by available seat miles over a set period of time.

Revenue passenger miles (RPMs) — The number of d miles flown by revenue-producing passengers.

Yield — The average revenue received for each mile a revenue passenger is carried. Determined by dividing total operating revenue by total revenue passenger miles.

Delta Air Lines News Abstracts

"Airline Chiefs Join to Block USAir Proposal." *Wall Street Journal,* 2 Oct. 1992.

"Atlanta Seeks to Lure Rival to Delta Air." *The Atlanta Journal-Constitution,* 11 Nov. 1992, sec. B, p. 1.

"Delta Air Lines and Pan Am Are Said to be Discussing Possibility of a Merger." *Wall Street Journal,* 18 April 1991, sec. A, p. 3, col. 2.

"Delta Air Reports $207.8 Million Loss for Its 2nd Quarter." *Wall Street Journal,* 24 Jan. 1991, sec. B, p. 5, col. 4.

"Delta Cutting Flights in California." *The Atlanta Journal-Constitution,* 14 Aug. 1992, sec. F, p. 7.

"Delta, Despite Victory in Pan Am Bid, Faces Some Big Challenges." *Wall Street Journal,* 13 Aug. 1991, sec. A, p. 1, col. 1.

"Delta Digs in for Long-term Prosperity." *Career Pilot,* May 1991, p. 18.

"Delta Flies High on Pan Am Deal." *USA Today,* 17 July 1991, sec. B, p. 1.

"Delta Gambles on Expansion Plans as Competitors Find Traffic Declining." *Aviation Week & Space Technology,* 4 March 1991, pp. 35-42.

"Delta Getting a Bargain on Pan Am Assets." *The Atlanta Journal-Constitution,* 12 July 1991, sec. F, p. 1.

"Delta Goes Global." *The Atlanta Journal-Constitution,* 1 Nov. 1991, sec. A, p. 1.

"Delta Has Profit but Expects Less in Year-End Quarter." *The Atlanta Journal-Constitution,* 25 Oct. 1991, sec. D.

"Delta is Ready for Life After Eastern." *Air Transport World,* June 1991, pp. 41-44.

"Delta Lashes Critics Over Pan Am Deal." *The Atlanta Journal-Constitution,* 11 Dec. 1991, sec. B, p. 1.

"Delta Launches $400-Million Program to Expand Maintenance, Support Operations." *Aviation Week & Space Technology,* 4 March 1991, p. 42.

"Delta Loses Its Attempt to Acquire Pan Am Route." *The Atlanta Journal-Constitution,* 11 Jan. 1991.

"Delta Makes a Difference." *Flight International,* 21-27 Aug. 1991, p. 20.

"Delta Makes Deal for 18 Gates, Other Assets." *The Atlanta Journal-Constitution,* 22 Jan. 1991, sec. A, p. 1.

"Delta Not Throttling Back on Major Expansion Plan." *The Atlanta Journal-Constitution,* 11 Jan. 1991.

"Delta Plans to Make $50 Million Offer for Pan Am Los Angeles-London Route." *Wall Street Journal,* 10 Jan. 1991, sec. A, p. 4, col. 1.

"Delta Says It's Talking With Pan Am Corp. Over Asset Purchases." *Wall Street Journal,* 24 April 1991, sec. A, p. 4, col. 2.

"Delta Sets Nov. 1 for Takeover of Overseas Routes." *The Atlanta Journal-Constitution,* 30 Aug. 1991.

"Delta to Raise Airfares 4.4 Percent." *The Atlanta Journal-Constitution,* 25 June, 1992.

"Delta, UAL Make Winning Eastern Bids." *Wall Street Journal,* 6 Feb. 1991, sec. A, p. 3, col. 3.

"Delta Wins More Atlanta Gates, United Buys Chicago Assets at Eastern Auction." *Aviation Week & Space Technology,* 11 Feb. 1991, p. 29.

"Delta Wins Pan Am Bidding, Gains on Larger Competitors." *Aviation Week & Space Technology*, 19 Aug. 1991, pp. 18-21.

"Delta's Expanding World." *The Atlanta Journal-Constitution*, 12 July 1991.

"Delta's New MD-11 Set for Takeoff." *The Atlanta Journal-Constitution*, 4 Feb. 1991.

"Delta's Pilots Agree to Extend Contract for 16-Month Period." *Wall Street Journal*, 5 Sep. 1991.

"Delta's Pilots Reject Request for Salary Cut." *The Atlanta Journal-Constitution*, 19 Jan. 1993.

"Eastern Airlines Sells Some Gates for $41.4 Million." *Wall Street Journal*, 22 Jan. 1991, sec. A, p. 4, col. 3.

"Eastern War Blamed for Record Delta Loss." *The Atlanta Journal-Constitution*, 24 Jan. 1991.

"Global Growth is a Learning Experience for Delta." *The Atlanta Journal-Constitution*, 26 Nov. 1992, sec. F, p. 1.

"High-Stakes Challenges on the Horizon for Delta." *The Atlanta Journal-Constitution*, 13 Aug. 1991, sec. D, p. 1.

"In the Wake of Eastern Airlines' Demise, Rival Carriers Swoop in for the Pieces." *Wall Street Journal*, 22 Jan. 1991, sec. B, p. 1.

"Inside Wall Street; Eastern's Demise is Delta's Rebirth." *Business Week*, 4 March 1991, p. 64.

"Londoner to Head Delta's Marketing Effort Overseas." *The Atlanta Journal-Constitution*, 28 Jan. 1993.

"New Transatlantic Battle Looms as Airline Balance of Power Shifts to Surging Big 3 American Carriers." *Aviation Week & Space Technology*, 22 July 1991, pp. 29-30.

"Pan Am Selling Europe Routes, Hubs and N.Y. Shuttle to Delta." *Aviation Week & Space Technology*, 15 July 1991, pp. 30-31.

"Pan Am Sets Sale to Delta of Assets, European Routes." *Wall Street Journal*, 12 July 1991, sec. A, p. 1, col. 1.

"Red Ink at Delta Hits Home." *The Atlanta Journal-Constitution*, 18 Dec. 1992.

"Taking off: The Delta Shuttle." *The Atlanta Journal-Constitution*, 30 Aug. 1991, sec. F, p. 1.

"UAL and Delta Post Big Losses for Quarter." *Wall Street Journal*, 26 April 1991, sec. A, p. 3, col. 1.

(Photograph by Airborne Express)

Airborne Express' fleet consists entirely of DC-8s, DC-9s and YS-11s. It buys used airliners and loads freight through the passenger doors in containers of its own design. Its fleet goal for 1993 is to add 10 more aircraft, including eight DC-9s.

America West began operations in 1983 with three B-737s. Its fleet grew to include 32 B-737s by the end of 1985. America West currently operates the A-320 and B-757 aircraft in addition to its B-737s.

(Photograph by America West Airlines)

(Photograph by American Airlines)

American Airlines operated a fleet of 80 aircraft by the time the United States entered World War II. Its fleet shrank to 55 aircraft in 1942 and 44 aircraft in 1943. Today, American's fleet totals 679 aircraft, including 70 B-757s.

Continental Airlines operates a 328-aircraft fleet. The A-300 is one of three widebody aircraft Continental flies. Currently the carrier has 23 A-300s including six Airbus planes acquired from Eastern Air Lines in 1991.

(Photograph by Continental Airlines)

(Photograph by Delta Air Lines)

Delta Air Lines offers its pilots the opportunity to fly a diverse fleet of aircraft including A-310s, B-727s, B-737s, B-757s, B-767s, L-1011s, MD-88s and MD-11s. Delta was the first U.S. carrier to fly the MD-11 in service, after taking delivery of two through a lease arrangement in December 1991.

(Photograph by FAPA)

Federal Express operates the largest all-cargo fleet in the world. The Memphis-based cargo carrier plans to modify its fleet of B-727-200s, the backbone of its domestic service since 1978, with "hush kits" to bring them into compliance with Stage III noise requirements.

(Photograph by Northwest Airlines)

The first of Northwest's B-747s, delivered on April 30, 1970, led to a Tokyo hub. By the mid-1980s, Northwest was the leading U.S. flag carrier in the Pacific with 77 B-747 flights per week out of six U.S. gateways to 11 Asian destinations.

Southwest's employees in 1991 volunteered a part of their salaries to help buy fuel for Southwest's fleet of B-737s. In 1992, a strong balance sheet allowed Southwest to buy aircraft while other, larger airlines canceled orders and options. The carrier took delivery of 13 new B-737s in 1992 and agreed that year to buy 34 new B-737-300s.

(Photograph by Southwest Airlines)

Trans World Airlines plans in 1993 to rebuild its aging fleet. Recently, TWA took delivery of six new MD-83s to add to its fleet of 39 MD-80s. The new aircraft include TWA's new "comfort class" seat spacing, which the carrier says nearly doubles legroom.

(Photograph by Trans World Airlines)

United Airlines was the industry leader in fleet quality in the early 1930s. United continues to set fleet trends in the 1990s as launch customer for the B-777, scheduled to arrive in May 1995. United's fleet in May 1993 totaled 548 aircraft, including 20 B-747-400s.

(Photograph by United Airlines)

(Photograph by United Parcel Service)

United Parcel Service's goal in 1993 is to bring 95 percent of its fleet to Stage III standards by 1995. The company also is making several upgrades to improve scheduling, weather forecasting and cockpit instrumentation. UPS' fleet currently totals 142 aircraft, including 11 B-747s.

(Photograph by USAir)

Mid-sized workhorses like the B-737-300, B-737-200 and DC-9 dominate USAir's fleet. The Pittsburgh-based carrier owns no B-747s or DC-10s; the biggest jet in its 444-aircraft fleet is the B-767 of which it has 12.

6

Federal Express

Federal Express, in its short history, survived early lean years and an uncertain future before a spectacular growth spurt in the 1980s made it an industry leader in overnight delivery.

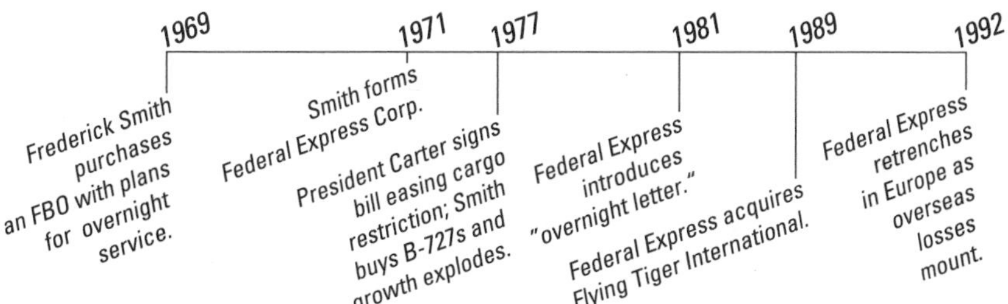

Federal Express is the brainchild of its chairman and CEO, Frederick W. Smith. His plan for an overnight delivery service grew from a term paper he wrote during his undergraduate days at Yale. Smith wrote in that paper, penned in 1965, that the route systems employed by passenger airlines of that era could not work for freight. What was needed was a system specifically designed for cargo—a hub-and-spoke system. Thus, in concept at least, Smith was contemporaneous with Delta Air Lines management in recognizing the potential power of the airline hub. Smith received a "C" on his term paper, but he never relinquished the belief that he was right.

On graduating from Yale in May 1966, Smith accepted a commission as a second lieutenant in the Marine Corps and went to Vietnam, where he learned many of the lessons of life he later employed at Federal Express. Smith served successively as a platoon leader, a battalion staffer and a company commander. After a seven-month tour of duty in Vietnam, he took a leave in Memphis, Tenn., his home, and then returned to the war—not, as he observed to a Memphis newspaper reporter, because he was all that patriotic, but because "there is a job I've been asked to do. I have had a year's experience, and I know I can do it better than any new officer they might send in to replace me."

Smith, returning with his wings, flew reconnaissance missions in one of the most fought-over regions of the war. When he was discharged on July 21, 1969, he held the rank of captain and received the Silver Star, the Bronze Star, two Purple Hearts, the Navy Commendation Medal and the Vietnamese Cross of Gallantry. He also learned from a platoon sergeant, a veteran of 14 years in the Marines, how to understand, years later, the concerns of rank-and-file Federal Express employees.

Smith, at age 25, put his considerable inheritance (a family trust, The Enterprise Corp., worth nearly $9 million) to work in August 1969 by purchasing controlling interest in a Little Rock company called Arkansas Aviation Sales. Under his grandfather, from whom he purchased his interest, the company was a money-losing fixed-based operator that provided maintenance services for corporate turboprop and jet aircraft. Smith turned it into an aggressive brokerage for corporate jets. He developed plans in his spare time to launch an overnight delivery service.

Federal Express

Aircraft fleet and purchase commitments

As of May 1993

Aircraft Type	Current Fleet	Firm Orders	Options
A-300-600	0	25	50
B-727	161	2	0
B-747	8	0	0
DC-10	30	3	0
MD-11	8	5	0
Total	207	35	50

That service turned out to be Federal Express, but it began haltingly. Smith formed Federal Express Corp. in June 1971 in anticipation of a contract with the Federal Reserve System to transport canceled checks. But, when the Fed decided not to award him a contract, Smith found plan B—an air taxi service—blocked by the fact that his company's two Dassault Falcon 20 business jets exceeded the weight restrictions for an air taxi operation.

Smith, convinced the government would change the weight requirements, plunged ahead, ordering 23 more Falcons in December 1971 and another eight in early 1972. He borrowed $13.8 million to finance these purchases. Fortunately, the Civil Aeronautics Board (CAB) revised its regulations and Federal Express was able to use its Falcons for air taxi operations. Federal Express began operations to 25 cities from its Memphis hub on April 17, 1973.

The company ran up massive losses as the sales growth Smith counted on failed to materialize. Conditions deteriorated while Smith looked desperately for new financing. In the fall of 1973, while Smith was in New York trying to arrange new financing, the carrier urged its employees not to cash their paychecks. Smith managed in November to get a recapitalization valued at $31.5 million.

Federal Express was blindsided in the midst of this crisis by a federal government edict that airlines would receive a 1973 fuel allotment based on their 1972 consumption. Federal Express had no 1972 consumption, so Smith set off to Washington for an intense lobbying session. Federal Express received a fuel allotment of 41 million gallons.

The $31.5-million recapitalization of November 1973 was nearly gone by January 1974. Discussions with lenders for further financing resulted in a condition that Howell M. Estes, Jr., a retired Air Force general, replace Smith as the company's CEO. Estes could not keep Federal Express from consuming the additional $6.4 million in financing too quickly, however, and by May the company was in default on loans and appealing again for more credit. Federal Express received another $3.9 million and a one-year grace period on paying the interest on its outstanding loans.

Federal Express looked like a bottomless pit for throwing away money, but a rate increase in early 1975 produced a profit by mid-year. Smith wanted more, however, than the Falcons, already flying near their capacity, could produce. Initial efforts to gain CAB approval for the operation of larger aircraft failed when major airlines rose in unison, crying that Federal Express was hurting their business. The company tried again and, in 1976, failed again. Smith did not quit. Finally, as the winds of deregulation began sweeping through the Congress, President Jimmy Carter signed a 1977 bill removing all controls from the air cargo industry.

With restrictions removed, Federal Express purchased seven B-727s from United. The company put its first B-727 into service on its Memphis-Los

Angeles route in January 1978. This was the beginning of the company's tremendous growth period.

Federal Express' lenders, seeing growth and profits, began to grow restive: They wanted their money. So Smith took Federal Express public in April 1978, selling 738,000 shares of its stock and raising $17.5 million in capital it used to pay off portions of debt and to finance new aircraft purchases.

Congress passed a law in 1979, authorizing private companies to carry letters. Federal Express seized the day and introduced its famous "overnight letter" in 1981. First-year results were a disappointing $56 million in revenues, but this service continued to grow in the years 1982 through 1988. Federal Express was the undisputed leader in the overnight delivery business by the beginning of 1987.

Federal Express achieved tremendous success from a troubled start. Gone were the days when Smith had to sell his own personal aircraft or make a desperation trip to Las Vegas to raise money for payroll.

The lion's share of credit for what Federal Express became goes to Smith, who stubbornly fought the good fight through enough adversity to floor lesser men. Smith was known widely for the pumped-up esprit de corps he brought to his company. He knew motivated employees were essential to success in the airline industry, and he built an outstandingly upbeat, loyal work force to carry the load at Federal Express. Smith also surrounded himself with good managers.

Arthur Bass was one of the consultants who conducted Federal Express' original marketing study. When the carrier got going, he came aboard to develop a marketing plan and handle industrial relations. He became president in 1975 after the resignation of General Estes, and Smith returned to his position as chief executive officer. Bass remained president until 1980 when he stepped aside to manage special projects. He left the company in 1982 to become president and chief executive officer of Midway Airlines.

Bass' replacement as Federal Express president in 1980 was Peter S. Willmott. Willmott joined the company in May 1974 as its senior vice president of finance and administration. He was instrumental in organizing the company's financial management structure. Smith assumed the role of president on Willmott's resignation in 1983 and promoted James L. Barksdale to executive vice president and chief operating officer. Barksdale had been in charge of the company's computer processing and telecommunications operations. The company's senior vice president for air operations, T. Allan McArtor, was a former Air Force pilot and Federal Express executive who also served as head of the FAA for a time before returning to Federal Express in 1988.

Federal Express
Aircraft fleet: 1983-1992

Aircraft	1983	1984	1985	1986	1987	1988	1989	1990	1991	1992
MD-11	—	—	—	—	—	—	—	—	4	8
B-727	38	47	53	53	60	68	106	114	135	152
B-747	—	—	—	—	—	—	21	20	12	11
DC-8	—	—	—	—	—	—	6	—	—	—
DC-10	6	10	11	15	19	21	24	25	27	30
Falcons	32	—	—	—	—	—	—	—	—	—
Total	76	57	64	68	79	89	157	159	178	201

Though Federal Express achieved heady success, it experienced a big failure along the way: ZapMail. ZapMail, introduced in 1984, called for customers to deliver their documents to a Federal Express office for electronic transmission to offices near the addressees. Consumers were not ready for this service and Federal Express suffered massive losses on ZapMail before canceling it in 1986.

Federal Express had new concerns by 1988. The rise of facsimile (FAX) machines combined with the maturing of Federal Express markets to retard sales growth. Additionally, United Parcel Service (UPS), an industry giant with 1989 sales of $12.4 billion, initiated a huge campaign to dislodge Federal Express from its overnight delivery market leadership.

In response to the growing threat of UPS, Federal Express began trying to work the kinks out of its disappointing overseas operations. The company lost approximately $74 million from its international operations between 1985 and 1989 because of inexperience in dealing with foreign customs agencies and in working with foreign freight forwarders. The quickest solution for such problems was to acquire an experienced major international freight carrier. Hence, the acquisition of Tiger International Inc. in February 1989.

Federal Express' $880-million purchase of Flying Tiger caught the airline industry by surprise. The marriage of the upstart overnight air express company with the pioneer of the air freight industry created a global airline with more than 56,500 employees, more than 160 aircraft and route authority to serve every part of the globe.

There were difficulties in merging Federal Express' non-union domestic air-express operation with Flying Tiger's unionized, heavy-freight, overseas business. Heading the list of details was the issue of seniority for 2,048 crew members, including 961 pre-merger Tiger captains, first officers and flight engineers.

The union issue came to the forefront soon after the merger. Tiger pilots were represented by ALPA for 40 years, and sentiment for an independent union from pre-merger Federal Express pilots stemmed from anger over broken management promises. Smith told pilots three years earlier that Federal Express crew members would go to the top of the seniority list if the company acquired another airline. However, the agreement with Flying Tiger specified the lists be subject to a mediator's ruling. The big worry for pre-merger Federal Express pilots was losing seniority to older Flying Tiger crew members. Nobody on the Federal Express roster had more than about 14 years seniority while the Tiger seniority list had dozens of pilots with 20 years or more.

Nevertheless, Federal Express pilots voted in October to reject representation by the Air Line Pilots Association as their collective bargaining agent. Of 2,022 eligible, 709 pilots cast ballots for representation. Smith won the fight, but not without damaging the esprit de corps he long worked to achieve with employees.

Operating as two separate airlines, which Federal had to do until the seniority question was decided, cost the carrier a bundle. The *Wall Street Journal* estimated Federal Express' inability to merge the pilot groups cost the company as much as $150 million a year in possible savings. Increased expenses, including inefficiencies in crew scheduling caused by the lack of an integrated pilot seniority list, negatively affected second quarter 1990 earnings—the first quarter of the two companies' consolidated operations. Federal Express reported an 11.8-percent increase in operating profit from the previous year, but net income dropped 29.5 percent. The merger also more than doubled Federal Express' long-term debt.

A government arbitrator's decision in May to merge the pilot seniority lists resulted in many longtime Federal Express pilots falling hundreds of places on the new merged list. Considerable grumbling from the Fed Ex side of the roster meant future union discussions almost were a certainty.

Federal Express established a new record in annual sales, $7 billion for its fiscal year ending May 1990, but its profits declined. The company reported a fiscal 1990 profit of $115.8 million vs. a 1989 profit of $184.6 million. The company blamed eroding profits on costs from its continued expansion overseas, increased airfreight competition and slow domestic growth.

Increased business activity to the Middle East and reduced competition at home caused by a threatened strike at UPS helped Federal Express report a $43.1-million net profit on sales of $1.9 billion the first quarter of fiscal 1991. Disappointing still, though, were its international operations. The company reported in March losses from its overseas operations doubled in nine months to more than $200 million. Analysts predicted that increased competition at home from UPS and Airborne Freight Corp., combined with continued losses overseas, would damage Fed Ex's domestic operations.

Adding to Smith's troubles, a second organizing effort by ALPA was under way. The union in May petitioned the National Labor Relations Board for an election, citing that more than two-thirds of Fed Ex pilots signed cards requesting an election. However, ALPA was 23 votes or 1 percent shy of the majority needed to become the bargaining agent when the ballots were counted. Elsewhere in the company were signs of turmoil. Within months James L. Barksdale, chief operating officer, and David D. Anderson, chief financial officer, resigned.

Federal Express' U.S. domestic operating income increased 10 percent for fiscal 1991 while international operations continued to post losses for the year. Federal Express' international operating loss totaled $157.5 million the first six months of fiscal 1992—17 percent more than the same period the previous year.

Federal Express' relatively late entry into the European market was the main cause of its problems overseas, according to some analysts. European firms TNT and DHL already were entrenched firmly in European business when Fed Ex expanded its operations. "Our domestic businesses in Europe have simply not provided the necessary synergies with our international business," understated Smith in an interview. Federal Express, after considering several options, agreed in February to co-load express freight with another carrier—TNT Express Worldwide. The agreement was a strong shift away from Smith's corporate philosophy of operating independently.

Federal Express also announced in March a major international retrenchment that, in effect, dismantled its hub-and-spoke system in Europe. Two competitors would deliver locally in European countries instead of Federal Express trucks and personnel. "Federal Express is coming full circle and acknowledging that the strategies that helped the company create the overnight delivery market in the U.S. didn't work in Europe," stated the *Wall Street Journal*.

Smith's strategies with the pilots also appeared to unravel when the National Mediation Board (NMB) in October ruled Federal Express interfered in a representation vote the previous summer. ALPA charged that the company tried to influence pilots by threatening employees with layoffs if the union won. In a subsequent election, 56.4 percent of pilots voted for union representation, with ALPA receiving the majority of votes. The company immediately contested the vote and filed an objection with the mediation board. The NMB overturned the company's objection, and in mid-June 1993 certified ALPA as the bargaining agent for Federal Express' pilots.

Federal Express reported a $113.8-million net loss in fiscal 1992 vs. a net profit of $5.9 million in 1991. Federal Express' international operating loss for the full year was $612.9 million while its domestic operating profit was $635.9 million.

Federal Express announced in July its 1993 fiscal fourth-quarter results. Net income improved 56 percent over the previous year's fourth quarter net income—$55.8 million in 1993 vs. $35.8 million in 1992. For the full year, net income in fiscal 1993 was $109.8 million before FAS 106 charges.

The officers responsible for Federal Express' decision-making, operations and maintenance at the time of publication are Frederick W. Smith, chairman, president and chief executive officer; William J. Razzouk, executive vice president of worldwide customer operations; Alan B. Graf, Jr., senior vice president and chief financial officer; and Theodore L. Weise, senior vice president of air operations.

Federal Express Financial Statistics[1]

(In millions)	1983	1984	1985	1986	1987	1988	1989	1990	1991	1992
Sales	1,008	1,436	2,016	2,573	3,178	3,883	5,167	7,015	7,688	7,550
Net Income (loss)	88.9	115.4	76.1	131.8	(65.6)	187.7	184.6	115.8	5.9	(113.8)
Assets	992	1,526	1,900	2,276	2,500	3,009	5,293	5,675	5,672	5,463
Liabilities	488	808	1,087	1,185	1,421	1,678	3,800	4,026	4,003	3,883
Net Worth	504	718	812	1,092	1,079	1,331	1,494	1,649	1,669	1,580

[1] All numbers are for Federal Express' fiscal year which ends May 31.

Federal Express Statistics

1992 Total Sales
Global/Major Airlines

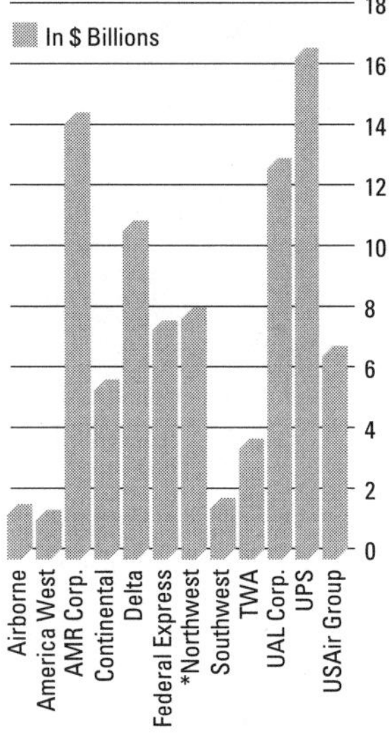

• Information is for Northwest Airlines only and not for parent company NWA Inc.

Federal Express' total sales for (its fiscal) 1992 were $7.55 billion, placing it sixth industrywide.

Federal Express experienced a 649-percent increase in total sales from June 1, 1983 to May 31, 1992.

Federal Express
Total Sales 1983-1992

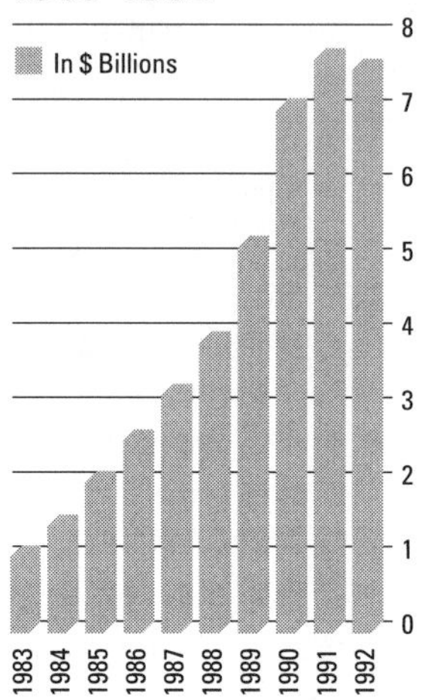

1992 Net Income
Global/Major Airlines

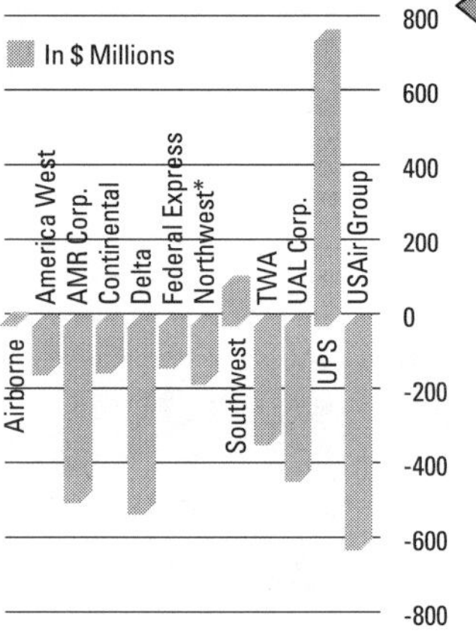

• Information is for Northwest Airlines only and not for parent company NWA Inc.

Despite its $113.8-million net loss, only three global/major airlines outperformed Federal Express in that area for 1992 (although the comparison is for calendar years for all airlines except Delta, which follows a July 1 through June 30 fiscal year; Federal Express' fiscal year ends May 31).

The fiscal 1992 loss was only Federal Express' second in the last 10 years, partially caused by a charge resulting from its pulling out of intra-European and intra-country markets.

Federal Express
Net Income 1983-1992

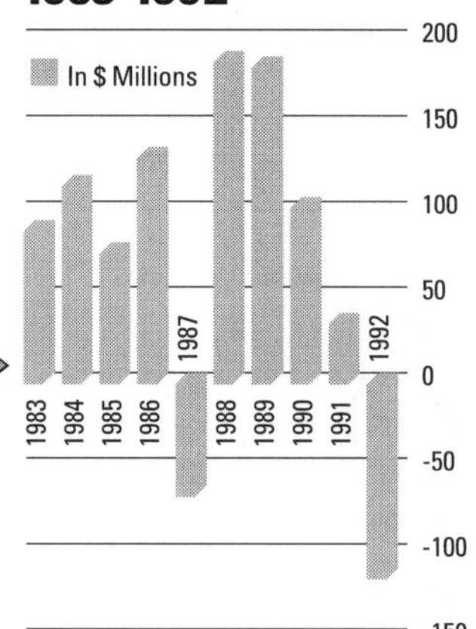

1992 Total Assets & Liabilities
Global/Major Airlines

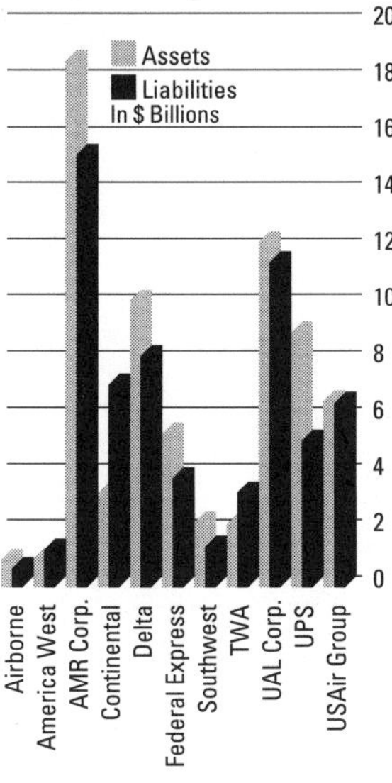

NWA Inc. is a privately held company and would not release 1990-1992 figures.

Federal Express placed sixth in 1992 among global/major airlines in the assets category, with a total of $5.46 billion. The carrier finished that same year with liabilities of $3.88 billion.

The value of Federal Express' assets and liabilities increased significantly between 1983 and 1992. The big jump in 1989 primarily is due to the Flying Tiger acquisiton. Federal Express' assets increased 81.6 percent to $5.463 billion in 1989 from $3.009 billion in 1988. Federal Express' liabilities jumped 131 percent to $3.883 billion in 1989 from $1.678 billion the previous year. The company's assets increased 451 percent, from $992 million in 1983 to $5.46 billion as of May 31, 1992.

Its liabilities increased 696 percent during the same period, from $488 million in 1983 to $3.88 billion in fiscal 1992

Federal Express
Assets & Liabilities 1983-1992

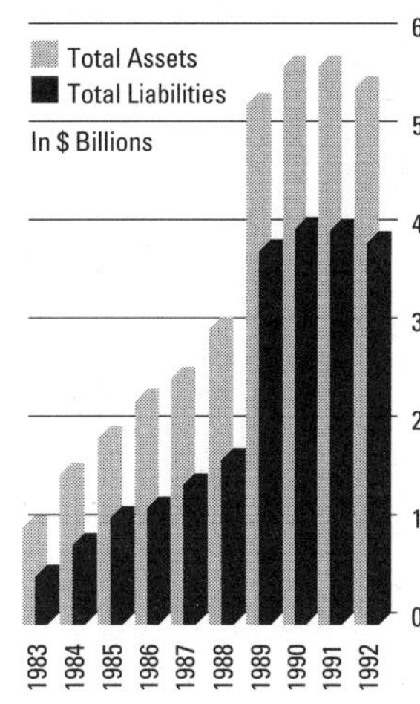

1992 Net Worth
Global/Major Airlines

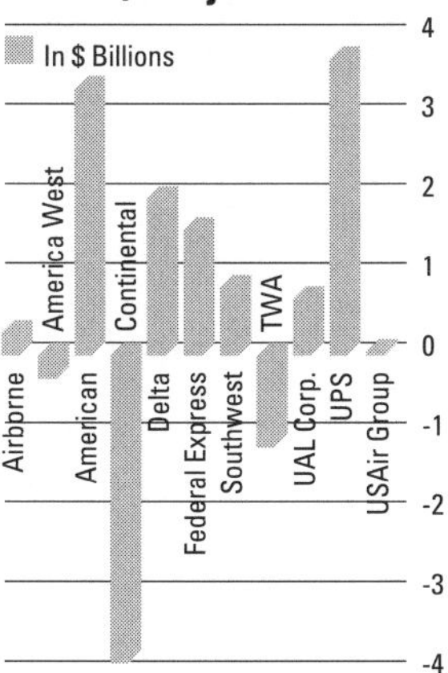

NWA Inc. is a privately held company and would not release 1990-1992 figures.

Federal Express had the industry's fourth-highest net worth in 1992 at $1.58 billion.

Federal Express also experienced phenomenal growth between 1983 and 1992. Its total assets increased 451 percent during the same period, from $992 million in fiscal 1983 to $5.46 billion as of May 31, 1992, while its total liabilities increased 696 percent. The company's net worth increased 213 percent, from $504 million in 1983 to $1.58 billion in fiscal 1992.

Federal Express
Net Worth 1983-1992

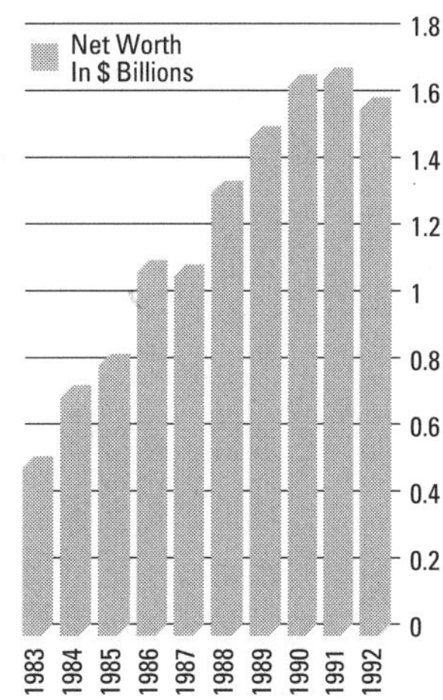

Statistics Related Terms

Assets — A resource having commercial or trade value that is owned (or which the company owns rights to) by a business. Typical examples for an airline include: Cash, securities, property, equipment, capital leases, landing slots and routes.

Cost per available seat mile — Represents operating and interest expense divided by available seat miles.

Financial accounting standard (FAS) 106 — A federally-mandated accounting change made to the way U.S. companies handle post-retirement benefits (other than pensions) to employees. FAS 106, for several U.S. global and major airlines, meant large, one-time, non-cash charges to earnings, further damaging their balance-sheet performance for 1992.

Leveraged buyout (LBO) — Takeover of a company using borrowed funds. Company assets often serve as security for the loans, although investors' assets also may be used.

Liabilities — The total amount the company owes to all creditors.

Net worth or stockholders' equity — The net assets (total assets minus total liabilities) of a company. For companies with more liabilities than assets, the result is a negative net worth or stockholders' deficit.

Federal Express News Abstracts

"Federal Express Corp. Names K.R. Newell, J.C. McCarty to Posts." *Wall Street Journal*, 4 Nov. 1991.

"Federal Express Earnings Plunge 79% But Firm, Some Others See Turnaround." *Wall Street Journal*, 20 March 1990.

"Federal Express Mulls Options to Stem Losses." *Wall Street Journal*, 12 Feb. 1992.

"Federal Express Orders Up to 75 Airbus Planes." *Wall Street Journal*, 8 July 1991.

"Federal Express Posts 5% Increase in Quarterly Profit." *Wall Street Journal*, 13 July 1990.

"Federal Express Still Dominant, But Not Absolutely, Positively." *Runways*, 5 Nov. 1990, p. 19.

"Federal Express to Cut 6,600 Jobs in European Units." *USA Today*, 17 March 1992.

"Federal Express to Take a Charge in its 3rd Period." *Wall Street Journal*, 7 Feb. 1991.

"New Soviet Air Service Rights Awarded to Alaska Airlines, Federal Express." *Aviation Week & Space Technology*, 10 Sep. 1990, p. 66.

"The Flying-Package Trade Takes Off." *U.S. News & World Report*, 2 Oct. 1989, pp. 47-50.

"'Trim' Growth." *Air Transport World*, Sep. 1991, pp. 74-78.

"Vindicated." *Forbes*, 9 Dec. 1991, pp. 198-202.

7

Northwest Airlines

Northwest quickly left behind its ties with mail service to establish an international reputation as the leading carrier to the Pacific. However, a leveraged buyout in 1989 made Northwest vulnerable to the industry downturn in the early 1990s.

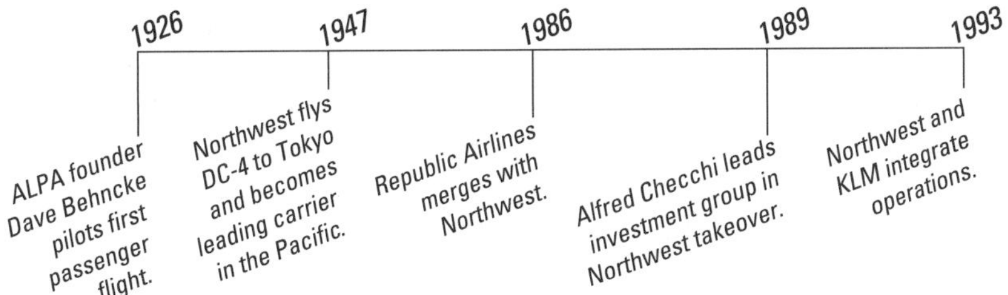

Northwest Airlines is the oldest continuously operated air carrier in the United States. It began in early 1926 as Dickenson Airlines, the property of Charles Dickenson, a Minneapolis entrepreneur who held the first private contract for airmail service to Chicago. Dave Behncke, the founder of the Air Line Pilots Association (ALPA), was the first airmail pilot Dickenson hired. Charles W. "Speed" Holman, a newly-hired pilot famous for racing and stunt flying, was among the first passengers of Dickenson Airlines. Holman was hitching a ride to his new job.

Much of airline history was prefigured in that first Dickenson/Northwest Airlines passenger flight that took Behncke and Holman from Chicago to St. Paul in late 1926. Dickenson Airlines soon became Northwest Airways with Col. Louis H. Brittin, developer of the St. Paul Airport, as its operations manager.

Dickenson/Northwest was typical of early-years airlines: hard-boiled toward labor. Holman, a daredevil, felt aerobatics was the natural employment for an aircraft and insisted on testing every airplane occasionally with a few loops. Conversely, Behncke was one of the first pilots to emphasize safety in the cockpit. It was daredevils like Holman who got aviation going;

nickel-watching airlines like Dickenson/Northwest that turned aviation into a true commercial enterprise; and safety-conscious, foresighted individuals like Behncke who won for airline employees a role in shaping commercial aviation policy and the working environment.

Northwest Airlines
Aircraft fleet and purchase commitments
As of May 1993

Aircraft Type	Current Fleet	Firm Orders	Options
A-320	50	16	0
B-727	57	0	0
B-747	39	0	0
B-747-400	12	6	0
B-757	33	40	0
DC-9	138	0	0
DC-10	29	0	0
MD-80	8	0	0
Total	366	62	0

Northwest Airways fired Behncke in early 1927 for refusing to fly an airplane Holman "warmed up" with a few loops. Holman then served as the carrier's chief pilot until 1931 when he lost his life in an airshow accident in Omaha, Neb.

Northwest moved quickly to establish itself as a full-service international airline. Hardly was the carrier airborne than it received three of the Stinson Detroiters it counted on for passenger service. Behncke, Detroiter manufacturer Eddie Stinson and Raymond Collins, an executive specializing in aviation finances, were the three pilots who picked up those first three Detroiters.

The carrier in 1928 introduced weekly international service between Fargo, N.D., and Winnipeg, Manitoba, Canada. Northwest flew to 10 cities by the end of 1929, and embarked on an ambitious aircraft purchase program: the company bought five Ford TriMotors and nine Hamilton Metalplanes over a period of three years starting in 1928. Control of Northwest effectively changed twice by 1929, with the company resting in the hands of a Minneapolis banker as the airline entered the 1930s.

The rapid expansion attracted notice, and in 1930 a group of Minnesota financiers bought the company and moved its headquarters to downtown St. Paul Airport. Northwest Airways Inc. reincorporated as Northwest Airlines Inc. on April 16, 1934. Conflicts with the fledgling pilots' union, ALPA, began that same year over Northwest's policy of paying pilots a flat monthly rate.

Northwest extended its route system over the Rockies to the West Coast by 1935, modernized its equipment with the introduction of the Lockheed 10A Electra and acquired a new president, Croil Hunter. Hunter guided the carrier through most of the Great Depression years, all of the World War II years and their immediate aftermath. Hunter also made the Douglas DC-3 a part of the Northwest fleet in early 1939.

Hunter's decision to buy DC-3s (36 of them, eventually) bore several kinds of fruit: First, it allowed Northwest to use flight attendants—great image builders for passenger service; second, it enabled passenger revenues to exceed airmail revenues for the first time; third, and partly because of the first two advantages, this large, modern aircraft allowed the company to seek equity financing through a public stock offering in 1941. The latter was crucial because access to capital markets is an essential in the life-or-death struggle of the airline industry.

Hunter's decision to buy the Lockheed 14H Super Electra bore another kind of fruit: The aircraft had a severe vibration problem, and Secretary of Commerce Daniel C. Roper suspended Northwest's operating certificate for several days in early 1938 following a fatal crash caused by the in-flight disintegration of a Super Electra's tail.

The Army appropriated almost half of Northwest's fleet for war duty with the onset of U.S. involvement in World War II. Northwest was chosen to establish an aerial supply route to Alaska and the Aleutian Islands because of its pilots' extensive experience flying in cold weather. Northwest pilots flew more than 21 million miles across the "Alaskan Air Bridge" by 1945. Other Northwest missions: The company operated a bomber modification plant in St. Paul where it outfitted more than 3,000 B-24s, B-25s and B-26s with special equipment; and, Northwest used 14 military transports to carry soldiers from the East Coast to the West Coast for redeployment to the Pacific Theater as the war in Europe ended.

Northwest set out after the war to capitalize on its Alaskan experience by operating over the Northwest Passage to the Orient. Northwest began flying to Alaska in 1946, followed quickly by service to Shemya Island in the Aleutians. Northwest earned the right to add "Orient" to its name when it completed its reach to the Orient on July 15 of the following year; a Northwest DC-4 landed in Tokyo after flying from Shemya Island to Tokyo, Seoul and Shanghai.

Northwest was the fourth-largest domestic airline and a leading international carrier to the Pacific by the end of the 1940s. The company began a major fleet modernization program to maintain its industry position, and the first of 10 Boeing 377 Stratocruisers joined the fleet in June 1949. The first of 24 Douglas DC-6s entered trans-Pacific service in 1954. Introduction of the Lockheed Super Constellation the following year gave Northwest further capability in the Pacific, and in 1957 the first of 17 DC-7Cs arrived. Nicknamed "The Seven Seas," the DC-7C was instrumental in Northwest's early efforts to establish its Pacific air freight business.

Meanwhile, the Korean War brought Northwest a new role: prime contractor for the Korean Airlift. Hunter left the airline in 1953 and Harold Harris, a former Pan Am vice president, took over for one year. Then, Donald W. Nyrop began a 22-year tenure in 1954 as the carrier's top officer. The 1950s also saw Northwest introduce service to points in Florida and Tokyo.

Northwest entered the Jet Age in 1960 by ordering five Douglas DC-8s. The carrier bought 17 B-720Bs in the next several years primarily for domestic service; 41 B-707s to meet international needs; and the first of 85 B-727s. Northwest removed all the propeller aircraft from the fleet in the years 1960 through 1971. The corporate logo changed in 1962 to the outline of a B-707 tail within a red circle to reflect Northwest's new identity as a jet airline.

Northwest's Pacific Basin service expanded in the 1960s. The first of Northwest's B-747s, delivered on April 30, 1970, led to a Tokyo hub, and by the mid-1970s Northwest flew to six Far Eastern cities from Tokyo. In fact, Northwest flew to Tokyo from six trans-Pacific gateways and to Seoul, South Korea, nonstop from Chicago, Los Angeles and Seattle by the end of 1986. Northwest became the leading U.S. flag carrier in the Pacific with 77 B-747 flights per week out of six U.S. gateways to 11 Asian destinations.

A new mix of leadership in 1976 brought a drive to develop Northwest's trans-Atlantic service. M. Joseph Lapensky became president and chief operating officer while Nyrop remained as chairman and chief executive. The first move involved B-747 freighters providing service from Boston and New York to Glasgow, Scotland and Copenhagen, Denmark. Passenger service began later in 1979 with flights from the United States to Stockholm, Copenhagen and Glasgow. Northwest's trans-Atlantic expansion was rapid from then on. Northwest ranked sixth in the number of passengers carried across the Atlantic by the end of 1986.

About this time, Northwest—like Continental, Delta and USAir—began casting about for the "critical mass" needed to survive in a deregulated environment; it sought a merger partner, an alliance to enhance an already powerful domestic structure and to swell the carrier to survivor dimensions. It found Republic.

Northwest Airlines
Aircraft fleet: 1983-1992

Aircraft	1983	1984	1985	1986	1987	1988	1989	1990	1991	1992
B-747-400	—	—	—	—	—	—	—	10	10	10
B-747	30	35	35	38	40	41	43	40	40	40
DC-10	22	19	19	20	20	20	20	20	20	29
A-320	—	—	—	—	—	—	2	11	11	40
B-757	—	—	13	29	28	33	33	33	33	33
B-727	65	65	65	80	76	71	71	71	71	69
MD-80	—	—	—	8	8	8	8	8	8	8
DC-9	—	—	—	126	130	139	139	140	140	143
Convair 580	—	—	13	13	—	—	—	—	—	—
Total	117	119	145	314	302	312	316	333	333	372

North Central Airlines/Southern Airways

Republic Airlines itself was the product of a merger: the 1979 merger of regional carriers North Central Airlines and Southern Airways. North Central was born of a Waco biplane that hauled executives of Four Wheel Drive Auto Co. of Clintonville, Wis., to Chicago and back. From the biplane came Four Wheel Drive's Wisconsin Central Airlines (1944), and from the Four Wheel Drive company airline came North Central Airlines (1952) headquartered at Minneapolis-St. Paul.

Frank Hulse founded Southern Airways Inc. in 1929 as a fixed-base operation. Twenty years later the Civil Aeronautics Board issued a temporary operating certificate to Southern and the new airline flew its first scheduled flight from Atlanta to Memphis in June 1949.

North Central Airlines had more than 4,100 employees by the end of 1978 and reported a profit of $22.1 million from revenues of $298.5 million. Southern had more than 3,000 employees and turned a profit of $2.4 million on revenues of $188.5 million.

Republic Airlines

These two healthy airlines merged in 1979 and called themselves Republic Airlines. The new entity then did an unhealthy thing: It acquired Hughes Airwest in 1980. The cost of this acquisition proved a terrible burden to Republic which lost $24.7 million in 1980 (interest expense: $48.3 million) and $46.3 million in 1981 (interest expense: $108 million). The bleeding continued over the next two years with 1982 bringing a $39.9-million loss and 1983 a $111-million loss.

Stephen M. Wolf, formerly of Texas Air, became president and chief executive officer of Republic in 1984. Wolf immediately took aggressive steps to stem the company's losses, including suspending service to 23 markets and negotiating new union contracts. The payoff came the same year: Republic showed a healthy profit of $29.5 million in 1984. The next year it finished with a record profit of $177 million.

Recovery in tow, Republic Airlines began looking for a merger partner. It found Northwest.

Not for a long time had Northwest been the fourth-largest U.S. airline. Northwest, while celebrating its 60th anniversary on July 29, 1986, acquired Republic and became once again the nation's fourth-largest carrier in terms of revenue passenger miles. The merger also gave Northwest hubs at Detroit and Memphis, Tenn., where Republic teamed up with regional airlines to establish powerful connecting systems. The Northwest fleet now stood at 314 aircraft; the service network, 135 cities in 18 countries.

NWA Inc., a holding company, formed in 1984 to manage Northwest's resources and protect its capital. NWA included Northwest Airlines Inc., Northwest Aircraft Inc., Northwest Aerospace Training Corp. (NATCO) and MLT Vacations Inc. Northwest Aircraft markets used aircraft from the Northwest fleet and acquires aircraft for Northwest and its regional airline partners. NATCO trains pilots for governments, corporations, Northwest and other airlines. MLT Vacations is a major wholesaler of travel and tour programs.

Steven G. Rothmeier succeeded Nyrop as chairman and chief executive officer and John F. Horn became president and chief operating officer. The new leadership was much like the old: dynamic, but autocratic and obsessed with cost containment. The latter paid off, but created takeover bait: NWA had a debt/equity ratio of .6:1 entering 1989 and a record of 39 straight years of profitability (with net earnings in fiscal 1988 of $135.1 million). Awash in cash, virtually debt-free, NWA was too strong a lure for Alfred A. Checchi, and in June 1989 NWA's board of directors agreed to sell to Wings Holdings Inc., an investor group led by Checchi, for $3.65 billion. Checchi and former Marriott colleague and equity partner Gary Wilson won after three months of intense bargaining, although two other suitors, investor Marvin Davis and Pan Am Corp., failed earlier in the year.

Checchi took over as chairman after Rothmeier left to go into investment banking. Wings Holdings partner Frederic Malek came in as president and the two men took NWA private. On the agenda: to lure back business travelers by earmarking $422 million over five years to improve passenger service and enhance Northwest's image.

NWA, in going private, also took on a whopping debt load of $3.6 billion, making it extremely vulnerable to an industry downturn. The slowdown came in August 1990 when Iraq invaded Kuwait: Air travel dropped off and fuel prices spiraled upward. Cost pressures forced Checchi to ask unions—the same groups who supported him in the takeover—for concessions.

Northwest reported a 47-percent drop in earnings the third quarter of 1990. The company posted in September net income of $91 million—down from $134 million the previous year. Northwest then named its third president since Checchi's buyout. John Dasburg, previously executive vice president of finance and administration, replaced Frederick Rentschler who succeeded Frederic Malek earlier in the year when Malek assumed the title of vice chairman.

With Dasburg at the helm, Northwest, already a key player in the lucrative Pacific market, sought to enhance its position and purchased for $20 million five key routes and a 25-percent stake in Hawaiian Airlines. With the purchase came rights to fly to the Pacific island of Saipan from major cities Nagoya and Fukuok, and into Australia via Honolulu.

The Hawaiian purchase was testament to Northwest's desire to grow. "We've made no secret of the fact that one way—and a very useful way of getting bigger—is by buying the assets of a domestic airline," said Northwest's vice president of law and public affairs, Elliott Seiden, in an interview. Already Checchi sent shock waves through the industry in mid-1990 with his proposal of a controlled liquidation of Eastern. Several months later, Northwest matched United's bid of $35.5 million and in February 1991 acquired all Eastern Air Lines' gates and facilities at National Airport in Washington, D.C. The sale gave Northwest five gates and 76 landing and takeoff slots, making Washington, D.C. Northwest's fourth-largest base of operations after Minneapolis, Detroit and Memphis. Northwest needed the Washington slots to feed Atlanta, earmarked as a possible hub to position Northwest for north-south routes along the East Coast.

Meanwhile, the recession and escalating fuel prices continued to erode profits; Northwest reported a fourth-quarter 1990 net loss of $121.4 million and a full-year loss of $10.4 million. The company reduced its international flight schedule 17 percent in January 1991 and Checchi informed workers he would look for a merger partner.

Continental was the front-runner when merger talks escalated in August 1991. A Northwest/Continental combination would create the U.S.' largest airline and allow Northwest to fly east-west in the Southern tier. The difficulty: merging Northwest's heavily unionized work force with a majority non-union force at Continental. Several other airlines also were the subject of acquisition discussions: the Trump Shuttle, Midway and America West.

Northwest continued its asset hunt and in August 1991 loaned America West $20 million in exchange for a two-year option to purchase its Honolulu-Nagoya route for $15 million. An ensuing code-share arrangement gave Northwest presence in the Southwest and West Coast markets where it was less known. Final approval for the Honolulu-Nagoya route exchange came in March 1992.

NWA Inc. Financial Statistics

(In millions)	1983	1984	1985	1986	1987	1988	1989	1990*	1991*	1992*
Sales	2,196	2,445	2,656	3,589	5,142	5,650	6,554	7,257	7,534	7,964
Net Income (loss)	50.1	55.9	73.1	76.9	103	135.1	355.3	(10.4)	(3.1)	(156)
Assets	1,602	1,754	2,320	4,323	4,269	4,372	5,347	–	–	–
Liabilities	748	861	1,373	3,217	2,746	2,738	2,894	–	–	–
Net Worth	854	893	947	1,106	1,523	1,634	2,453	–	–	–
ASMs*	29,511	32,664	37,149	48,408	61,420	61,275	70,250	77,317	80,827	89,142
RPMs*	17,712	19,772	22,341	28,815	39,550	40,148	45,660	51,490	53,196	58,226
Load Factors*	60%	60.5%	60.1%	59.5%	64.4%	65.5%	56.5%	66.6%	65.8%	65.3%

*Information is for Northwest Airlines only.

After cementing transactions with Hawaiian, Eastern and America West, Northwest failed to make good on several pacts, including a proposed hub operation in Atlanta and possible management of the Trump Shuttle. Merger talks with Continental also ended. Yet the most serious admission to Northwest's growing reputation as a failed deal maker came with its abrupt withdrawal from a tentative pact with Midway. Northwest in October 1991 paid $20 million in cash and agreed to assume $4.7 million of Midway's obligations for 21 gates at Chicago Midway. Northwest also would pay $150 million more in cash, notes and assumed liability for the remaining assets. Chicago-based Midway, then operating under Chapter 11 bankruptcy reorganization, immediately shut down after the transaction failed, blaming Northwest for its demise.

Midway chairman David R. Hinson in an interview in *Aviation Week & Space Technology* accused Northwest of reneging on its commitment to acquire remaining assets after it completed the acquisition of Midway's 21 gates at the airport. Analysts speculate Northwest initiated the transaction to keep Southwest out of the Chicago area; Northwest's approved $140-million to $170-million buyout plan came at the expense of Southwest's competing offer of $109 million. Northwest claimed in its defense it based its initial offer on allegedly misleading traffic and revenue information. A review by the DOT inspector general several months later showed Midway did report inaccurate data, although there was no indication Midway deliberately misrepresented the information.

Northwest reported in February 1992 a fourth-quarter 1991 net loss of $79.2 million and a net loss of $3.1 million for the year. Parent NWA Inc. suffered a fourth-quarter 1991 net loss of $164.3 million and a full-year net loss of $316.9 million. Such losses forced Northwest in March to ground flights between Atlanta's Hartsfield International and Washington National. The majority of those flights—former Eastern Air Lines' routes—operated at less than 25 percent occupancy.

Good news came in March when Minnesota officials signed the final documents giving the airline $665 million in financing, allowing it to build aircraft maintenance facilities in the state. The package comprised $835 million in loan guarantees, general obligation and revenue bonds, grants and tax breaks. The financing failed, however, to insulate Northwest from diluted revenues from an ill-conceived promotion: Northwest's grown-ups-fly-free fare sale, offered in response to American's value pricing plan. The promotion and the summer fare wars that ensued largely were responsible for the carrier's dismal performance during a traditionally strong financial quarter. Checchi, forced to announce in June 1992 the first of a string of layoffs at the company, then went to the unions for help and issued a request to pilots for $500 million in concessions. The pilots responded with an analysis of the company's finances, and in September 1992, offered a counterproposal with pay and work rule concessions totaling $100 million in annual savings over three years.

Rumors of a possible Chapter 11 filing surfaced in November after Northwest reportedly depleted a $600-million credit line scheduled to last through the winter. Northwest had on hand enough cash—$300 million—to operate for 60 days, according to an article in *USA Today*. KLM Royal Dutch Airlines responded with a $50-million loan, provided other investors would commit $250 million more. Lenders and suppliers contributed the additional funds and allowed the airline to delay $340 million in principal payments on debt due. Northwest's six unions then pledged $900 million in concessions to be achieved through separate negotiations.

KLM, which held a 49-percent equity stake in Northwest, offered the $50 million after the government approved the two airlines' request to link operations more closely. The linkup was possible due to the open-skies pact signed in September 1992 allowing KLM and U.S. carriers to fly without restriction between points in the U.S. and the Netherlands. Northwest and KLM received the official go-ahead to operate as one airline when the DOT granted the carriers immunity from antitrust laws in January 1993.

The KLM alliance, however, was not a panacea, though it provided emergency funds to the financially-ailing carrier and would bring growth to Northwest's route structure. Northwest management, in response to mounting financial problems, in June 1993 threatened to file for bankruptcy-law protection unless its three unions agreed to $886 million in wage and benefit cuts.

The officers responsible for the carrier's operations, maintenance and decision-making at the time of publication are John Dasburg, president and chief executive officer; Michael E. Levine, executive vice president of marketing; William Slattery, executive vice president of operations; and John Kern, executive vice president of maintenance and flight operations.

Northwest Airlines Statistics

1992 Total Sales
Global/Major Airlines

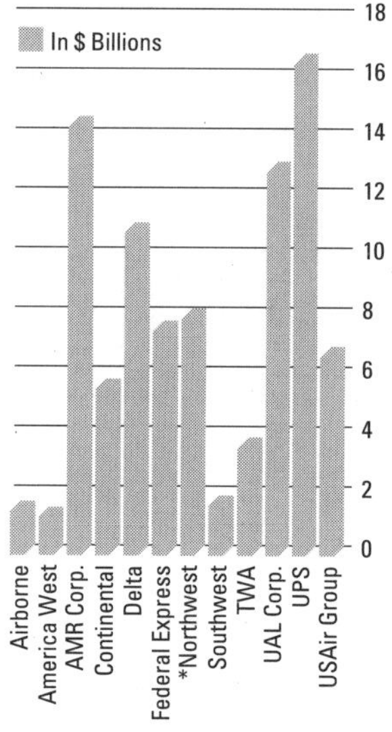

• Information is for Northwest Airlines only and not for parent company NWA Inc.

Northwest Airlines placed fifth in the industry with total 1992 revenues of $7.964 billion, trailing AMR, Delta, UAL and UPS.

Northwest's revenues increased 263 percent during the period 1983 to 1992. The increase in sales, $3.6 billion in 1986 to $5.1 billion in 1987, mainly is due to Northwest's merger with Republic in 1986. Revenue growth for 1991 and 1992 measured 3.8 percent and 5.7 percent, respectively.

Northwest
Total Sales 1983-1992

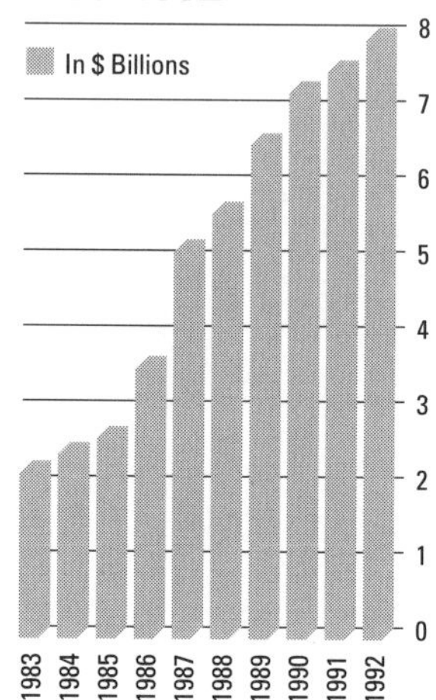

1992 Net Income
Global/Major Airlines

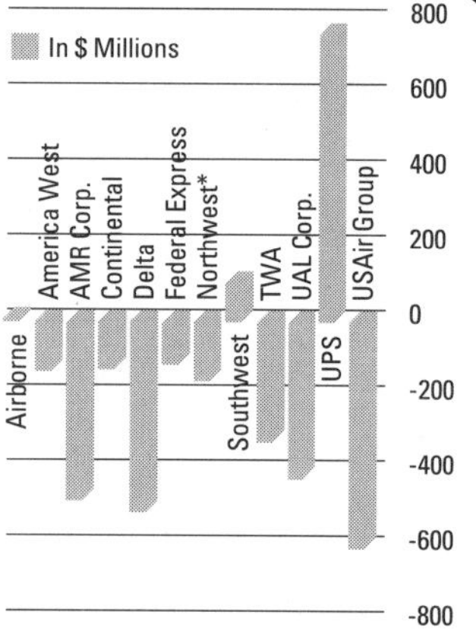

• Information is for Northwest Airlines only and not for parent company NWA Inc.

Northwest's pre-FAS-106 net loss of $156 million was less severe than several other airlines' losses. Its parent company, NWA Inc., lost $405.1 million in 1992 before its FAS-106-related charge.

NWA Inc. earned nearly $850 million in profits from 1983 to 1989. The airline itself lost $169.5 million during the first three years of the 1990s, with the losses of parent NWA Inc. even more severe ($722 million for 1991 and 1992).

Northwest
Net Income 1983-1992

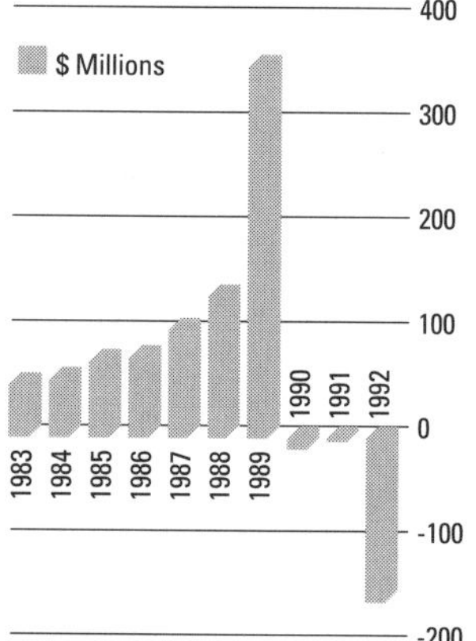

NWA Inc.
Net Worth 1983-1989

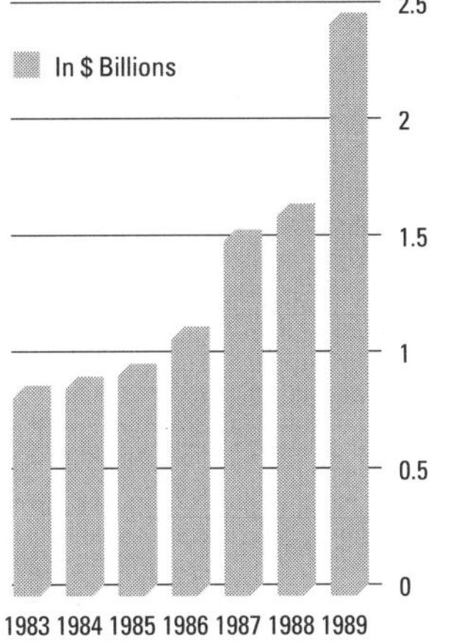

NWA Inc. ranked third in net worth in 1989 behind AMR Corp. and Delta, with a net worth of $2.45 billion. Figures for 1990 through 1992 were unavailable.

NWA was the fifth-largest company based on total assets in 1989 with assets of $5.347 billion. Figures for 1990 through 1992 were unavailable from Northwest.

NWA Inc.
Assets & Liabilities 1983-1989

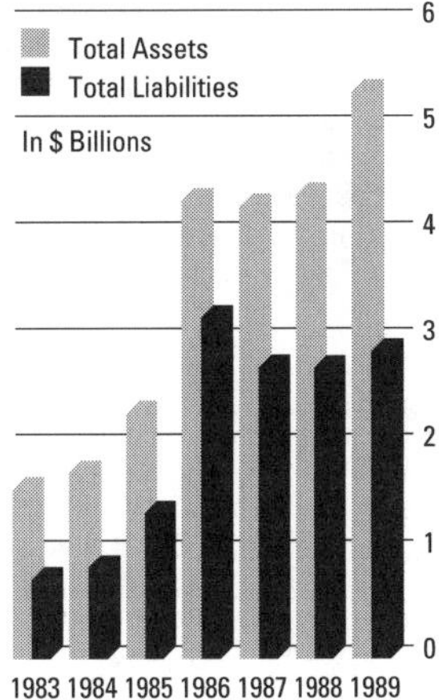

1992 ASMs & RPMs
Global/Major Airlines

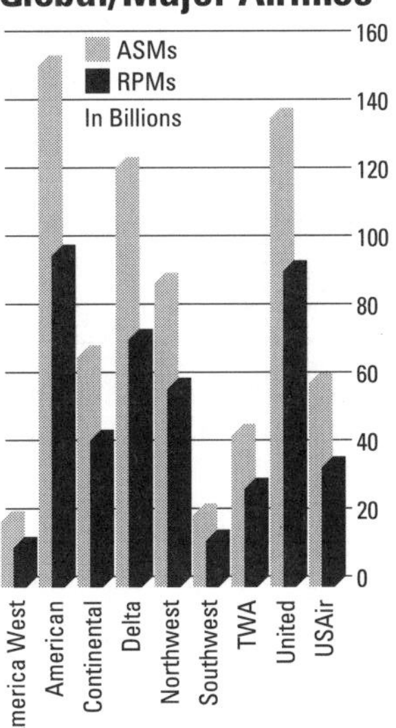

Northwest finished 1992 as the fourth-largest airline in terms of capacity. Northwest trailed third-place Delta by 33.96 billion available seat miles (ASMs; Delta's figures are for its fiscal year).

Northwest had 89.142 billion ASMs in 1992, a 202-percent increase over its 1983 figures. Its revenue passenger miles (RPMs) increased 229 percent over the same period. Its 1992 increases in ASMs and RPMs were 10.3 percent and 9.5 percent, respectively. Northwest's 58.226 billion RPMs gave it a 1992 load factor of 65.3 percent, down one-half of one point from 1991, but still good enough for second place behind United's 67.4-percent load factor.

Northwest
ASMs & RPMs 1983-1992

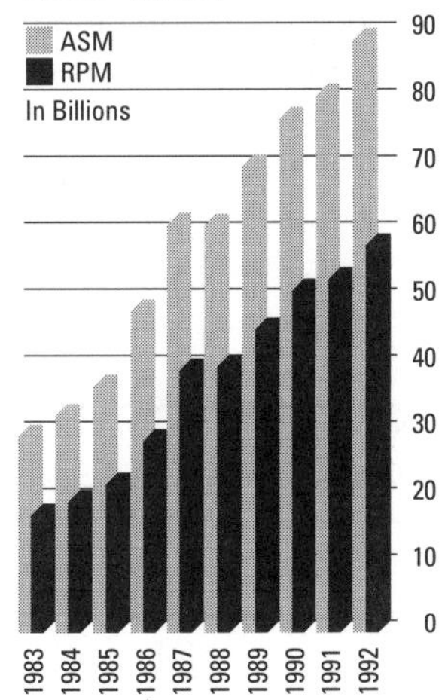

Statistics Related Terms

Assets — A resource having commercial or trade value that is owned (or which the company owns rights to) by a business. Typical examples for an airline include: Cash, securities, property, equipment, capital leases, landing slots and routes.

Available seat miles (ASMs) — Represent the number of seats available for passengers multiplied by the number of scheduled miles those seats are flown.

Cost per available seat mile — Represents operating and interest expense divided by available seat miles.

Financial accounting standard (FAS) 106 — A federally-mandated accounting change made to the way U.S. companies handle post-retirement benefits (other than pensions) to employees. FAS 106, for several U.S. global and major airlines, meant large, one-time, non-cash charges to earnings, further damaging their balance-sheet performance for 1992.

Leveraged buyout (LBO) — Takeover of a company using borrowed funds. Company assets often serve as security for the loans, although investors' assets also may be used.

Liabilities — The total amount the company owes to all creditors.

Net worth or stockholders' equity — The net assets (total assets minus total liabilities) of a company. For companies with more liabilities than assets, the result is a negative net worth or stockholders' deficit.

Passenger load factor — Revenue passenger miles divided by available seat miles over a set period of time.

Revenue passenger miles (RPMs) — The number of miles flown by revenue-producing passengers.

Yield — The average revenue received for each mile a revenue passenger is carried. Determined by dividing total operating revenue by total revenue passenger miles.

Northwest Airlines Abstracts

"All Al Checchi Needs Now is Cash." *Business Week,* 25 Feb. 1991, p. 39.

"AMR Advances in Bid to Run Trump Shuttle." *Wall Street Journal,* 20 Sep. 1991, sec. A, p. 4.

"Flying Circus: Northwest Goes Gunning for Delta in Detroit." *The Atlanta Journal-Constitution,* 7 Feb. 1992.

"Midway Clears Way for Northwest Air to Sell Airport Gates." *Wall Street Journal,* 22 Nov. 1991, sec. B, p. 3.

"Northwest Air Cancels Airbus Order, Delays Boeing Delivery to Cut its Costs." *Wall Street Journal,* 28 Jan. 1992, sec. A, p. 3.

"Northwest Air Drops Plan to Service Route Suspended by Pan Am." *Wall Street Journal,* 10 April 1991, sec. A, p. 4, col. 1.

"Northwest Air Plans to Lay Off 2.2% of its Work Force in Move to Trim Costs." *Wall Street Journal,* 5 Jan. 1993.

"Northwest Air, KLM Agree to Meld More Activities." *Wall Street Journal,* 10 Sep. 1992, sec. A, p. 3.

"Northwest Airlines Gets New Loans, Realigns Orders With Aircraft Makers." *The Atlanta Journal-Constitution,* 8 Dec. 1992, sec. F, p. 3.

"Northwest Airlines Renews its Attempt to Acquire Troubled Continental Air." *Wall Street Journal,* 22 Aug. 1991, sec. A, p. 3.

"Northwest Airlines Traffic Down." *Wall Street Journal,* 11 March 1991, sec. B, p. 7, col. 6.

"Northwest Cuts 565 More Jobs." *USA Today,* 17 Nov. 1992, p. 1.

"Northwest Locked in Battle to Survive in '90's." *The Atlanta Journal-Constitution,* 29 June 1992.

"Northwest Looks to High Tech for Competitive Gain." *Professional Pilot,* Jan. 1992, pp. 78-82.

"Northwest Pilots Reject Cuts, Propose Buying Stake." *Wall Street Journal,* 5 March 1991, sec. A, p. 4, col. 5.

"Northwest Pursues Labor Cuts, Discounts to Improve Balance Sheet." *Aviation Week & Space Technology,* 20 July 1992, p. 34.

"Northwest Seeks Midway Documents in Bid to Prove Records Were Falsified." *The Atlanta Journal-Constitution,* 27 Nov. 1991.

"Northwest Sues American Alleging Predatory Pricing." *Wall Street Journal,* 15 June 1992, sec. A, p. 5.

"Northwest's Captain Leaves on the Seat-Belt Sign." *Wall Street Journal,* 12 March 1991, sec. A, p. 19, col. 3.

"Northwest, TWA Announce Layoffs." *The Atlanta Journal-Constitution,* 2 Oct. 1992.

"NWA in Talks to Operate, Buy Trump Shuttle." *Wall Street Journal,* 8 March 1991, sec. A, p. 3, col. 4.

"NWA Weighs Sale of Routes, Merger Option." *Wall Street Journal,* 11 Feb. 1991, sec. A, p. 3, col. 3.

"NWA's Northwest Sets $744 Million Financing Accord." *Wall Street Journal,* 12 Nov. 1991.

"Sam Skinner's Game of Darwin-in-the-Sky." *Business Week,* 25 March 1991, p. 28.

"'Scrambling Well.'" *Air Transport World,* July 1991, pp. 57-60.

"Skinner Eases Curbs on Stakes in U.S. Airlines." *Wall Street Journal,* 24 Jan. 1991, sec. A, p. 5, col. 1.

"U.S. Airlines Try to Attract Fliers With Mile Awards." *Wall Street Journal,* 8 Sep. 1992.

"U.S. Gives Delta Temporary Rights to Pan Am Route." *Wall Street Journal,* 6 Dec. 1991.

"Who's News; NWA Inc." *Wall Street Journal,* 9 Jan. 1991, sec. B, p. 4, col. 5.

8

Southwest Airlines

Southwest from its inception stirred its competitors' ire with fares designed to lure passengers from their cars. The Texas-based airline through time always remained true to its short-haul, low-fare niche.

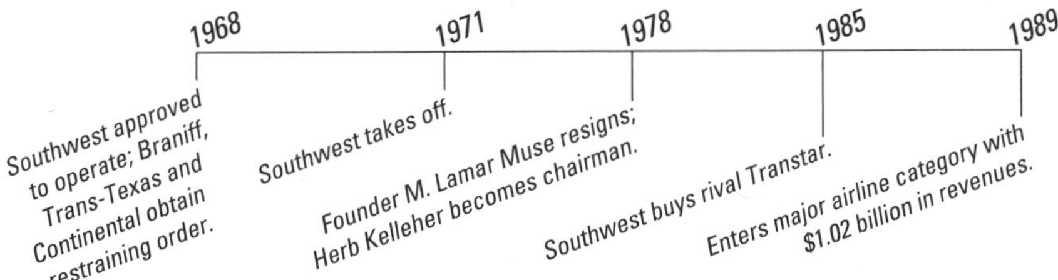

Rollin King started Southwest Airlines down the highway of time, but it was Herb Kelleher, the genius of the crossroads, who rescued the company in its times of trial and spirited the short-haul, no-frills carrier onto the fast lane. M. Lamar Muse was the airline's muse for a while. Then Kelleher took over that role, too.

King, while shutting down a small commuter airline he owned in 1966, began exploring the idea of a bigger carrier to serve Texas' three largest metropolitan areas. King completed his marketing and feasibility studies and decided in early 1967 to go forward with a company. He asked Kelleher, his attorney, to take the necessary legal steps to incorporate. Kelleher, initially skeptical of King's idea, agreed to do the legal work anyway, gratis.

Kelleher, however, became so enthralled with the idea he invested his own money in it. Kelleher arranged for initial capital and filed an application with the Texas Aeronautics Commission (TAC) for the new airline, named Air Southwest Co., to fly between Dallas and Houston, Dallas and San Antonio and Houston and San Antonio. (The company's application did not fall under jurisdiction of the Civil Aeronautics Board since the business plan called for Air Southwest to fly only within the state of Texas.)

TAC approved the application on Feb. 20, 1968, but the next day three airlines, Braniff, Trans-Texas (later Texas International) and Continental, obtained a temporary restraining order preventing the commission from giving Southwest a certificate. These airlines argued in court that Southwest's proposed markets already were saturated and would not support added competition. Southwest lost this trial and its appeal to the state Court of Civil Appeals. Kelleher, undismayed, appealed to the Texas Supreme Court which, in March 1970, overturned the lower court rulings and decided in Southwest's favor.

The original complainants still were unwilling to share Texas with an upstart and took their case to the U.S. Supreme Court. But, the high court refused to hear the appeal and finally, in December 1970, Southwest could refocus its energies on raising the capital to begin operations. Muse became Southwest's president the following month.

Muse inherited a company with only $142 in the bank and bills totaling more than $80,000 in the winter of 1971. Paying the bills and raising enough capital to get the airline off the ground was the immediate task. Muse succeeded on all points after garnering $6.5 million from a stock offering and $1.25 million in promissory notes. The carrier took off on June 18, 1971, after one final legal thrust from Braniff and Texas International. The name under which it flew was Southwest Airlines, the same name formerly carried by the commuter King shut down five years earlier.

Southwest Airlines
Aircraft fleet and purchase commitments
As of May 1993

Aircraft Type	Current Fleet	Firm Orders	Options
B-737	146	59	53
Total	146	59	53

Five years: That's how long it took to create Southwest Airlines under airline regulation. There was no basis for the Braniff-TI-Continental legal action without regulation, and voices favoring deregulation began to sound.

Kelleher, King and Muse recognized their decision to make Southwest an intra-Texas short-haul carrier put them in direct competition with the automobile. Their answer: make flying both quicker and cheaper than driving. Old-guard airline people thought the strategy quixotic: Airline fares could not be cheaper than driving, and Southwest's short routes could not be quicker.

But Muse and Co. were inspired. The airline flew with only a single class of passenger seat and very low fares, point-to-point. Destinations, each with only a 10-minute stop, were at airports close to business centers to attract the frequent traveler. Thus, Dallas' Love Field and Houston's Hobby Airport became the focal points of Southwest's operations.

Southwest's innovative two-tier fare system began after only five months in the air. The idea was born of the necessity of ferrying planes from Houston back to Dallas for servicing. Rather than fly empty planes, Muse charged $10 for a ticket to catch an evening flight to Dallas. Southwest had to turn people away by the end of the second week.

The first six months of operations, though successful, must have seemed like a gimmick to competitors Continental, Texas International, Braniff and American. Southwest's operations from the outside had all the signs of a sweatshop. Morale was high on the inside—so high that from its inception Southwest established the best productivity per employee in the airline industry.

Southwest entered 1973 with a two-tier fare system of $26 by day and $13 by night. Even these low fares were not low enough in the San Antonio-Dallas market, so Southwest dropped its fares on that route to $13 a seat, night or day. Angered, Braniff responded with $13 one-way daytime fares on Southwest's most lucrative flights, Dallas to Houston. The blow infuriated Southwest's management. The company had less than $350,000 in cash and management felt Southwest would go out of business if it reduced its fares to match Braniff's.

Muse challenged Braniff by raising public consciousness of the stakes. He began a campaign—the cornerstone of which was newspaper advertising—in Dallas and Houston that began, "Nobody's going to shoot Southwest Airlines out of the sky for a lousy $13!" Southwest offered passengers a choice: Pay the matching Southwest fare of $13 or pay the full fare of $26 and receive a gift. The gift was liquor. Braniff withdrew from the Dallas Love-Houston Hobby market a little more than two months later.

Southwest survived its first major challenge by vanquishing a competitor, realizing its first quarterly profit and becoming the largest-volume distributor of Chivas Regal, Crown Royal and Smirnoff in Texas. Meanwhile, Kelleher kept busy preparing Southwest's defense against a lawsuit: The cities of Dallas and Fort Worth wanted to force Southwest to move from Love Field to the soon-to-open Dallas/Fort Worth International Airport. A federal court ruled in July 1973 that Southwest could operate at Love Field while the field remained open. The cities appealed, and in January 1975, the U.S. Supreme Court let the original decision stand.

The TAC's approval of Southwest's request (of July 1973) to add Harlingen, Texas, as a destination landed the carrier in court again the very next month when Texas International sought a restraining order against the new service. Southwest started flying the route under TAC authority as the litigation began its slow march. Meanwhile, a strike grounded Texas International, weakening TI's arguments against the Southwest service. Then came a federal indictment of TI and Braniff for conspiring to put Southwest out of business. A district court in October 1976, no doubt influenced by the strike and indictment, sustained the TAC's decision to allow Southwest to serve Harlingen.

Southwest had 517 employees and six B-737-200s by the end of 1976. Revenues and net income grew from \$2.13 million and a loss of \$3.75 million, respectively, in 1971 to \$30.9 million and a profit of \$4.94 million in 1976. Southwest proved an airline could profit while providing quality air transportation at low fares. Congress hailed Southwest's track record as an example of a deregulated airline industry. Southwest, the argument went, accomplished its wonders despite regulatory barriers to free-wheeling competition; imagine what the industry could accomplish if the government removed those barriers.

President Jimmy Carter signed the Deregulation Act in October 1978 and Southwest took advantage of the act's provision that a carrier could enter one route a year without CAB permission. It immediately added Houston-New Orleans to its route system and, in January 1979, requested approval to fly from Dallas to New Orleans. The Dallas-New Orleans request caught the attention of Jim Wright, majority leader of the House of Representatives. Wright's concern was that service at Dallas/Fort Worth International could face threats if interstate travel took place out of Love Field. When the CAB approved Southwest's request, Wright responded with a bill (which later became law) to restrict passenger service from Love Field to states adjacent to Texas.

Southwest Airlines
Aircraft fleet: 1983-1992

Aircraft	1983	1984	1985	1986	1987	1988	1989	1990	1991	1992
B-737	44	52	56	63	75	85	94	106	123	142
MD-80	—	—	68	—	—	—	—	—	—	—
DC-9	—	—	—	88	—	—	—	—	—	—
B-727	22	—	—	—	— —	—		—	—	—
Total	66	52	124	151	75	85	94	106	123	142

Muse resigned in 1978 after a dispute with the board of directors, and founded his own airline, Muse Air, in 1981. Kelleher became chairman of the board and Howard Putnam, formerly at United, became the new president.

Muse's departure did not affect Southwest. The company earned profits in 1978, 1979 and 1980, respectively, of \$17 million on revenues of \$81 million; \$16.7 million on revenues of \$136.1 million; and \$28.4 million on revenues of \$213 million. The company had 1,839 employees and a fleet of 23 B-737s by the end of 1980.

Putnam's tenure at Southwest ended in late 1981 when he left to become president of Braniff. Kelleher became Southwest's president and guided the carrier into Kansas City, Las Vegas, Los Angeles, Phoenix, San Diego and San Francisco. He increased the fleet to 37 aircraft to handle the expansion.

Southwest bought rival Transtar in 1985, which Lamar Muse originally founded in 1981 under the name Muse Air. Transtar accumulated more than

$50 million in losses trying to compete against Southwest in its strongest markets. Transtar remained a subsidiary of Southwest until June 1987 when Southwest shut it down because it was not profitable. Southwest reported a 1987 profit of only $20.2 million on sales of $778.3 million primarily because of Transtar's poor performance.

Southwest led the airline industry in productivity in 1987 by carrying 2,344 passengers per employee (nearest rival: USAir, with 1,499 per employee), employing just 74 people per aircraft (against Braniff's 75, Continental's 91 and American's 157) and placing second to long-haul Braniff in revenue passenger miles per employee.

Southwest, given such productivity, began 1988 confident its lackluster 1987 performance was no index of its potential. Southwest finished the year with a record $57.9-million profit on sales of $860.4 million. Fellow airline CEOs during the year chose Kelleher to chair the Partnership for Improved Air Travel. The broad-based, Washington-headquartered organization formed to develop a better understanding of the needs of the air travel system and to build private and public support to ensure the needs are met.

Southwest's success also attracted the attention of some of the nation's largest news networks. CBS's 60 Minutes, Turner Broadcasting's Cable News Network and NBC's Today Show featured Southwest in major stories in 1989. *Texas Monthly* magazine profiled Kelleher in its April 1989 issue. Southwest's ability to deliver quality (if bare-bones) service at the industry's lowest prices, the charismatic nature of Kelleher's leadership and the fact that Southwest could accomplish such large profits on such puny fares while paying high wages attracted the attention. Southwest has its own unions—SWISA (Southwest Independent Stewardesses Association) representing flight attendants, SWAPA (Southwest Airlines Pilots Association) representing pilots—but no labor-management conflict.

Morale at Southwest may be the best in the airline industry. Kelleher constantly tells his employees how much he loves them—in his 1989 message to shareholders he called them the "finest, most loving and lovable people in the airline industry"—and the Southwest labor force seems to reciprocate Kelleher's sentiments. The esprit de corps helps Southwest achieve a productivity that its competitors find killing because such low fares can result.

Southwest, like America West, achieved "major airline" status by the end of 1989, earning $1.02 billion in revenues. America West was a child of deregulation; Southwest, one of deregulation's forerunners. America West used the freedoms of deregulation to build itself around a hub at Phoenix; Southwest helped create those freedoms by behaving from the start as though a free market already existed.

Southwest's consistent first-place rankings in productivity, on-time performance and passenger satisfaction together with its high profitability make it one of the U.S.'s most successful airlines. Only the master of motivation himself, Herb Kelleher, could hustle a $47.1-million profit out of the business climate of fare battles, recession, war and terrorism fears, and revenue-eating fuel prices that wracked the airline industry in 1990.

The spiraling costs and cutthroat competition (much of it initiated by Kelleher) in the fourth quarter of 1990 knocked Southwest Airlines into the red—a $4.6-million loss on sales of $301.6 million. But that lone quarter of very slight loss propelled Southwest's gung-ho employees into further self-sacrifice. Already enjoying the lowest costs in the industry, Kelleher got from his employees in January 1991 a new cost-savings program: Employees volunteered a part of their salaries to help buy fuel for Southwest aircraft.

Southwest added its 30th destination (Burbank, Calif.) during 1990, but refocused its energies on short-haul markets, the hallmark of its success. Kelleher continued to pester America West in its own back yard, Phoenix. Through all this, Southwest had total revenues in 1990 of $1.19 billion, a 19-percent increase over the $1 billion in revenues of 1989.

In short, very little changed at Southwest in 1990 despite industry turmoil that saw the demise of Eastern and the bankruptcies of Continental and Pan Am (not to mention desperate maneuvering at TWA and cash shortages at Northwest and USAir). It finished the year as the same lean, hungry and efficient carrier that made Southwestern U.S. markets some of the nation's most competitive ever since deregulation in 1978.

Shrewd financial planning during profitable periods allowed Southwest to expand its route system when opportunities arose—even during a recession. Cost-cutting measures instituted in mid-1989 in anticipation of a recession also helped fuel the expansion. "We have a lot of liquidity; we can sustain a loss and we're planning to conduct 1991 just like any other year," said Kelleher in an interview.

Southwest increased operations steadily by 10 percent from 1985 through 1990, but in 1991 it grew 16 percent with added flights in the Midwest and California. Southwest quickly moved into vacant facilities at Oakland Airport when USAir reduced about a third of its flights in the California corridor. And when Midway shut down, 20 midwestern cities in 1991 begged the Dallas-based airline for replacement service. Southwest launched a bid for Midway gates and related airport facilities at Chicago's Midway Airport in October 1991, but lost to Northwest. Midway ceased operations and liquidated when Northwest backed out of an agreement to buy the bulk of Midway's assets. Southwest then picked up eight additional gates at Chicago's Midway Airport and added daily flights between Midway and Indianapolis and Cleveland to existing service between Midway and Detroit, Kansas City, Mo., Nashville and St. Louis.

Despite these large gains, Southwest maintained its commitment to grow at a deliberate pace. Sacramento, Calif., was the only new city added to Southwest's service structure in 1991 despite service requests from more than 50 cities. Southwest began service in Cleveland in February 1992, and Columbus, Ohio, became the airline's 34th city in 15 states in June 1992. The company gauges the potential of new city service via a proven formula before opening in new areas. "We use it [the formula] to determine where we think we can stimulate the most new traffic in the shortest period of time," Kelleher said in an interview. "We have a limited number of airplanes coming in and, after we satisfy existing service responsibilities, we might have three or four additional airplanes we can use to open new cities. Maybe we could be profitable in six new cities, but we pick the two that will do the best for us so we get the highest immediate return."

Overall, Southwest in 1991 was the largest airline operating from Kansas City in terms of daily flights. It increased market share at St. Louis by 18.6 percent and ranked first or second in terms of originating boardings at 27 of the 34 airports the airline served at year-end. Southwest was the only major passenger airline to post a profit in a year when the industry lost $2 billion. The airline recorded a 1991 net profit of $26.9 million, a decline of about 42.8 percent from 1990.

A strong 1992 balance sheet allowed Southwest to buy aircraft while other, larger airlines canceled orders and options and scaled back operations. The airline negotiated a $250-million low interest rate line of credit in late 1991, and in the first quarter of 1992 it sold new stocks to raise another $88 million in equity capital. Southwest took delivery of 13 new

Southwest Airlines Financial Statistics

(In millions)	1983	1984	1985	1986	1987	1988	1989	1990	1991	1992
Sales	448	536	680	769	778	860	1,015	1,187	1,314	1,685
Net Income (loss)	40.9	49.7	47.3	50	20.2	57.9	71.6	47.1	26.9	103.6
Assets	587	646	1,002	1,061	1,043	1,308	1,415	1,471	1,837	2,293
Liabilities	272.7	284.4	536.4	549.5	528.3	741	827.8	866.3	1,208.8	1,438.7
Net Worth	314.6	361.8	466	511.9	514.3	567.4	587.3	604.9	628.5	854.3
ASMs	6,324	7,983	9.885	12,574	13,331	13,309	14,797	16,411	18,491	21,367
RPMs	3,894	4,669	5,971	7,388	7,789	7,676	9,282	9,959	11,296	13,787
Load Factors	61.6%	58.5%	60.4%	58.8%	58.4%	57.7%	62.7%	60.7%	61.1%	64.5%

B-737s in 1992 and agreed that year to buy 34 new B-737-300s in an order valued at $1.2 billion.

Southwest's third-quarter 1992 net earnings jumped 71 percent with a net profit of $26.9 million. Southwest recorded its 20th consecutive year of profitability in January 1993, with a fourth-quarter 1992 profit of $27.2 million and a year-end profit of $103.6 million compared to $26.9 million the previous year.

The Southwest officers responsible for the carrier's operations, maintenance and decision-making at the time of publication are Herbert D. Kelleher, chairman, president and chief executive officer; Gary A. Barron, executive vice president and chief operations officer; Gary C. Kelly, vice president of finance and chief financial officer; Paul E. Sterbenz, vice president of flight operations; and John A. Vidal, vice president of maintenance.

Southwest Airlines Statistics

1992 Total Sales
Global/Major Airlines

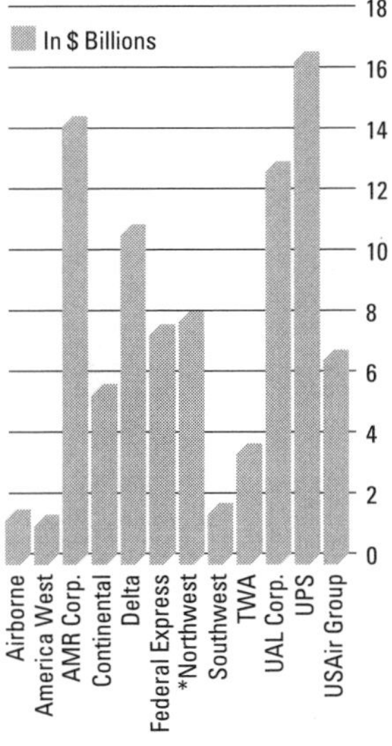

• Information is for Northwest Airlines only and not for parent company NWA Inc.

Southwest finished 1992 with total sales of $1.685 billion.

The company's sales increased 276 percent during the period 1983 to 1992. Southwest's expansion is the major contributor to this increase.

Southwest Total Sales 1983-1992

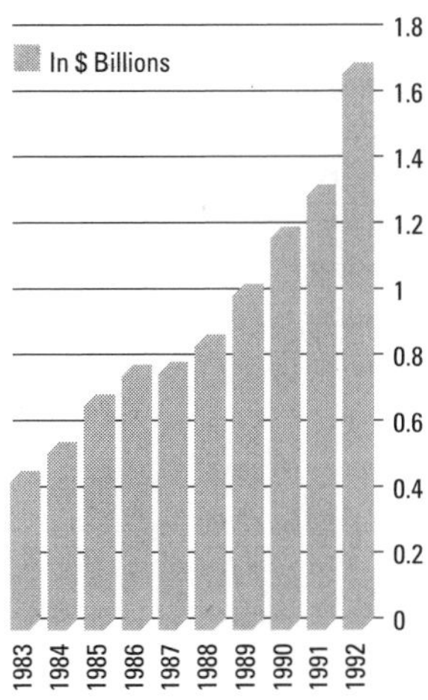

1992 Net Income
Global/Major Airlines

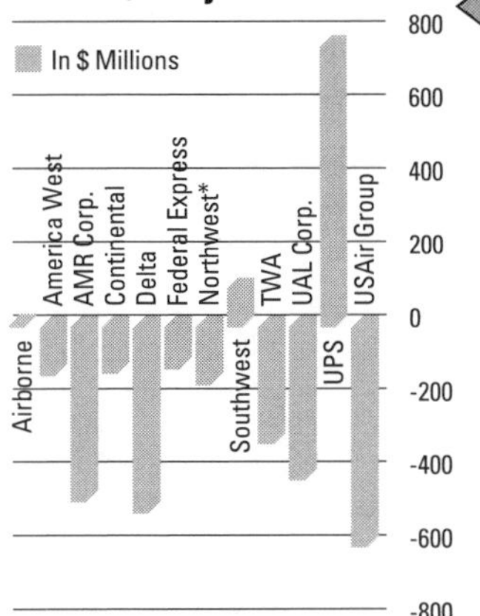

• Information is for Northwest Airlines only and not for parent company NWA Inc.

Southwest's profit of $103.6 million was the industry's second-highest in 1992 and first among airlines flying passengers.

Southwest earned a profit in every year since 1973.

Southwest continued earning profits while methodically adding new service and aircraft through the first few months of 1993.

Southwest Net Income 1983-1992

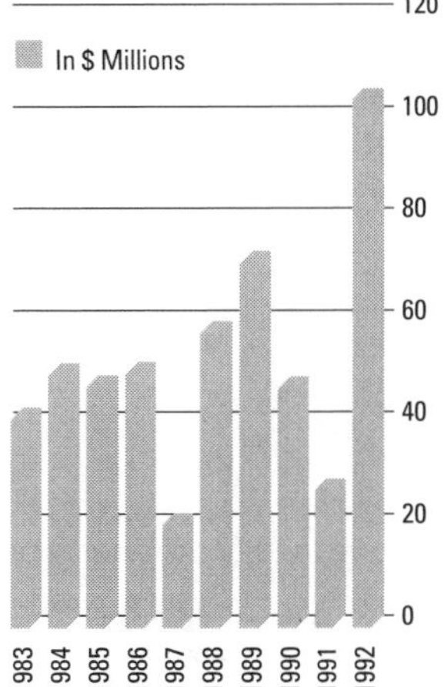

1992 Total Assets & Liabilities
Global/Major Airlines

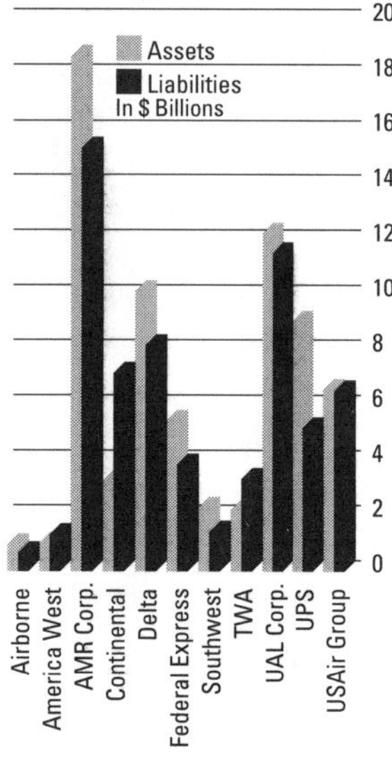

NWA Inc. is a privately held company and would not release 1990-1992 figures.

In 1992 Southwest had total assets valued at $2.29 billion and total liabilities of $1.44 billion.

Southwest's assets have increased 291 percent from $587 million in 1983 to $2.29 billion in 1992.

The company's liabilities grew 428 percent during the same period, from $272.7 million in 1983 to $1.44 billion in 1992.

Southwest had $699.1 million in long-term debt at the end of 1992 and a total shareholders' equity of $854.3 million.

Southwest
Assets & Liabilities 1983-1992

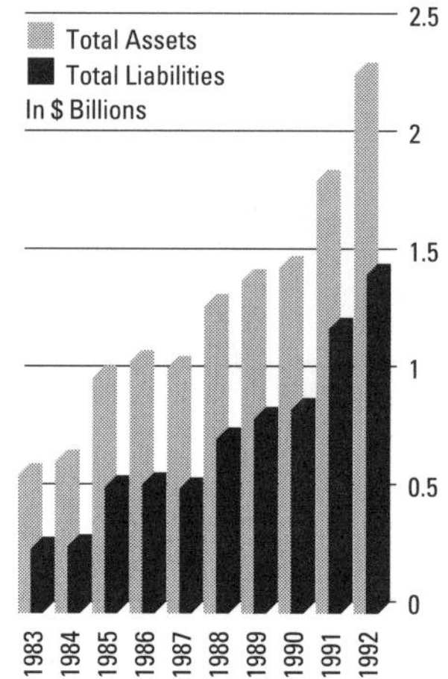

1992 ASMs & RPMs
Global/Major Airlines

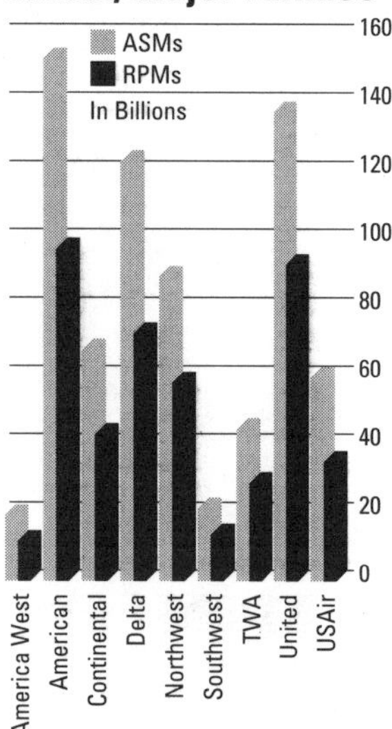

Southwest had 21.37 billion available seat miles (ASMs) in 1992 and filled 64.5 percent of these seats with revenue-producing passengers.

Southwest's capacity, as measured in ASMs, grew from 6.32 billion in 1983 to 21.37 billion in 1992—an increase of 238 percent.

Its revenue passenger miles (RPMs) increased 254 percent during the same period, from 3.9 billion in 1983 to 13.79 billion in 1992.

Southwest
ASMs & RPMs 1983-1992

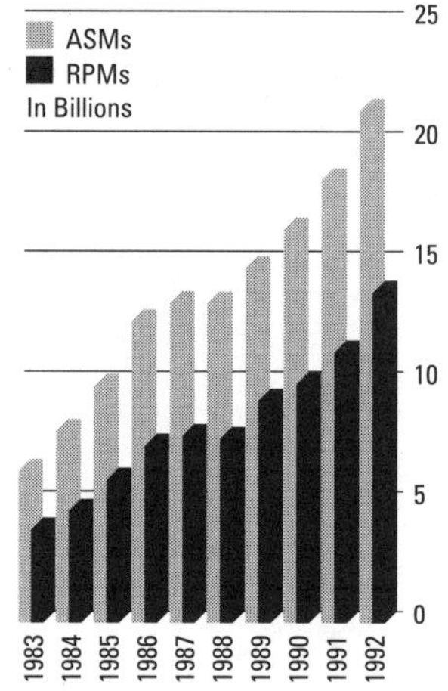

1992 Net Worth
Global/Major Airlines

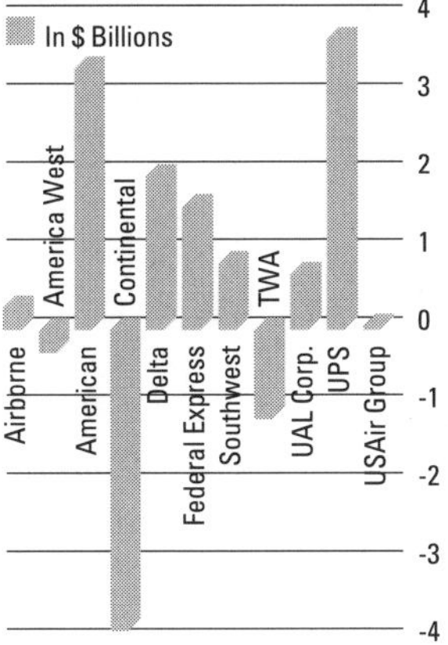

NWA Inc. is a privately held company and would not release 1990-1992 figures.

Southwest completed 1992 with a net worth of $854.3 million which placed it fifth in relation to the other global/major carriers.

Between 1983 and 1992 Southwest's assets increased 291 percent from $587 million to $2.29 billion. Southwest's liabilities grew from $272.7 million in 1983 to $1.44 billion at the end of 1992. Southwest's net worth increased 172 percent during this period, from $314.6 million in 1983 to $854.3 million in 1992.

Southwest Net Worth 1983-1992

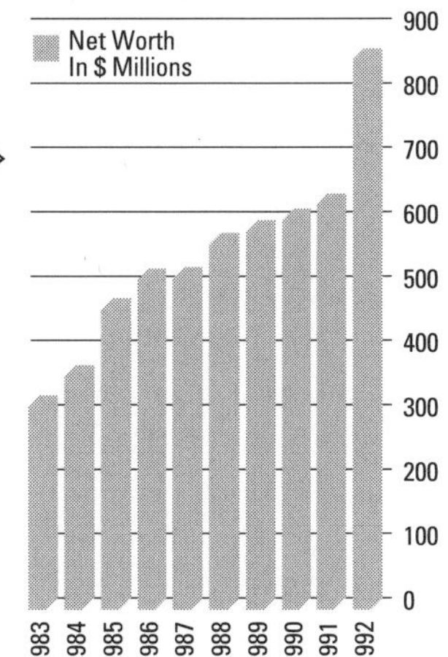

Statistics Related Terms

Assets — A resource having commercial or trade value that is owned (or which the company owns rights to) by a business. Typical examples for an airline include: Cash, securities, property, equipment, capital leases, landing slots and routes.

Available seat miles (ASMs) — Represent the number of seats available for passengers multiplied by the number of scheduled miles those seats are flown.

Cost per available seat mile — Represents operating and interest expense divided by available seat miles.

Financial accounting standard (FAS) 106 — A federally-mandated accounting change made to the way U.S. companies handle post-retirement benefits (other than pensions) to employees. FAS 106, for several U.S. global and major airlines, meant large, one-time, non-cash charges to earnings, further damaging their balance-sheet performance for 1992.

Leveraged buyout (LBO) — Takeover of a company using borrowed funds. Company assets often serve as security for the loans, although investors' assets also may be used.

Liabilities — The total amount the company owes to all creditors.

Net worth or stockholders' equity — The net assets (total assets minus total liabilities) of a company. For companies with more liabilities than assets, the result is a negative net worth or stockholders' deficit.

Passenger load factor — Revenue passenger miles divided by available seat miles over a set period of time.

Revenue passenger miles (RPMs) — The number of d miles flown by revenue-producing passengers.

Yield — The average revenue received for each mile a revenue passenger is carried. Determined by dividing total operating revenue by total revenue passenger miles.

Southwest Airlines News Abstracts

"Advertisers' Fights Don't Usually Involve Such Strong-Arm Tactics." *Wall Street Journal,* 11 March 1992.

"Herb Kelleher's Jet Set." *Dallas Life Magazine,* 12 Jan. 1992, pp. 8-13.

"Hit'em Hardest With the Mostest." *Forbes,* 16 Sep. 1991, pp. 48-51.

Southwest Air Posts Loss of $4.8 Million for Fourth Quarter." *Wall Street Journal,* 29 Jan. 1991, sec. B, p. 3, col. 6. (Note: The headline states a loss of $4.8 billion, but the body of the article reports $4.6 million. Also a press release from Southwest reports a net loss of $4.6 million.)

"Southwest Air Posts Loss of $8.2 Million for the First Quarter." *Wall Street Journal,* 23 April 1991, sec. C, p. 8, col. 5.

"Southwest Airlines Flies High With Offbeat Style." *The Atlanta Journal-Constitution,* 24 March 1991, sec. H, p. 6, col. 1.

"Southwest Airlines is a Rare Air Carrier: It Still Makes Money." *Wall Street Journal,* 26 Oct. 1992, p. 1.

"Southwest Luvs Passengers, Employees, Profits." *Air Transport World,* July 1991, pp. 32-41.

9

Trans World Airlines

TWA's early days highlight a famous duo's coast-to-coast flight, the "spoils conference" of the 1930s and tycoon Howard Hughes. With the 1960s came TWA's reputation as a global airline. Recent history, however, depicts a shrinking carrier mired in labor and financial strife.

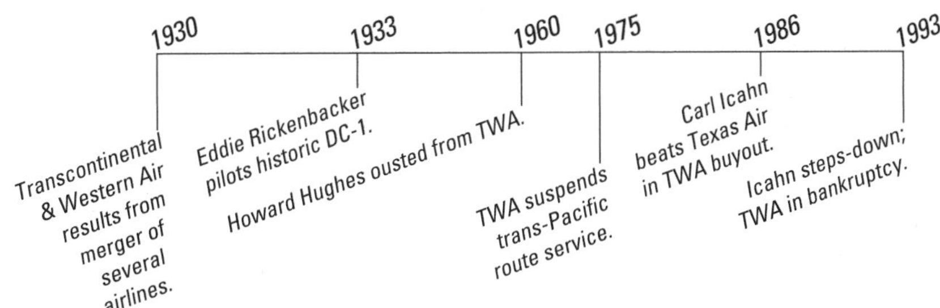

Several tiny airlines formed part of Trans World Airline's genealogy in the years 1925 through 1928. But, the largest presence was a holding company, North American Aviation Inc., which General Motors controlled.

Western Air Express, founded in 1925 to fly mail between Los Angeles and Salt Lake City via Las Vegas, was the first of the tiny airlines. Maddux Air Lines which began operations in 1927 in an attempt to survive on passenger service using the Ford 5-AT TriMotor was the second. Standard Air Lines, founded in 1927 to provide service between Los Angeles and Phoenix, was the third and Transcontinental Air Transport (TAT), formed in 1928 as a subsidiary of North American Aviation, was the fourth. (North American achieved control of several air carriers at this time, including Eastern and a number of airlines that eventually combined as TWA.)

Maddux Air Lines did not last long without a mail contract and TAT swallowed it in 1929. TAT implemented a new concept in transcontinental travel that same year: passengers traveled by air during the day and by train at night since aircraft were not available yet for nonstop transport across the country. The weary voyagers finally reached their destinations after nearly two days and two nights of constant travel.

Western Air Express acquired Standard Air Lines, controlled by North American Aviation, in 1930. Jack Frye, one of Standard's two founders, became Western's new vice president of operations. A part of Western (including the old Standard Air Lines) merged with TAT and Pittsburgh Aviation Industries Corp. (a fifth TWA predecessor) the same year to form a new company, Transcontinental & Western Air (T&WA). Dick Robbins, president of Pittsburgh Aviation, became T&WA's new president.

The new company promptly eliminated the railroad service and provided the nation's first coast-to-coast, all-air service by flying longer hours during the day and resting overnight in Kansas City. Trip time was an impressive 36 hours, but Robbins was determined to reduce it further.

Trans World Airlines
Aircraft fleet and purchase commitments
As of May 1993

Aircraft Type	Current Fleet	Firm Orders	Options
A-330	0	20	0
B-727	55	0	0
B-747	11	0	0
B-767	10	0	0
DC-9	46	0	0
L-1011	19	0	0
MD-80	39	0	0
Total	180	20	0

T&WA's engineers worked with aircraft designer Donald Douglas to develop a larger and faster plane. An experimental aircraft labeled the DC-1 resulted, though only one of these planes ever was built. T&WA made aviation history after taking delivery of the DC-1 in 1933 for tests. The experimental plane flew coast-to-coast in 13 hours and four minutes with Frye at the controls and famous World War I pilot Eddie Rickenbacker in the second seat. (This was a high-altitude flight, indeed, since Frye soon controlled T&WA and Rickenbacker controlled Eastern not long after.) Aircraft testing resulted in several modifications implemented on the Douglas DC-2. This plane, the fastest airliner of its time, was delivered to T&WA in 1934.

Meanwhile, Alabama Sen. Hugo L. Black began an investigation to determine if the methods used to award airmail contracts and airline routes were legal. Black, later a U.S. Supreme Court justice, uncovered evidence of a covert 1930 meeting between leaders of the major airlines and Walter Brown, postmaster general under President Herbert Hoover, before the awarding of airmail contracts. Jim Farley, the new postmaster general, anticipated a fair redistribution of airmail money and urged President Franklin Delano Roosevelt to cancel the 1930 airmail contracts.

FDR did cancel the contracts in January 1934. He then sent the U.S. Army Air Corps to fly mail in open-cockpit tactical planes without sufficient training in all-weather and night flying, and without the instrumentation to deal with blizzards and rainstorms. Rickenbacker denounced Roosevelt for "legalized murder" after a rash of fatalities; Charles Lindbergh refused his support for "the operation by military forces of American business and commerce"; and the New Deal suffered its first serious setback. FDR restored the airmail service to private operators after just two months of the Air Corps debacle.

T&WA, as one of the major airlines involved in the 1930 contracts scandal, fell under all of Roosevelt's stipulations for contract reassignments. First, like all other airlines that participated in the Walter Brown "spoils conference," it had to reorganize itself under a new name. Second, if it wanted a mail contract, it had to get rid of Robbins because he participated in the Brown conference and no contract would go to an airline employing a person thus tainted. Third, any new airmail contract had to specify pilot wages and working conditions.

Transcontinental & Western Air simply added "Inc." to its name to meet stipulation No. 1; T&WA forced Robbins' resignation and Frye replaced him for stipulation No. 2; and, T&WA chose confrontation for stipulation No. 3.

FDR's reward to Dave Behncke of ALPA for Behncke's support during the Air Corp. experiment was to require that new airmail contracts specify pilot wages and working conditions. It set Frye, T&WA's new president, in direct opposition to both ALPA and many of the airline's own pilots.

Frye bitterly opposed paying pilots less or more according to what equipment they flew; ALPA wanted wages based on aircraft speed and productivity. Frye opposed any limits on monthly flight time; ALPA advocated them. Frye succeeded in getting his pilots to leave ALPA and create a company union, the T&WA Pilots Association; ALPA succeeded in getting the National Labor Board's Decision 83, which set monthly maximum flight time at 85 hours and tied the pay system to speed of aircraft with a mileage increment, a productivity measure.

T&WA flew under Decision 83 when it acquired the central transcontinental mail route. It also flew into losses in 1936 and 1937. The company's board of directors blamed Frye and looked for a replacement. Frye blamed the directors for failing to let him run the airline as he wished, and he sought an investor to help him buy the company. He found multimillionaire Howard Hughes. Hughes, with Frye's assistance, acquired a controlling interest by 1939 and purchased the company. The airline had its first tycoon.

T&WA, like other major carriers, expanded service and sought greater speed and capacity in its aircraft in the years 1935-1941. The world's first pressurized commercial airliner—the Boeing 307 Stratoliner—was one project that allowed T&WA to fly above the weather and take advantage of upper-altitude winds. The airline inaugurated coast-to-coast service in the Boeing 307 in July 1940, thus reducing flying time to 13 hours, 40 minutes.

T&WA ordered the advanced, long-range Lockheed Constellation in 1939, anticipating the day it might shatter Pan Am's monopoly on international flying. World War II was the proving ground for the airline's international operations. T&WA turned half its fleet over to the armed forces in December 1941; the next month it formed the Intercontinental Division and operated an air route across the Atlantic to Europe and then on to Africa and India. The company performed aircraft modifications and trained radio operators, mechanics and military flight crews.

As Constellations began rolling off the assembly line in 1943, T&WA agreed to turn its orders over to the military as they became available. The second Connie off the assembly line was T&WA's first. This Constellation flew from Burbank to Washington, D.C., for delivery to the Air Transport Command, in just six hours, 57 minutes with Frye at the controls. Hughes, tycoon, airline owner and amateur pilot, relieved him.

Trans World Airlines

Aircraft fleet: 1983-1992

Aircraft	1983	1984	1985	1986	1987	1988	1989	1990	1991	1992
B-747	18	19	21	17	18	19	19	17	15	11
L-1011	35	33	35	33	33	33	33	34	33	15
B-767	10	10	10	10	11	11	11	11	9	10
B-707	19	—	—	—	—	—	—	—	—	—
B-727	82	82	82	78	76	72	69	66	63	54
MD-80	11	15	19	23	29	33	33	33	29	33
DC-9	—	—	—	46	46	46	48	48	48	46
Total	175	159	167	207	213	214	213	209	197	169

The Civil Aeronautics Board (CAB) awarded T&WA its first overseas route in 1945, and in February 1946 the company began New York to Paris service using its recently returned Constellations. The airline's route structure stretched from the United States to India by 1950. T&WA's flight system stretching more than halfway around the globe, but denial of the carrier's request to transit China thwarted an effort to complete an around-the-world route structure. The airline changed its name from Transcontinental & Western Air to Trans World Airlines in May 1950, and the cumbersome '&' dropped out of TWA.

The Howard Hughes of later legend emerged during the '50s: eccentric, erratic billionaire. Frye resigned the presidency in 1947 and his replacement left the following year. The next president, Ralph Damon, remained until his death in 1956, but Carter Burgess resigned after only a year in office. Burgess' replacement, Charles Thomas, lasted just three years. Hughes, in the eyes of the board of directors, was responsible for such rapid turnover in the president's office; he completely dominated TWA's affairs. The company, lacking consistent direction, lost money.

The solution was to remove Hughes, but he owned 78 percent of the company. How to accomplish Hughes' ouster?

The answer came through a contractual technicality in jet purchases from Boeing. Hughes purchased new aircraft through his subsidiary, Hughes Tool Co., intending to lease them back to TWA. He resorted to outside financing to pay Boeing on the condition that then-president Thomas remained in office for at least 60 days after the approval of financing or Hughes must forfeit the voting rights on his stock to a three-man trust. (Lending institutions would choose two members of the trust; Hughes Tool Co. would provide the third.) Thomas resigned before 60 days and the board of directors persuaded the lenders to invoke the voting rights condition. Hughes squirmed, but was trapped, and the trustees took control in December 1960.

Fortunately, one among them was an able leader. Ernest Breech, an old hand in TWA affairs, was chairman of the board for North American Aviation in 1934 when Hughes acquired TWA. He engineered the earlier merger between Transcontinental Air Transport and Western Air Express. Breech remained at North American Aviation after the sale of TWA and later served as a vice president at General Motors, as president of a GM subsidiary, Bendix Aviation Co., and as chairman of the board at Ford Motor Co.

Breech, as a TWA trustee, recruited a new management team to restore the airline's profitability. Selecting Charles Tillinghast as president was his first move.

Tillinghast was a vice president at Bendix. His previous experience hadn't prepared him fully for the challenge ahead, but Tillinghast was a quick study with a keen eye for details. He recognized that recent turmoil caused the company to lag far behind its competitors in jet deliveries. He ordered 20 medium-range and six long-range Boeing jets for delivery the following year. He trimmed operating costs and refocused the carrier's energies on re-establishing its international and domestic presence. The company again was profitable by the end of 1962.

The years 1964 through 1972 were good ones for TWA. The airline finally became an around-the-world airline during this period with a trans-Pacific route award in 1968 (service actually began in 1969). These years also saw TWA put the B-727 into service for its domestic system and the B-747 and L-1011 into service on its international routes.

The Lockheed L-1011, with all of its early problems, arrived at TWA in 1972. TWA's flight attendants struck in 1973—a 45-day strike that inflicted severe financial damage. The Arab oil embargo knocked the wind out of TWA the next year, hitting it harder than any other U.S. carrier except Pan Am because overseas fuel prices were significantly higher than prices in the U.S. The CAB denied TWA's request for a federal subsidy to cover its increased fuel costs. TWA then sold nine of its B-747s to Iran, grounded four B-747s and two L-1011s, laid off thousands of employees and began talks with Pan Am about a possible merger. The CAB clearly disapproved a merger, so Pan Am and TWA agreed to exchange several routes. The CAB OK'd the swap, ending quite suddenly TWA's experiment as a global carrier: TWA suspended its trans-Pacific route service in 1975.

The worst of this particular storm was behind TWA by the end of 1975. It lost $86.3 million in 1975, but Tillinghast resigned and a new management with new eyes and hands arrived to reorganize and rebuild around yet another strategy. L. E. Smart became the new chairman of the board; C. E. Meyer became president. Trans World Corp. was created in 1979 as a holding company for the airline and other subsidiaries, including the Hilton International Co. acquired in 1967; Canteen Corp., a food service company acquired in 1973; and Spartan Newfoods Corp., acquired in 1969 (Spartan is known for its Hardee's and Quincy's Family Steak House subsidiaries). The purpose of Trans World Corp. was to diversify the company's resources and protect profits from the airline industry's extreme volatility. The only major new acquisition of this period was the Century 21 real estate firm (1979).

The diversification plan proved ill-conceived and the airline separated from the rest of the corporation in 1981. Trans World Airlines Inc. was created and TWA again was an independent operating entity.

However, the airline suffered from bloated costs, and the rapid deployment of the hub-and-spoke system by rival airlines caught TWA by surprise. TWA's shrinking fleet in the early 1980s as the company sold off assets to cover losses exacerbated TWA's competitive disadvantage from the lack of a true hub; the aircraft retained were big, long-distance planes like the B-747 and L-1011, leaving TWA without aircraft to operate economically over domestic routes. The route expansion undertaken from New York's JFK International in 1984 mostly was long-distance: Atlanta, Memphis, Tenn., Jacksonville, Fla., and Milwaukee, and Amsterdam, Brussels, Munich, Zurich and Kuwait, with only Raleigh-Durham, N.C., and Norfolk, Va., considered short-haul.

TWA management's tardiness in recognizing the power of code-sharing arrangements with commuter airlines aggravated the situation. TWA management failed to see the advantage of scouring a 280-mile radius for long-haul transfer traffic.

Discouraged, the company's directors put the airline up for sale in 1985. TWA's pilot and mechanic unions rebuffed the first suitor, Frank Lorenzo. The unions actively courted Carl Icahn and gave him hundreds of millions of dollars in last-ditch labor concessions to thwart a TWA-Texas Air merger already sanctioned by TWA and Texas Air directors. Icahn gained the advantage with union support. His buyout of TWA became effective Jan. 3, 1986.

TWA knew no peace under its second tycoon. The flight attendants, represented by the Independent Federation of Flight Attendants, struck the airline on March 7, 1986, after failing to agree with management on a new contract. Pay and work benefits were the major issues. The airline already hired 1,600 replacement workers when the flight attendants called off their strike. The series of court decisions regarding the rights of strikers was the most lasting effect of the strike; the Supreme Court ruled in 1989 that once a strike is settled, companies are not required to replace workers who cross picket lines with returning strikers with more seniority.

TWA immediately began doing some things right with D. Joseph Corr, former president of ACF Industries, as president. TWA acquired Ozark Air Lines in February 1986 to complement its weak domestic system and to stop the blood-letting at St. Louis where TWA finally began building a real hub to battle Ozark. TWA also built a true hub at New York's JFK International using TWExpress partners at both St. Louis and New York to siphon off traffic from communities within the airport region. And Corr, with Icahn's advice and consent, began squeezing the fat out of TWA operations.

"Our main problem was costs," Corr said in mid-1987. "The major problem that we had was that there were just too many people who did not understand the importance of spending our money carefully." Foul-tasting coffee specially ground for TWA at a high price was the example Corr gave. Corr junked the coffee deal and ordered "a better-tasting product" that saved more than $1 million a year.

However, Corr's changes also meant stripping out "layer after layer of bureaucracy" between top management and on-line employees, and shrinking the airline quickly in Europe. Corr said, concerning the management cuts, "I would much rather have that money down on the floor fixing planes than for staff in the general office." International terrorism dried up the European market, so TWA axed more than 20 percent of its European operation.

Trans World Airlines Financial Statistics

(In millions)	1983	1984	1985	1986	1987	1988	1989	1990	1991	1992
Sales	3,354	3,657	3,867	3,185	4,056	4,361	4,507	4,606	3,660	3,634
Net Income (loss)	(12.4)	29.9	(193.1)	(106.3)	106.2	249.8	(298.5)	(237.6)	34.6	(317.7)
Assets	2,739	2,879	2,763	3,361	4,254	4,056	3,759.2	3,277	2,683	2,218
Liabilities	2,019	2,150	2,223	3,119	3,964	4,087	4,103.9	3,989	3,481	3,368
Net Worth	719.3	729.4	539.5	241.4	292.4	(31.3)	(344.7)	(712)	(797.9)	(1,150)
ASMs	42,501	45,510	49,178	46,880	51,811	56,102	57,230	54,958	43,188	44,651
RPMs	27,261	28,297	32,047	27,334	32,861	34,700	35,046	34,236	27,962	28,882
Load Factors	64.1%	62.2%	65.2%	58.3%	63.4%	61.9%	61.2%	62.3%	64.7%	64.7%

The Corr and Icahn leadership worked for awhile. TWA earned a profit of $106 million in 1987 and strong earnings continued through the third quarter of 1988. But Icahn took TWA private in October with a spate of negative results: his president resigned (although Corr agreed to remain on the board of directors), all three major unions at TWA erupted into open revolt and TWA began losing money hand over fist. Reasons for the losses: a steep drop in operating income and cash flow, a sharp rise in costs and a mountain of new debt added by Icahn in taking TWA private. TWA's pilots filed suit, charging Icahn with "milking $665 million of TWA's assets" and "emptying this company completely to a shell company." The Independent Federation of Flight Attendants filed a petition with the Department of Transportation requesting a DOT investigation of Icahn's fitness to run an airline. The International Association of Machinists refused to come to terms with Icahn over pay. This labor-management standoff added $50 million to the payroll as machinists' wages returned to their level before the IAM gave Icahn concessions to help him take over TWA.

Icahn reorganized TWA after Corr resigned so that all seven top-ranking vice presidents reported to an "office of the chairman." The office consisted of Icahn, Alfred D. Kingsley (a director) and Jerry Nichols (formerly TWA's vice president for ground operations).

TWA lost $298.5 million in 1989, plagued by high interest payments on debt, declining revenues, rising costs and labor strife. It lost another $237.6 million in 1990 despite a $36-million extraordinary gain and a $205-million credit from asset sales. The company sold assets as fast as possible.

TWA's management claimed the company needed wage concessions from employees to survive. ALPA and the IAM claimed the only way TWA could survive was through an ownership change. ALPA and the IAM worked separately and sought a new owner to buy out Icahn. The two unions put together a concession package in March 1991 clearing the way for billionaire investor Kirk Kerkorian to bid for TWA. However, the sale of three TWA London routes to American Airlines doused Kerkorian's interest.

Trans World Airlines (TWA) in the first half of 1991 fought off a fate many believed inevitable as other old-line majors, such as Pan Am and Continental, crumbled into Chapter 11. Industry observers, judging TWA's debt too heavy and its best markets too cyclical, foretold the end of the Mount Kisco, N.Y.-based carrier in 1991. TWA's supply of cash and securities dwindled to $290 million by early April, down from about $1 billion a year earlier. The company ended 1991 with an operating loss of nearly $354 million The airline's net income was $34.6 million with tax credits for the year.

Some Wall Street analysts felt Icahn could yet rescue TWA by buying Pan Am, though Pan Am broke off all talks with TWA in early 1991. A viable offer from the financially-ailing carrier seemed unlikely until American came forward; together the two airlines bid $310 million for Pan Am's European routes and its shuttle operation. The offer rose to $1.3 billion when United joined to block a bid from Delta Air Lines. Pan Am creditors eventually rejected the three-carrier bid in favor of Delta's $1.4 billion offer.

TWA survived the cash crunch to raise $700 million in cash and securities to launch a debt buy-back plan. The $445 million the carrier received on May 3 from the sale of three London routes to American Airlines was a large portion of TWA's cash kitty. The price tag originally was to cover six routes, but when the Department of Transportation ruled that TWA could sell only three routes to American, Icahn held out for the full $445 million anyway. American buckled, facing competitive pressures from United which bought Pan Am's London routes.

Icahn's plan to pay down TWA's $1.2 billion in debt hinged on note holders accepting 73 cents on the dollar for equipment trust certificates due in 1991 and 1996; 65 cents on the dollar for 15-percent senior secured notes due in 1994; 35 cents on the dollar for both 16-percent senior unsecured notes due in 1992 and 17-percent senior unsecured notes due in 1993; and 17.5 cents on the dollar for 12-percent junior subordinated unsecured notes due in 2001 and 2008. All told, TWA proposed buying about $1.37 billion in debt for roughly $483 million (including fees and expenses). The debt-repurchase plan fell through in July when a judge required settlement with senior noteholders before paying junior bondholders.

Icahn tendered another proposal in late July 1991,

a debt-for-equity swap that essentially reduced his 90-percent ownership in the airline by at least half. Icahn personally was liable for any pension obligations to workers the airline itself couldn't finance because his personal stake in the airline exceeded 80 percent. The restructuring program, if approved, released Icahn's personal holdings from liability for TWA's underfunded pension plans. The restructuring program also required filing for Chapter 11 bankruptcy protection in early 1992.

Icahn ignored the Chapter 11 curse and instead concentrated on finding a merger candidate. A TWA/Continental combination, Icahn mused, would produce a strong, low-cost, low-fare airline with the vast market it needed to thrive. TWA would gain access to Continental's domestic route system while Continental could take advantage of TWA's international presence. Analysts speculated labor unions at both carriers and the Pension Benefit Guaranty Corp.—the self-financed government pension agency that insures privately-run pension plans—strongly would oppose a partnership. Continental, a Chapter 11 carrier, and TWA both had underfunded pensions, and integrating TWA's unionized work force with non-union employees at Continental would be difficult at best.

Merger talks with Continental continued as Icahn worked to expand TWA's operation at New York's JFK International Airport. A domestic hub at Kennedy, Icahn felt, would help TWA's weak domestic route system. TWA acquired Pan Am's commuter operation, Pan Am Express—renamed Trans World Express—days before Pan Am folded, hoping to feed more domestic overseas-bound passengers into Kennedy. Proceeds from the sale of TWA's three remaining London routes—Philadelphia-London Gatwick and Baltimore/Washington-London Gatwick—to USAir would fund the expansion.

Then in February, Icahn surprised the industry by filing for Chapter 11 bankruptcy protection earlier than expected. TWA's filing brought under federal bankruptcy protection almost one-fifth of the U.S. airline industry's capacity. The filing erased $1 billion of debt—almost two-thirds of what TWA owed—saving the airline $150 million a year in interest payments. Icahn retained a 15-percent to 40-percent equity stake in the airline as a result of the reorganization and would head the company for at least one year, after which he would control five of the 11 board seats while the company's creditors controlled six.

TWA had about $200 million in cash on hand when it filed for bankruptcy protection, with an additional $100 million expected from asset sales. Analysts gave the carrier a 50-50 chance of reorganizing successfully since three of five recent major airline bankruptcies failed. Icahn, however, upped TWA's survival chances to 90-10. "I'm a fighter and a competitive guy, but I'm also a realist, and if I thought that TWA was a lost cause, I would say 'to heck with it' and break it up to obtain the maximum value," Icahn told *Aviation Week & Space Technology* in an interview. Icahn's financial interest in keeping the carrier afloat heightened when Congress made Icahn's other companies liable for the shortfall in TWA's pension plans which were underfunded by as much as $933 million. An accord with TWA's machinists' union and a plan with creditors to save the carrier $234 million annually in aircraft lease and debt payments worked in Icahn's favor.

Icahn then pledged to redefine TWA as a low-cost, no frills niche carrier. He targeted competitors' major hub cities, such as Delta's Atlanta, for expansion. TWA's cash position improved when a U.S. bankruptcy court in July approved TWA's request to sell its remaining Chicago O'Hare assets to American for up to $221 million. TWA was operating as a scaled-down airline by late October 1992. It cut the U.S. cities served to 62 from 70 and eliminated service to four of 22 international cities.

Meantime, Icahn negotiated with creditors and union officals to end his tenure as chairman and owner. Labor leaders agreed to a 15-percent concession in wages, benefits and work rules by all employees for a 45-percent equity stake in the airline. Creditors agreed to forgive about two-thirds of TWA's $1.5-billion debt and restructure the remaining debt for 55 percent of the common equity plus debt securities and preferred stock. Icahn in turn agreed to forfeit claim on some $170 million in TWA bonds and to loan the airline $200 million. The Pension Benefit Guaranty Corp. (PBGC), however, insisted the reorganization plan address TWA's $1.2 billion in underfunded pensions. The PBGC threatened lawsuits that would deplete Icahn's reported $989-million personal fortune. Icahn eventually agreed to pay a minimum of $80 million and as much as $240 million over eight years to TWA's pension fund. Analysts estimate Icahn over time will lose more than $200 million from his investment in TWA.

TWA's new chairman and chief executive, William Howard, a former chairman of Piedmont Airlines, officially took control in July 1993. Howard replaced interim managers Robin Wilson, a union representative, and Glenn Zander, who represented the creditors. Zander and Wilson were named vice chairman and, in conjunction with Howard, form TWA's current management team.

TWA filed its official reorganization plan in February with a tentative date of late spring 1993 to emerge from bankruptcy. The new management's focus: abandon the strategy of cut-rate fares, replace and expand TWA's aging fleet and gradually expand its shrunken route system over the next five years by strengthening hubs in St. Louis, New York and Atlanta, and internationally at Charles de Gaulle International Airport in Paris.

TWA posted a $33.2-million net loss for December 1992, down from the $59.3 million the company lost the previous month. It's fourth-quarter net loss was $144 million and the airline's cash position deteriorated from more than $44.9 million at the end of November to $14.6 million at the end of December. TWA's full year 1992 net loss was $317.7 million.

Trans World Airlines Statistics

1992 Total Sales
Global/Major Airlines

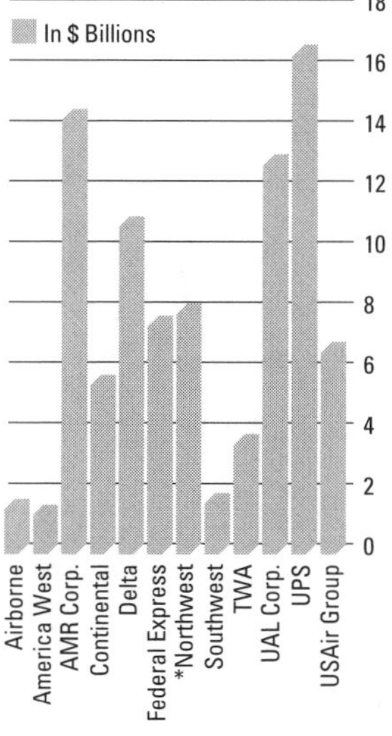

• Information is for Northwest Airlines only and not for parent company NWA Inc.

TWA finished 1992 ranked ninth in total sales.

TWA's sales during the period 1983 to 1992 increased only 8.3 percent.

After peaking in 1990, TWA's sales declined in 1991 before leveling off in 1992 after filing for Chapter 11 bankruptcy protection in January.

The 1986 decline in total sales was due primarily to the reduction in international revenues caused by increased terrorist activity in Europe.

TWA
Total Sales 1983-1992

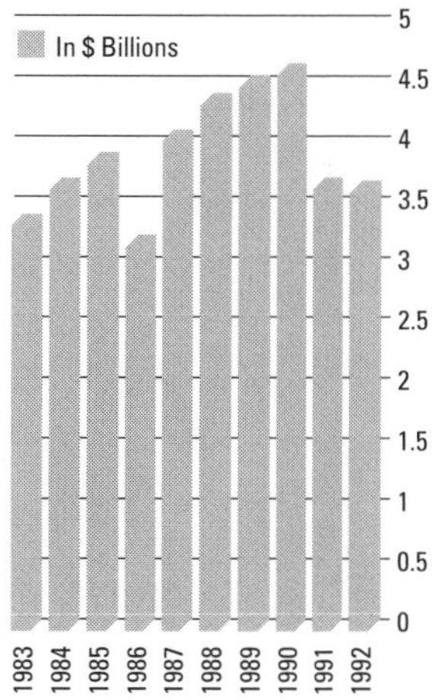

1992 Net Income
Global/Major Airlines

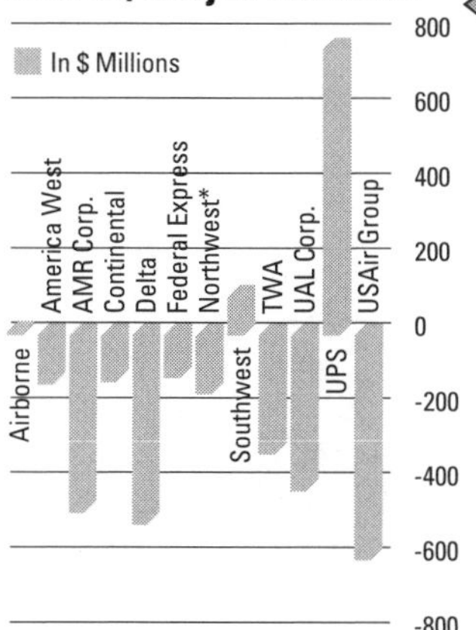

• Information is for Northwest Airlines only and not for parent company NWA Inc.

TWA lost $317.7 million in 1992. Four U.S. airlines lost more money than TWA for the year (before FAS 106 charges).

TWA earned record profits in 1987 and 1988. However, the company had $190.5 million in one-time earnings in 1988. These earnings resulted from the company's sale of all its Texaco common stock from which the company gained $140.6 million, and a $49.9-million gain from a cash judgment received from a lawsuit.

TWA lost $819.2 million from 1989-1992, including $520.7 million during the first three years of this decade.

TWA
Net Income 1983-1992

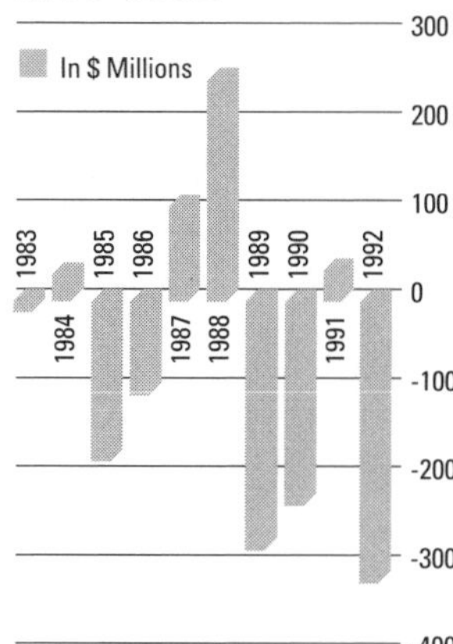

1992 Total Assets & Liabilities
Global/Major Airlines

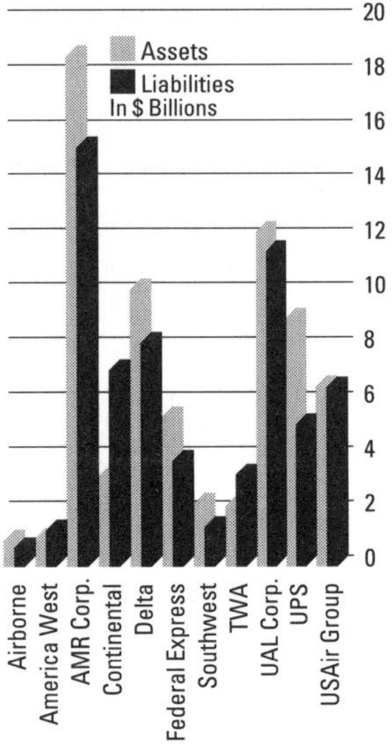

NWA Inc. is a privately held company and would not release 1990-1992 figures.

TWA was the ninth-largest global/major airline in 1992 based on total assets.

TWA's assets increased 55.3 percent between 1983 and 1987. Its assets shrunk 45.3 percent from 1987 to 1992. Its assets decreased 19 percent over the full 10-year period, from $2.74 billion in 1983 to $2.22 billion in 1992.

TWA's liabilities increased 66.8 percent from 1983 to 1992, from $2.02 billion to $3.37 billion.

TWA
Assets & Liabilities 1983-1992

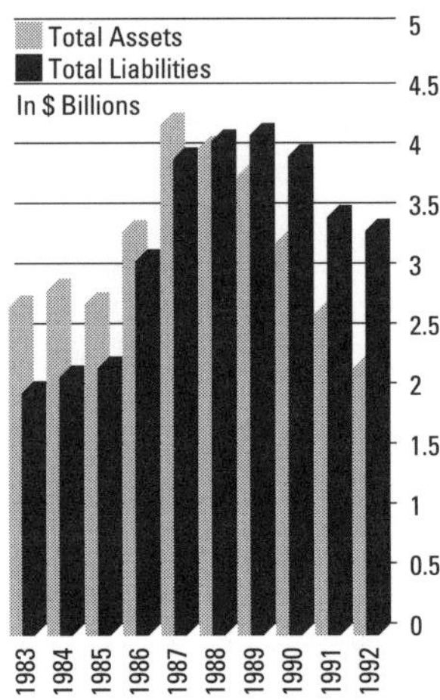

1992 ASMs & RPMs
Global/Major Airlines

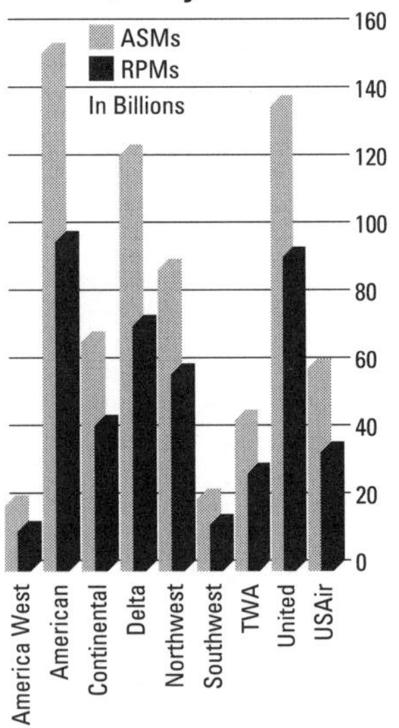

TWA finished 1992 with a systemwide capacity of 44.7 billion available seat miles (ASMs) which made it the seventh-largest airline in 1992 based on ASMs.

Between 1983 and 1992, TWA's available seat miles and revenue passenger miles increased 34.7 percent and 28.6 percent, respectively. From 1989 to 1992, however, its ASMs and RPMs decreased 22 percent and 17.6 percent, respectively. For the full 10-year period, TWA's ASMs increased 5.1 percent while its RPMs increased 5.9 percent.

TWA
ASMs & RPMs 1983-1992

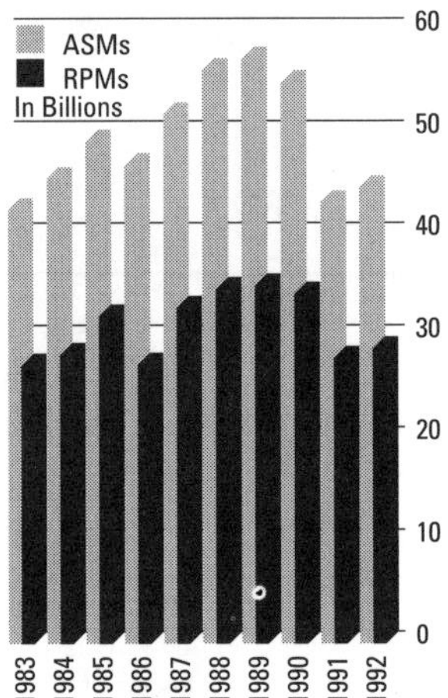

1992 Net Worth
Global/Major Airlines

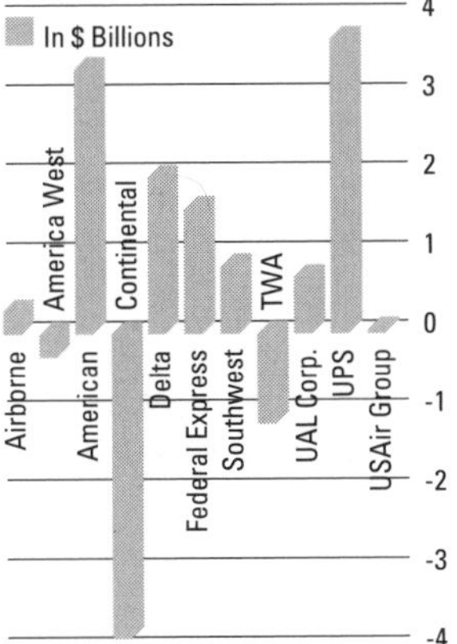

NWA Inc. is a privately held company and would not release 1990-1992 figures.

TWA finished 1992 with a stockholders' deficit of $1.15 billion, the fifth straight year TWA finished with a negative net worth.

TWA's net worth declined from a positive $719.3 million in 1983 to a negative (stockholders' deficit) $1.15 billion in 1992.

TWA's liabilities increased substantially as a result of the Icahn purchase and subsequent privatization of the company. Its liabilities increased 66.8 percent between 1983 and 1992—from $2.02 billion to $3.37 billion. TWA's assets decreased 19 percent during this same period—from $2.74 billion in 1983 to $2.22 billion in 1992.

TWA's liabilities, however, are on the decline: a decrease in liabilities of 17.9 percent over the first three years of the 1990s has TWA with its lowest liability since 1986.

TWA
Net Worth 1983-1992

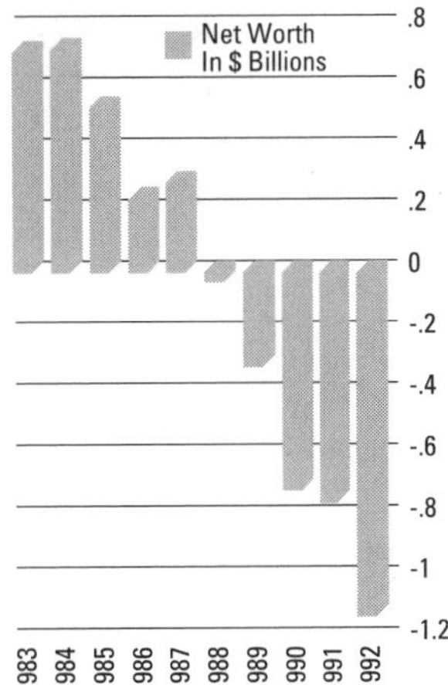

Statistics Related Terms

Assets — A resource having commercial or trade value that is owned (or which the company owns rights to) by a business. Typical examples for an airline include: Cash, securities, property, equipment, capital leases, landing slots and routes.

Available seat miles (ASMs) — Represent the number of seats available for passengers multiplied by the number of scheduled miles those seats are flown.

Cost per available seat mile — Represents operating and interest expense divided by available seat miles.

Financial accounting standard (FAS) 106 — A federally-mandated accounting change made to the way U.S. companies handle post-retirement benefits (other than pensions) to employees. FAS 106, for several U.S. global and major airlines, meant large, one-time, non-cash charges to earnings, further damaging their balance-sheet performance for 1992.

Leveraged buyout (LBO) — Takeover of a company using borrowed funds. Company assets often serve as security for the loans, although investors' assets also may be used.

Liabilities — The total amount the company owes to all creditors.

Net worth or stockholders' equity — The net assets (total assets minus total liabilities) of a company. For companies with more liabilities than assets, the result is a negative net worth or stockholders' deficit.

Passenger load factor — Revenue passenger miles divided by available seat miles over a set period of time.

Revenue passenger miles (RPMs) — The number of miles flown by revenue-producing passengers.

Yield — The average revenue received for each mile a revenue passenger is carried. Determined by dividing total operating revenue by total revenue passenger miles.

Trans World Airlines News Abstracts

"Business Traveler Discounts Isolate TWA From Big Three." *Aviation Week & Space Technology*, 21 Oct. 1991, pp. 24-25.

"Congressional Battle Looming Over Airline Route Purchases." *Aviation Week & Space Technology*, 22 April 1991, p. 34.

"Crandall vs. Icahn." *USA Today*, 22 April 1992, sec. B, p. 2.

"Delta Air, USAir Are Poised to Grab TWA's Remaining Routes to London." *Wall Street Journal*, 18 March 1991, sec. A, p. 3, col. 1.

"Iacocca, Who Has Held Talks on TWA, Indicates Doubt He Would Take Top Job." *Wall Street Journal*, 11 Dec. 1992, sec. B, p. 10.

"Icahn Discloses Smaller Supply of TWA Cash." *Wall Street Journal*, 1 April 1991, sec. A, p. 3, col. 4.

"Icahn Officially Ends Stint as the Chairman of TWA." *Wall Street Journal*, 11 Jan. 1993.

"Icahn to Cede Majority Stake in TWA With 'Prepackaged' Chapter 11 Filing." *Wall Street Journal*, 31 July 1991, sec. A, p. 3.

"Icahn Wins Reprieve From TWA's Bondholders." *The Atlanta Journal-Constitution*, 26 July 1991.

"Judge OKs Deal Between TWA's Icahn, Creditors." *The Atlanta Journal-Constitution*, 31 Dec. 1992.

"Kerkorian Asked by U.S. to Justify His Bid for TWA." *Wall Street Journal*, 11 April 1991.

"Kerkorian Gives Details of TWA Rescue Proposal." *Wall Street Journal*, 15 April 1991, sec. C, p. 16, col. 4.

"Kirk Kerkorian Reportedly Fails to Buy TWA." *Wall Street Journal*, 21 March 1991, sec. A, p. 3, col. 4.

"Negotiations for Control of TWA Focus on Pilots, Protection for Pension Plans." *Wall Street Journal*, 4 Aug. 1992.

"Northwest, TWA Announce Layoffs." *The Atlanta Journal-Constitution*, 2 Oct. 1992.

"Pan Am: TWA-American Bid Likely to Boost Price." *The Atlanta Journal-Constitution*, 23 July 1991, sec. C, p. 1.

"Pension Agency and Icahn Reach Accord on TWA." *Wall Street Journal*, 8 Dec. 1992, sec. A, p. 3.

"Poker Without Chips." *Forbes*, 13 May 1991, p. 44.

"Skinner Only Partly Clears TWA's Sale of London Routes to American Airlines." *Wall Street Journal*, 26 April 1991.

"Trans World Airlines Inc.; Carrier Planning to Restore Prewar Overseas Schedule." *Wall Street Journal*, 4 April 1991, sec. A, p. 2, col. 3.

"Trying to Save TWA, Carl Icahn is Facing Intractable Problems." *Wall Street Journal*, 29 April 1991, sec. A, p. 1.

"TWA 3rd-Period Loss More Than Tripled to $51.3 Million." *Wall Street Journal*, 11 Nov. 1991, sec. A, p. 8, col. 1.

"TWA, American Air Join to Fight Kerkorian Bid." *Wall Street Journal*, 16 April 1991, sec. B, p. 10, col. 6.

"TWA Chief Wary of Delta, But Hopeful About Atlanta." *The Atlanta Journal-Constitution*, 28 May 1992, sec. D, p. 7.

"TWA Cleared to Sell 3 London Routes to AMR." *Wall Street Journal*, 15 March 1991, sec. A, p. 3.

"TWA Close to Ending Bankruptcy Case." *The Atlanta Journal-Constitution*, 8 Dec. 1992, sec. F, p. 3.

"TWA, Continental Talk of Merger, Despite Debit." *Wall Street Journal*, 13 Dec. 1991.

"TWA Creditors, U.S. Pension Agency Reach Pact; Icahn's Bailout Plan Gains." *Wall Street Journal*, 9 Oct. 1992.

"TWA Defaults on $75.5 Million of Bond Debt." *Wall Street Journal*, 4 Feb. 1991, sec. A, p. 5, col. 1.

"TWA Filing Says Survival Depends on Sale." *Wall Street Journal*, 29 Jan. 1991, sec. B, p. 3, col. 4.

"TWA Hearing Delayed." *USA Today*, 26 July 1991.

"TWA in Search for 'Pizazz', Meets With Iacocca." *The Atlanta Journal-Constitution*, 11 Dec. 1992, sec. D, p. 9.

"TWA London Route Sale Curbed." *Flight International*, 2 April 1991, p. 11.

"TWA Making $420 Million Bid for Pan Am." *Wall Street Journal*, 22 July 1991, sec. A, p. 3.

"TWA May Go to Creditors, Employees." *USA Today*, 4 Aug. 1992, sec. B, p. 1.

"TWA May Seek Chapter 11 Status, Even in Routes Sale." *Wall Street Journal*, 3 April 1991, sec. A, p. 4, col. 3.

"TWA Plans Small Atlanta Hub." *The Atlanta Journal-Constitution*, 23 April 1992, sec. D, p. 1.

"TWA Proposes to Buy Back All of its Debt." *Wall Street Journal*, 16 May 1991, sec. A, p. 2.

"TWA Says Pilots Union Agreed to Pact." *Wall Street Journal*, 25 Aug. 1992, sec. A, p. 3.

"TWA Scraps Most of its Earlier Offer to Repurchase Securities at a Discount." *Wall Street Journal*, 23 July 1991.

"TWA to Halve Overseas Service, a Victim of Gulf Fears." *Wall Street Journal*, 21 Jan. 1991, sec. B, p. 1, col. 3.

"TWA Unions Set Concession Package, Clearing Way for a Bid by Kerkorian." *Wall Street Journal*, 25 March 1991.

"TWA Urges U.S. to Bar Kerkorian Bid, Repeating Threat of Bankruptcy Filing." *Wall Street Journal*, 17 April 1991, sec. A, p. 4, col. 2.

"TWA, USAir Have Talks About Joining Forces." *The Atlanta Journal-Constitution*, 30 June 1992.

"TWA's Icahn: Airline Industry a Costly Con Game." *The Atlanta Journal-Constitution*, 14 May 1992, sec. D, p. 8.

"Unions Offer Cost-Cutting Plan to Enable Kerkorian to Gain Control, Overhaul TWA." *Aviation Week & Space Technology*, 8 April 1991, p. 28.

10

United Airlines

United Airlines, a current member of the "Big Three" fraternity, throughout history remained a dominant carrier despite periods of financial turmoil, labor strife and its short association with the name "Allegis Corp."

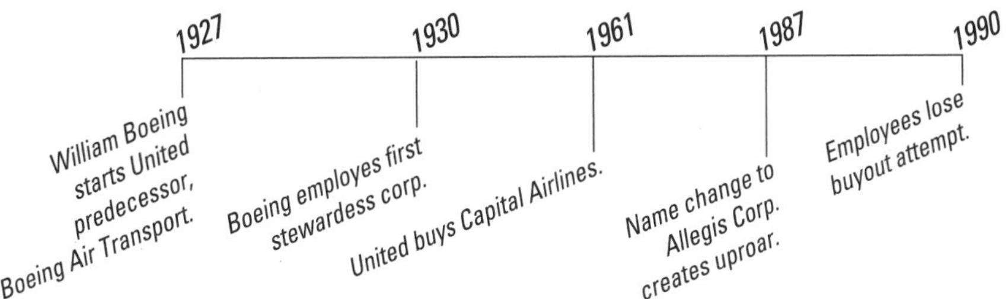

Two very different men appear in United's genealogy. One is the same Walter Varney who founded Varney Speed Lines, a predecessor of Continental. The other is William Boeing, who founded Boeing Aircraft Co. in 1916.

Varney's Varney Air Lines won the fifth route ever offered to a commercial carrier by the U.S. Post Office Department: Salt Lake City-Pasco, Wash., mail service. Varney started four airlines: two of them he sold, two of them failed, and Varney went on to other things (flying as a test pilot, for example). Varney belongs to United's genealogy because United Aircraft and Transport Corp., an early version of the major airline, acquired his Varney Air Lines in 1929.

William Boeing is more meaningful in the history of United by far. Boeing put together the elements of United Air Lines in the mid-1920s. He first acquired an airmail route from Chicago to San Francisco after passage of the Kelley Airmail Act of 1925. Then he created a subsidiary, Boeing Air Transport, to fly the mail. Its first flight was July 1, 1927.

This was the Roaring Twenties when companies were made and unmade at the blink of an eye. Boeing went with the prevailing winds and changed directions in 1928. He formed a holding company, Boeing Airplane and Transport Corp., to handle the acquisitions he foresaw. In the space of only two years, Boeing acquired Pratt & Whitney, Vought Airplane Co.,

Hamilton Standard Propeller Co., Sikorsky Aircraft Co., Stout Air Services, Stearman Aircraft Co., National Air Transport, Varney Air Lines and Pacific Air Transport. He changed the name of his company to United Aircraft and Transport Corp. halfway through that round of acquisitions. He created a second holding company, United Air Lines, in 1931 to manage the diverse airline holdings separately from the manufacturing concerns. Philip G. Johnson, who became president of Boeing Air Transport in 1926, helped Boeing lead the company through this period of acquisitions and early growth.

The Airmail Act of 1934 prohibited companies receiving airmail contracts from holding any interest in another aviation industry. As a result, United Aircraft and Transport Corp. divested itself of United Air Lines which then became an independent operating company.

United benefited from a powerful stroke of fortune at this critical juncture in its life: William A. Patterson became its president. He remained in that position until 1966. Patterson, throughout his tenure, easily could adopt the motto later used by Hinson at Midway: "Good guys finish first."

United Airlines

Aircraft fleet and purchase commitments
As of May 1993

Aircraft Type	Current Fleet	Firm Orders	Options
A-320	0	50	*
B-727	96	0	0
B-737	222	10	*
B-747	37	0	0
B-747-400	20	4	*
B-757	81	16	*
B-767	38	8	*
B-777	0	16	*
DC-10	54	0	0
Total	548	104	408

*United reports 408 aircraft options but would not release aircraft types.

Patterson began his career as a loan officer at the Wells Fargo Bank in San Francisco. One of his early challenges was arranging a line of credit for Vern Gorst's new Pacific Air Transport Co. Patterson later accepted Gorst's offer to become financial advisor to Pacific Air Transport. Patterson went to Seattle as an assistant to Johnson after Boeing acquired Pacific. He was a vice president by 1934 and was a natural choice for president after the breakup.

Patterson made United a service-oriented airline. Boeing already set a precedent by employing stewardesses (those first flight attendants were all trained nurses since their primary purpose was to reassure potential passengers who were afraid to fly). United also became the first airline to install two-way radios in all its aircraft and have inflight kitchens.

Patterson continued his efforts to make passengers feel safe and comfortable. He recognized that employees were the key to service and only well-treated employees render topnotch service. Accordingly, he worked hard at good labor-management relations. He was not an aloof boss. Tradition holds that Patterson visited each employee at least once a year to listen to complaints and solicit ideas on how to make the company better.

The record shows that Patterson created the industry's first internal medical department. The department provided screening physicals for job applicants along with day-to-day employee medical needs. Patterson also believed in promoting people from within and United for years had one of the lowest turnover rates among its top managers.

High employee morale and experienced management were two reasons for United's extraordinary success; Patterson's thorough belief in the future of commercial air transportation was another. He was instrumental in coordinating the efforts of major carriers of the day, including those of designer and builder Donald Douglas, to finance and construct a four-engine aircraft capable of traversing the continental United States nonstop.

The history of the airlines to a large extent boils down to a history of their aircraft. United took an early lead in fleet quality in the early 1930s, and was the undisputed industry leader when Patterson took the reins of United. Patterson bought the new 10-passenger Boeing 247D, the first all-passenger, all-metal plane used commercially, to improve United's already dominant market share. This move sent competitors scurrying for equipment to rival or surpass United's.

C. R. Smith, E. L. Cord's right-hand man at American Airlines, emerged as Patterson's main competitor for best-fleet honors. American's engineers, led by Smith, worked with Douglas to design a new aircraft to compete with the Boeing 247D. The DC-1 was unveiled in 1933; then Douglas developed the DC-3 in 1936, a 21-passenger aircraft superior to anything then flying. The DC-3 turned the tide and American Airlines overtook United as the industry leader in market share by the end of 1937. The Boeings remained uncompetitive despite efforts to modify them.

Thus, United wasted no time in testing and placing an order for the DC-4 when Douglas introduced the new four-engine aircraft at the end of 1938. But World War II diverted the DC-4s to military deployment before delivery was complete.

United, like all the other airlines, sacrificed 50 percent of its fleet for military service. United also performed contract air transport for the Army's Air Transport Command. The company carried more than 20,000 tons of men and material a total distance of 21 million miles by war's end, mainly in the Pacific and Alaskan theaters.

United focused its energies on re-establishing its route system and resuming the rivalry with American as peace drew near. Patterson made a tactical error at this point. With the war over, Patterson cast about for a two-engine aircraft to replace the aging DC-3. He settled on Glenn Martin's model 303 and ordered 50 planes with deliveries scheduled between 1947 and 1948. United initiated DC-4 service in 1946 and DC-6 service in 1947 to improve service along its transcontinental routes. But, United began accumulating excessive losses and, at the end of 1947, Patterson decided canceling the $16-million Martin order was in United's best interests.

Meanwhile, Smith went on a shopping spree at American and ordered 75 of the new Convair 240s with an option for 25 more. These aircraft arrived in 1948 and Smith rapidly deployed them on American's short-haul routes. Smith gained an advantage over Patterson and United where the DC-3s still flew its short-haul routes. Smith maintained that advantage for the next decade.

Patterson had fortune on his side when he decided not to follow American's lead and begin trans-Atlantic service. He directed his staff to study the potential profitability of this new market, and United's studies indicated existing demand for trans-Atlantic service would not support additional carriers. Therefore, Patterson elected to stay out of the trans-Atlantic race and pursue routes from the mainland to Hawaii instead. United handled almost half of the total traffic between California and Hawaii by the end of 1950.

Patterson was no more pro-union than other top airline managers of the time and United did have occasional labor trouble, especially with its pilots. An 11-day pilot strike hit the carrier in 1951. The pilots wanted their pay based on miles flown rather than hours flown since aircraft were getting faster. ALPA tried to lock in a contract to protect pay. Patterson refused and the pilots struck. The post-World War II attitude toward "gold-plated" unions like ALPA resulted in public condemnation of the pilots, but Patterson issued a company-wide bulletin urging other employees not to demonstrate any antagonism toward the pilots. Instead, fellow employees should help the pilots salvage their dignity, he wrote.

United Airlines
Aircraft fleet: 1983-1992

Aircraft	1983	1984	1985	1986	1987	1988	1989	1990	1991	1992
B-747-400	—	—	—	—	—	—	—	—	12	18
B-747	18	18	13	24	31	31	34	41	38	37
DC-10	47	50	51	55	55	55	55	54	55	54
L-1011	—	—	—	6	6	2	—	—	—	—
B-767	19	19	19	19	19	19	19	19	24	34
DC-8	42	29	29	29	29	29	27	18	—	—
B-757	—	—	—	—	—	—	5	24	45	63
B-727	154	154	154	154	154	147	140	128	116	104
B-737	49	49	59	77	88	122	149	179	193	209
Total	329	319	325	364	382	405	429	463	483	519

United continued modernizing its fleet with the Boeing Stratocruiser, DC-6B, DC-7 and Convair CV-340. Patterson also worked with engineers on United's specifications for the new generation of jet aircraft then on the drawing boards. Patterson ordered the new Douglas DC-8 after Boeing refused to modify its B-707 to meet United's needs. Specifically, Patterson wanted a fuselage wide enough to seat six across, a 30-degree wing sweep for more stability than Boeing's 35-degree wing sweep and a special landing gear to allow the plane to turn more sharply on the runway. Boeing built a lightweight, medium-range B-707 look-alike and dubbed it the B-720. United bought several of them. United's first DC-8 arrived in September 1959. Also, United became the first airline to install weather radar on all its aircraft during the 1950s.

Patterson's last five years with United were not vintage ones. He led United's 1961 purchase of financially-troubled Capital Airlines. The acquisition expanded United's air service to 116 cities in 32 states, but it also expanded debt and brought a demand for aircraft. United introduced the B-727 to its fleet in 1962 to handle the greater short-haul traffic.

George Keck replaced Patterson in 1966. Keck in his four-year tenure never came to grips with United's escalating problems. He did inaugurate routes to Hawaii from cities in the Northeast, Midwest and Great Lakes regions; ordered the B-747 and DC-10; and purchased Western International Hotels (1970) where his successor ran the show.

United faced serious financial difficulties by the end of the 1960s. The company undertook a reorganization and created a holding company, UAL Inc. United Airlines and the other businesses became wholly-owned subsidiaries of UAL, and Edward E. Carlson became United's new president. Carlson, who came to United as president of Western International Hotels, was what the doctor ordered. His disciplined management style forced lower-level managers to be more accountable for their decisions. And, he began an aggressive cost-cutting campaign that whipped United into a more streamlined, efficient company by the time deregulation became law in 1978. United seized the day and rapidly expanded its service and fleet, snaring record 1978 profits while other carriers struggled.

Percy Wood replaced Carlson in 1978 when Carlson retired, and Richard J. Ferris became chairman of the board. Ferris emerged the real power but lost most of the Carlson-era gains over the next nine years. The first blow came immediately, although it was not the fault of anyone in United's executive offices. An American Airlines DC-10 crash grounded the nation's entire DC-10 fleet (including United's). The Carter Administration recession deepened, further eroding revenue. A 58-day strike by United's pilots was the crowning blow. All told, these events served United a $99.6-million loss for 1979.

United fared better in 1980, earning a $21-million profit. But by this time, Wood's fate was sealed. He resigned in 1981, replaced by James J. Hartigan. Ferris remained chairman and became CEO as well. United lost $70.5 million in 1981 but generated profits in 1982, 1983 and 1984.

United became a true international carrier by adding routes between Seattle and Tokyo and Seattle and Hong Kong in 1983. The next year the airline earned the distinction as the first U.S. carrier to provide service in all 50 states. Nineteen eighty-five was a watershed year. It was the year when Ferris' plans for United became manifest. The company purchased Pan Am's Pacific routes; it bought Hertz Corp.; it started negotiations to purchase the Hilton Hotel chain. The handwriting was on the wall: Ferris wanted to mold UAL into a travel empire, not just a preeminent airline. A May 1985 pilot strike over the two-tier wage scale management wanted to implement foretold the internal warfare that soon tore United apart. The 29-day strike disrupted operations and United lost $48.7 million in 1985.

Ferris, in addition to the Hertz Corp. rental car agency, the Hilton International hotel chain and Pan Am's Pacific routes, accumulated the Westin Hotel chain and the Apollo Services computer reservations systems to complete his travel empire. Now he had to market it. Ferris planned to emphasize the company's new one-stop travel shopping concept, but he went one step too far in his marketing strategy. He changed the name of UAL Corp. to Allegis Corp. in 1987.

Rarely has a name attracted so much adverse reaction. The name "Allegis" symbolized to United employees the company's increasing divergence from the business of air transport. They pressured the board of directors to redirect the company's resources to the airline business, convinced that their recent pay concessions were squandered by purchasing Hertz Corp. and the Hilton hotels. Allegis Corp. felt the traveling public's resistance to Ferris' vision, aware of the derision excited by the name "Allegis" itself. The directors, under pressure from all sides, decided in 1987 to sell all non-airline-related businesses. Hilton International, Hertz and Ferris were gone that year and Westin departed in early 1988.

Stephen M. Wolf, of airline turnaround fame, was the new chairman, president and CEO who entirely erased the footprints of Ferris. Wolf was the only cohort of Frank Lorenzo to have notable success running airlines. Wolf's track record included service as senior vice president for marketing at Pan Am (1981-82), president of Continental Airlines (1982-83), president and CEO of Republic Airlines (1984-86), president and CEO of Flying Tiger Line (1986-87) and president and CEO of Tiger International (1987).

Wolf's reputation as a turnaround artist came with the revivals of Republic and the Tiger lines. He applied his skills to United by junking the name "Allegis" in favor of "UAL Corp." (May 26, 1988) and strengthening the company's finances by reducing total debt and increasing the cash balance. His work fostered a $1.124-billion profit in 1988, an enormous improvement over the $335.1-million net profit of 1987.

Wolf's handiwork did not go unnoticed by the financial community. Several investors made overtures to purchase UAL Corp. in 1989 as the leveraged buyout (LBO) frenzy once again heated up with regard to airlines. Investor Marvin Davis made the first substantial offer of $5.4 billion in August 1989. Later, a group led by Wolf and backed by United's pilots offered $300 a share. When this deal collapsed, the pilot, flight attendant and mechanics' unions teamed up with Coniston Partners to offer $201 a share or $4.38 billion in April 1990. This group, United Employee Acquisition Corp. (UEAC), hired former Chrysler vice chairman Gerald Greenwald to lead its buyout offer. Many banks backed out of this deal during the crisis in the Persian Gulf, and UEAC canceled the agreement with Coniston Partners. UEAC failed to have an offer ready for United by the Oct. 9 deadline and business returned to normal.

United faced its future with an adept managerial team, a strong financial position, a solid (and expanding) route structure and half ownership in a superior computer reservations system (CRS). It was coming off a year (1990) in which it earned a profit of $94.5 million on sales of $11.04 billion while other airlines lost money hand over fist. It entered 1991 dueling with American to become the world's dominant global airline.

United stuck to its aggressive five-year expansion plan which called for $18.7 billion in capital outlays on behalf of business growth in every sector of the globe. United scored a raft of points in the final months of 1990 and early months of 1991 in its contest to assume overall industry leadership in

United Airlines Financial Statistics

(In millions)	1983	1984	1985	1986	1987	1988	1989	1990	1991	1992
Sales	5,373	6,219	5,306	7,119	8,305	8,982	9,794	11,037	11,663	12,890
Net Income (loss)	142	282	(48.7)	12	335	1,124	324.2	94.5	(331.9)	(417.2)
Assets	4,689	4,683	5,924	6,549	8,389	6,701	7,207	7,983	9,876	12,257
Liabilities	3,084	2,780	4,124	4,257	5,467	5,475	5,642	6,312	8,279	11,551
Net Worth	1,605	1,903	1,800	2,292	2,922	1,226	1,564	1,671	1,597	706
ASMs	68,711	77,192	66,119	91,409	101,454	101,721	104,547	114,995	124,100	137,491
RPMs	43,794	46,687	41,640	59,312	66,348	69,101	69,639	76,137	82,290	92,690
Load Factors	63.7%	60.5%	63%	64.9%	65.4%	67.9%	66.6%	66.2%	66.4%	67.4%

global growth. It got U.S. and Japanese authority for a new Chicago-Tokyo route after competing head-on against American. It ordered up to 128 Boeing aircraft, including firm orders for 30 B-747-400s and 34 of the new B-777s. It paid $54 million for Eastern gates and departure slots in Chicago. It made a $400-million deal to take over Pan Am's London routes to New York, San Francisco, Washington, Los Angeles, Seattle-Tacoma and Newark. With new authority in London, United laid plans to begin service between London and the European cities of Paris, Amsterdam, Brussels, Munich, Frankfurt, Berlin and Hamburg. It increased service from all four of its U.S. hubs (Chicago O'Hare, Denver Stapleton, San Francisco International and Washington Dulles). It accepted delivery of 54 new aircraft scheduled to join its fleet in 1991.

That's not to say that United and its parent company, UAL Corp., were without problems. United, like virtually all airlines, was hit hard financially by the increase in fuel costs and the steep drop in traffic resulting from the Persian Gulf crisis and the nation's economic recession. United also was in the throes of negotiating new labor contracts with its pilot, flight attendant and machinists' unions. Also, Wolf increasingly was under fire for his hefty annual compensation package—$18 million in 1990, the same year UAL profits fell 71 percent.

Resentment lingered among pilots over the failed attempts by the pilots' union to take over the airline. Relations with management improved when Wolf & Co. agreed to a generous contract that guaranteed senior pilots raises of more than 15 percent by 1993 and pay hikes of 30 percent to 70 percent for lower-paid junior pilots. The three and a half-year pact also contained substantial improvements in job security provisions including a guarantee the contract would remain in effect if United was bought. United's flight attendants, after some conflict and informational picketing, also reached agreement with the carrier on a new contract. Negotiations with the Machinists' union remained in federal mediation until Machinists approved a new five-year labor contract on Dec. 23, 1992.

United flew one-third of its capacity on international routes by Aug. 1991, cementing its position as a major world player. Its inaugural flights to London's Heathrow Aiport marked a significant expansion of United's reach into the European market, and the next logical step in United's international growth strategy was expansion to South America. United accomplished this by edging out American and Delta to buy Pan Am's Latin American operation for $135 million at an auction in December 1991.

United's earnings continued their trend downward and the company's third-quarter 1991 net earnings of $25 million were substantially lower than anticipated. The results, Wolf said, were especially disappointing "in that the third quarter traditionally is the strongest operating period for United and for the U.S. airline industry in general." Wolf blamed United's ills on its substantial Midwest presence and thus its heavy exposure to the discount pricing practices of Chapter 11 carriers Midway, Continental and America West.

United, after reporting its worst year-end loss ever—$331.9 million in 1991—announced a $3.6-billion cut in capital expenditures. The carrier revamped its fleet-growth plan to take delivery of 122 fewer planes during the 1992-1995 period, cutting spending by about 22 percent. Wolf, in a letter dated Feb. 18, 1992, warned employees that large-scale layoffs and fleet cutbacks were inevitable unless financial performance improved significantly. "We cannot continue to incur the magnitude of losses we are experiencing and not do anything," he wrote. Wolf reiterated his message to employees in July 1992 after the airline reported second-quarter losses of $95.1 million.

Financial woes, however, did not stop United from continuing its battle with American for dominance at Chicago O'Hare, the world's busiest airport, where the two airlines operate hubs and compete extensively. United bid $66,000 a month and beat out American for 16 TWA takeoff and landing slots in Chicago in March. United already increased its lead over American in Chicago a year earlier by purchasing Express partner Air Wisconsin and gaining additional jet slots. United, however, lost its bid for 40 takeoff and landing slots and three gates when TWA agreed to sell its Chicago assets to rival American for $221 million in June.

United flew 92.7 billion RPMs in 1992, a 13-percent increase from 1991, and its load factor increased to 67.4 percent from 66.3 percent. United ran a close second to American's 97.4 billion RPMs and its traffic was up 20.6 percent in January 1993 compared to January 1992. Much of United's growth in the international sector came from operations in South America where it added more new flights there than to Europe in 1992. United in May reshaped its organizational structure to reflect the carrier's increasing global presence and created an international division. Additionally, Jack Pope, formerly the carrier's executive vice president and chief financial officer, was promoted to president and chief operating officer to help manage the rapid growth. Pope became second-in-command to Wolf who continued in his dual roles of chairman and chief executive officer of United and UAL Inc.

"United lost $957 million in 1992, including a $540-million, one-time, non-cash charge for accounting changes. United's pre-FAS 106 loss was $417.2 million. Wolf referred to the environment as "chaotic" and cited competitors operating indefinitely under bankruptcy law protection as one of the industry's "fundamental flaws." Wolf announced United would lay off 2,200 workers by mid-February 1993, eliminate 10 executive positions, cancel plans to hire 1,900 workers and retire 40 older aircraft in 1993 to stem the red ink.

As expected, United then turned to its unions for relief. Wolf set the example and took a 15-percent pay cut. He also imposed 5-percent and 10-percent salary cuts on company officers and directors. United's unions, however, balked at Wolf's request for similar sacrifices from contract workers; labor groups fought bitterly in 1991 for wage and benefit improvements that many felt were long overdue. Additionally, union representatives believed the massive layoffs and requests for wage and benefit reductions were unjustified. ALPA requested the carrier turn over its financial records and business plan to the union for review before the pilots would consider wage reductions. Wolf threatened that without concessions, United would have to sell its 17 U.S. flight kitchens, eliminating 5,600 jobs.

The carrier continued to post losses in the first quarter of 1993. The company reported a loss before charges of $138 million, a 28-percent increase from the year-earlier loss before charges of $108 million.

The officers responsible for the operations, maintenance and decision-making at United Airlines at the time of publication are Stephen M. Wolf, chairman and chief executive officer; John C. Pope, president and chief operating officer; Joseph R. O'Gorman Jr., executive vice president of operations; Hart A. Langer, senior vice president of flight operations; and Rono J. Dutta, senior vice president of maintenance operations.

United Airlines Statistics

1992 Total Sales
Global/Major Airlines

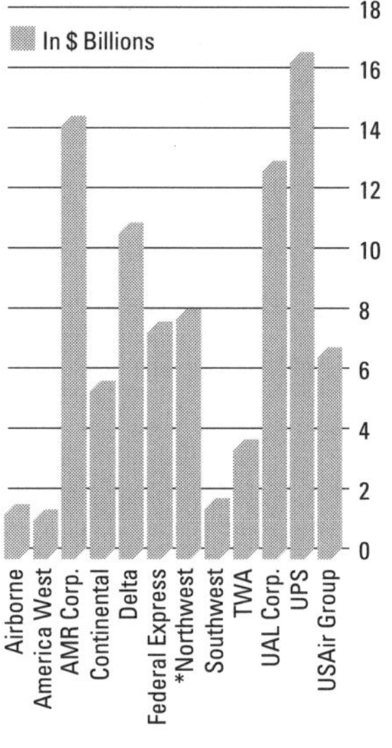

• Information is for Northwest Airlines only and not for parent company NWA Inc.

UAL Corp. finished 1992 with total revenues of $12.89 billion. This placed it third, behind UPS' 1992 revenues of $16.5 billion and AMR Corp.'s $14.4 billion in total sales.

United was the third-largest U.S. airline in 1992 in total revenues and second in total revenue passenger miles (RPMs) flown. The company flew 92.7 billion RPMs in 1992. AMR Corp. was first in 1992 in total RPMs flown and second in total revenue. AMR had total 1992 revenues of $14.4 billion and flew 97.4 billion RPMs.

UAL's sales increased 140 percent between 1983 and 1992. This sales increase primarily was due to United's tremendous expansion. The company increased its capacity from 68.7 billion available seat miles in 1983 to 137.5 billion in 1992, an increase of 100 percent. A 29-day pilot strike in 1985 adversely affected UAL's revenue and net income.

UAL Corp.
Total Sales
1983-1992

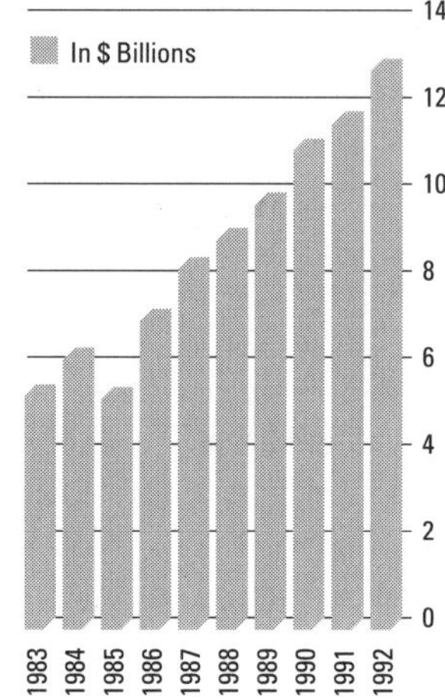

1992 Net Income
Global/Major Airlines

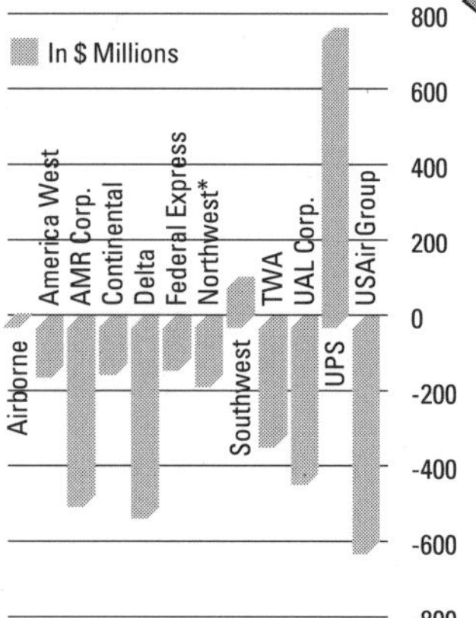

• Information is for Northwest Airlines only and not for parent company NWA Inc.

UAL finished 1992 with the fourth-worst net loss in the industry.

Before 1991, UAL made a profit in seven of its previous eight years.

The loss in 1985 is attributed to a 29-day pilot strike that significantly disrupted operations.

After posting a combined profit of $2.1 billion in the 1980s, including $1.12 billion in 1988 alone, UAL lost $654.6 million from 1990-92 (before charges due to Financial Accounting Standard 106 for 1992).

UAL Corp.
Net Income
1983-1992

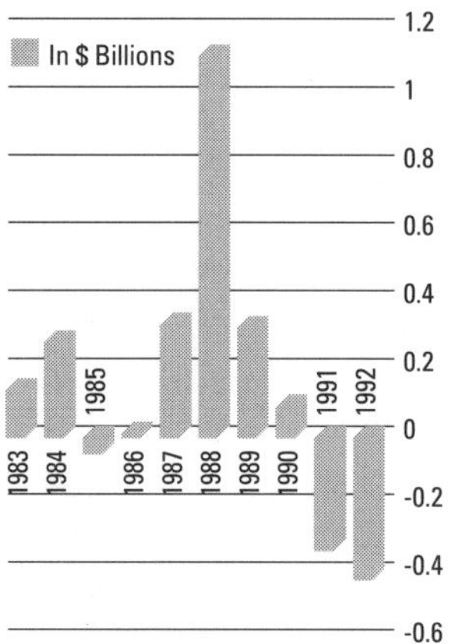

1992 Total Assets & Liabilities
Global/Major Airlines

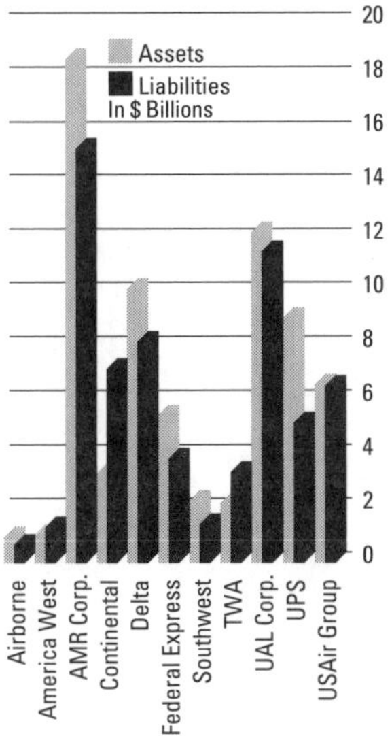

NWA Inc. is a privately held company and would not release 1990-1992 figures.

UAL finished 1992 with assets valued at $12.26 billion, second only to AMR Corp.'s $18.7 billion in assets.

UAL had total liabilities of $11.55 billion at the end of 1992, of which $3.78 billion was long-term debt.

UAL's assets increased 161 percent between 1983 and 1992 primarily as a result of the company's acquisitions of Pan Am's Pacific routes, the Hertz Corp., various hotel interests and general growth.

The sale of Hertz Corp., Hilton Hotels and Westin decreased the company's equity in 1988, but its liabilities did not decrease correspondingly.

The company's total liabilities increased 275 percent from $3.08 billion in 1983 to $11.55 billion in 1992.

UAL Corp.
Assets & Liabilities 1983-1992

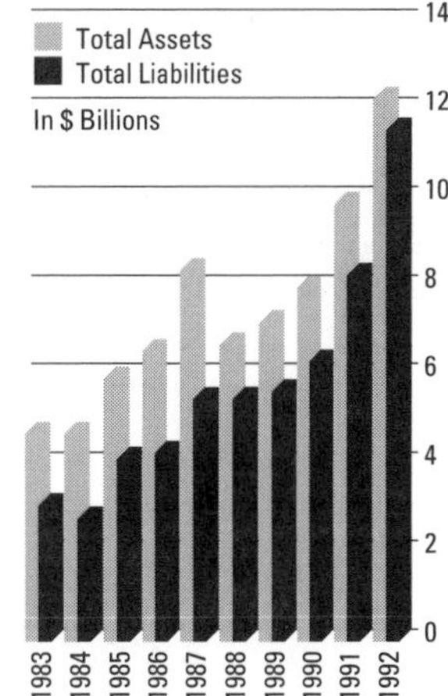

1992 ASMs & RPMs
Global/Major Airlines

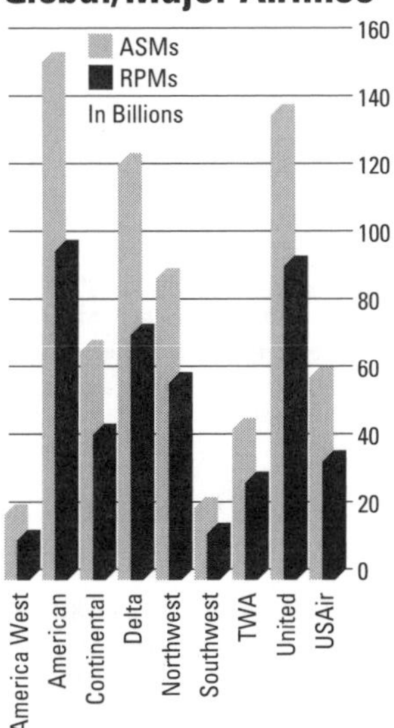

United had the second-largest capacity, measured in available seat miles (ASMs), in the industry in 1992.

The company's 92.7 billion RPMs flown in 1992 was second only to AMR.

United's capacity, measured in ASMs, increased 100 percent between 1983 and 1992.

The company's RPMs grew from 43.8 billion in 1983 to 92.7 billion in 1992, an increase of 112 percent.

The capacity decline in 1985 was due to a 29-day pilot strike that disrupted operations at the airline.

United's load factor for 1992 was 67.4 percent, highest among global and major airlines.

United
ASMs & RPMs 1983-1992

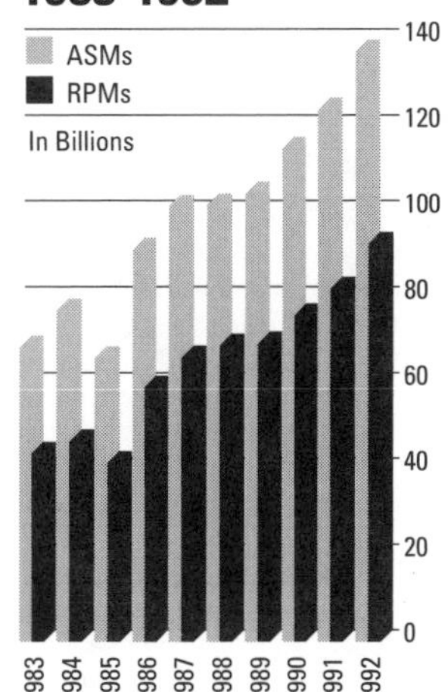

1992 Net Worth
Global/Major Airlines

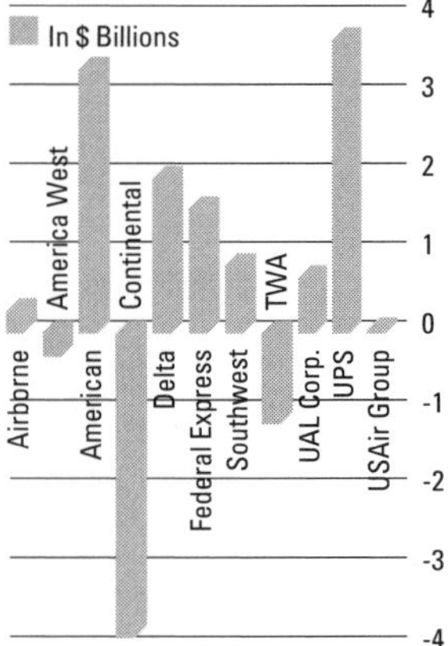

NWA Inc. is a privately held company and would not release 1990-1992 figures.

UAL Corp., the holding company of United Airlines, finished 1992 with a net worth of $706 million which placed it sixth in the industry.

UAL's drop in net worth between 1987 and 1988 partially can be attributed to the sale of Hertz, Hilton Hotels and Westin, which resulted in the company losing equity without a corresponding loss of liabilities, depressing its net worth in 1988.

UAL's net worth decreased in 1992 for the second consecutive year.

UAL Corp.
Net Worth 1983-1992

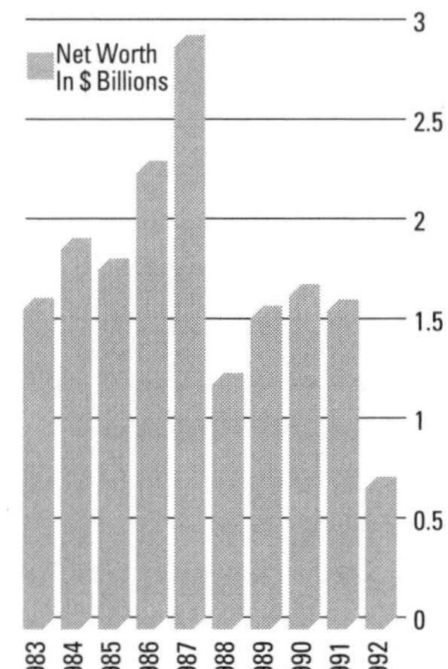

Statistics Related Terms

Assets — A resource having commercial or trade value that is owned (or which the company owns rights to) by a business. Typical examples for an airline include: Cash, securities, property, equipment, capital leases, landing slots and routes.

Available seat miles (ASMs) — Represent the number of seats available for passengers multiplied by the number of scheduled miles those seats are flown.

Cost per available seat mile — Represents operating and interest expense divided by available seat miles.

Financial accounting standard (FAS) 106 — A federally-mandated accounting change made to the way U.S. companies handle post-retirement benefits (other than pensions) to employees. FAS 106, for several U.S. global and major airlines, meant large, one-time, non-cash charges to earnings, further damaging their balance-sheet performance for 1992.

Leveraged buyout (LBO) — Takeover of a company using borrowed funds. Company assets often serve as security for the loans, although investors' assets also may be used.

Liabilities — The total amount the company owes to all creditors.

Net worth or stockholders' equity — The net assets (total assets minus total liabilities) of a company. For companies with more liabilities than assets, the result is a negative net worth or stockholders' deficit.

Passenger load factor — Revenue passenger miles divided by available seat miles over a set period of time.

Revenue passenger miles (RPMs) — The number of miles flown by revenue-producing passengers.

Yield — The average revenue received for each mile a revenue passenger is carried. Determined by dividing total operating revenue by total revenue passenger miles.

United Airlines News Abstracts

"3 Airlines Criticize USAir-British Airways Deal." *The Atlanta Journal-Constitution*, 2 Oct. 1992, sec. G, p. 1.

"AMR Sues UAL Over Plan to Buy Air Wisconsin." *Wall Street Journal*, 20 Nov. 1991, sec. A, p. 11.

"Analysts See Airline Stocks Soaring." *USA Today*, 30 Jan. 1991, sec. B, p. 3.

"Bidders Shun Eastern Hub at Hartsfield." *The Atlanta Journal-Constitution*, 1 Feb. 1991.

"Boeing Misses United Deal, May Lose Another Big Order." *The Atlanta Journal-Constitution*, 9 July 1992.

"Britain, U.S. Fail to Decide if United Air Can Take Over for Pan Am at Heathrow." *Wall Street Journal*, 16 Jan. 1991.

"British Aviation Agency Wants to Open Heathrow Airport to Additional Airlines." *Wall Street Journal*, 23 Jan. 1991.

"Delta Main Buyer of Eastern Assets." *The Atlanta Journal-Constitution*, 6 Feb. 1991, sec. C, p. 1.

"Delta Questions United/Pan Am Deal." *Flight International*, 2-8 Jan. 1991, p. 5.

"Delta, UAL Make Winning Eastern Bids." *Wall Street Journal*, 6 Feb. 1991, sec. A, p. 3, col. 3.

"Delta Will Again Try to Stall Pan Am Route Sale so it Can Make Bid." *The Atlanta Journal-Constitution*, 10 Jan. 1991.

"Dogfight; United and American Battle for Global Supremacy." *Business Week*, 21 Jan. 1991, pp. 56-62.

"In the Wake of Eastern Airlines' Demise, Rival Carriers Swoop in for the Pieces." *Wall Street Journal*, 22 Jan. 1991, sec. B, p. 1.

"Justice Department Clears Sale of Pan Am Routes." *Wall Street Journal*, 18 Jan. 1991, sec. A, p. 10, col. 5.

"Major U.S. Airlines Bid for Eastern's Remains." *USA Today*, 5 Feb. 1991, sec. B, p. 2.

"New UAL Aid for Pan Am Possible Soon." *Wall Street Journal*, 7 Jan. 1991, sec. A, p. 3, col. 3.

"Pan Am Seeks Chapter 11 Shield, Gets UAL-Backed Cash Infusion; Fuel Costs Are Cited; Carrier Will Maintain its Usual Schedule." *Wall Street Journal*, 9 Jan. 1991, sec. A, p. 3, col. 1.

"Pan Am to Cut its Work Force by 15% and Further Reduce Service to Europe." *Wall Street Journal*, 6 Feb. 1991.

"Sam Skinner's Game of Darwin-in-the-Sky: The New Air Treaty Heats up Competition on Both Sides of the Atlantic." *Business Week*, 25 March 1991, p. 28.

"States Offer Big Bucks to Land United Hub." *USA Today*, 21 March 1991.

"This is Stage of Recession to Fly to Airline Stocks, Some Advise." *The Atlanta Journal-Constitution*, 28 Jan. 1991, sec. G, p. 1.

"U.S. Agency Gives United Air Use of Pan Am Route." *Wall Street Journal*, 2 April 1991, sec. A, p. 2, col. 3.

"U.S. Will Oppose UAL Offer to Buy Eastern Assets." *Wall Street Journal*, 15 Feb. 1991, sec. A, p. 4, col. 2.

"UAL Agrees to Change Executive-Pay Disclosures." *Wall Street Journal*, 9 Jan. 1992.

"UAL Lashes Out at Japanese Moves Against New Route." *Wall Street Journal*, 14 Oct. 1992, sec. B, p. 11.

"UAL Stock Sale Seeks Proceeds of $225 Million." *Wall Street Journal*, 6 March 1991, sec. A, p. 3, col. 1.

"UAL to Trim Capital Outlays by $3.6 Billion." *Wall Street Journal*, 11 Feb. 1992, sec. A, p. 3.

"UAL's Deficit in Quarter Was $123.5 Million." *Wall Street Journal*, 1 Feb. 1991.

"UAL's United Airlines Names Two to Head New Operating Groups." *Wall Street Journal*, 22 Feb. 1991, sec. B, p. 6, col. 1.

"UAL's United Seeks the Pan Am Route of Miami-London." *Wall Street Journal*, 26 March 1991.

"United Airlines Bids for Pan Am Routes, Planes." *Wall Street Journal*, 11 July 1991.

"United Airlines Renews its Bidding for Some Pan Am Assets." *The Atlanta Journal-Constitution*, 9 Aug. 1991.

"United Airlines' Wolf Takes Huge Cut in Pay for 1991." *The Atlanta Journal-Constitution*, 31 March 1992, sec. E, p. 7.

"United, American Cleared for Landing at London's Heathrow as New Era Dawns." *Wall Street Journal*, 12 March 1991, sec. B, p. 1, col. 3.

"United Awaits UK Approval for Proposed Pan Am Purchase." *Flight International*, 19 Dec. 1990-1 Jan. 1991, p. 8.

"United Backs Loan to Help Pan Am Continue Operations." *Aviation Week & Space Technology*, 14 Jan. 1991, pp. 27-28.

"United Begins Chicago-Tokyo Flight, But Japanese Threaten to Close Route." *Wall Street Journal*, 9 Jan. 1991, sec. A, p. 2, col. 1.

"United Bids $625M for Pan Am Assets." *USA Today*, 9 Aug. 1991, p. 1.

"United Continues International Drive." *Flight International*, 5-11 June 1991, p. 11.

"United, Delta Get Eastern Asset Nod." *USA Today*, 6 Feb. 1991, p. 1.

"United Flies to Heathrow With Flourish." *USA Today*, 3 April 1991.

"United is Fastest Growing Major Air Carrier in U.S." *Professional Pilot*, Sep. 1991, pp. 26-30.

"United Lands Pan Am's London Landing Rights." *USA Today*, 12 March 1991, sec. B, p. 2.

"United Offers Spin Around Globe." *USA Today*, 13 Aug. 1992.

"Wolf Pads UAL Stake." *The Atlanta Journal-Constitution*, 24 March 1992.

"World's Major Airlines Scramble to Get Ready for Competitive Battle." *Wall Street Journal*, 14 Jan. 1992, sec. A, p. 1.

"United Air Cleared for Washington Link to Rome and Milan." *Wall Street Journal*, 24 March 1992.

11

United Parcel Service

UPS' air operation is a success despite its youth. An old company with an upstart air group, UPS experienced rapid growth in air express when it began operating its own air cargo line in 1988.

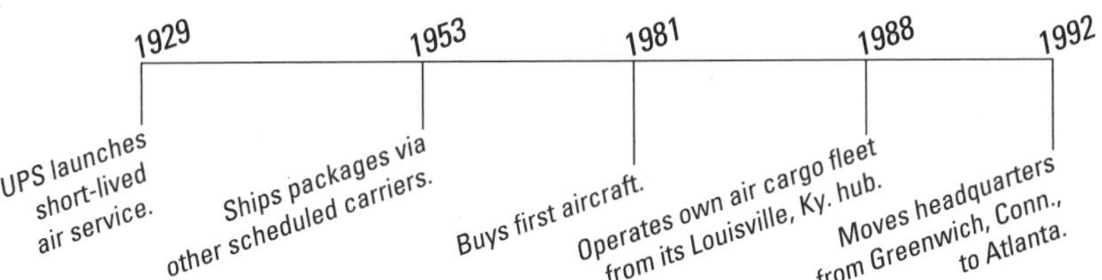

United Parcel Service traces its history to the early days of aviation, but not as an air carrier. James E. Casey borrowed $100 to start a messenger delivery service in Seattle in 1907. Soon the company thrived as a delivery service for downtown department stores. Later, renamed United Parcel Service (UPS), the company became an alternative to the post office when it switched from serving merchants to delivering packages for anyone. United Parcel Service launched its first air service on the West Coast in 1929, but quit after the great stock market crash; it didn't try again until the early 1950s when it started leasing space for shipments on other carriers' aircraft.

UPS in 1953 used scheduled airlines to ship two-day air service packages between major cities to support the company's ground delivery business. The company bought its first aircraft in 1981 and moved its air operation from Chicago to Louisville. UPS initiated Next-Day air service in 1982 after Federal Express created the market for overnight letters and small packages.

UPS, in late 1983, expanded its express package business by adding 12 Fairchild Expediters to its large jet fleet. The small aircraft, operated through contract by Merlin Express, flew from UPS' large hub cities to smaller cities throughout the Eastern U.S.

The high-flying, overnight express market fueled UPS' growth. Consultants' estimates put Federal Express with 58 percent of the air express market and UPS with 15 percent in 1986. However, it still did not run an airline, opting instead to employ contract air carriers to operate its aircraft.

The proliferation of air carrier contracts, some of them with competitors, grew burdensome as UPS expanded its air service, so the company decided in 1987 to operate its own air cargo fleet. First, UPS took control of International Parcel Express (IPX), a consortium-owned international air company, and acquired its airline operating certificate. Next, it allowed contracts to expire with several independent carriers that provided crews for UPS-owned jets. Each month through 1988, a UPS-trained crew waited to climb aboard when the company took back control of one of its aircraft. UPS hired a majority of its first pilots and engineers from contract carriers, including 26 pilots UPS "inherited" from IPX. Altogether, the company hired and trained 844 pilots between January and February of 1988.

United Parcel Service
Aircraft fleet and purchase commitments
° As of May 1993

Aircraft Type	Current Fleet	Firm Orders	Options
B-727	52	0	0
B-747	11	0	0
B-757	30	25	41
B-767	0	30	30
DC-8	49	0	0
Total	142	55	71

The transition of weaning itself from the contract carriers and starting its own airline took almost a year. UPS operated its own airline by the end of 1988 with 780 pilots and a 95-plane fleet. Almost overnight UPS was the tenth-largest airline in the U.S. The company earned steadily increasing revenues that reached $11 million in 1988. Net profit that year was $759,000.

UPS was in solid second place with about 25 percent of the market share in 1988, behind Federal Express which had at least half the market. An estimate in 1990 put Federal Express' share at 48 percent and UPS at 26 percent.

There were no prima donnas at UPS. The company imposed on its pilots the same fanatical devotion to efficiency that characterized all the rest of its operations. Watches synchronized, every step counted and timed, UPS continued its zealous expansion pace in 1990 despite a threatened Teamsters strike and $200 million in overseas losses (over a 15-month stretch). UPS managed to keep up its double-time pace throughout all of the challenges. Its delivery truck drivers continued their march at the company-prescribed three feet per second, its pilots continued their takeoffs at intervals that eliminated the need to touch the brakes and UPS continued to acquire routes and smaller companies.

The expansion pace was what might be expected of a $12.4-billion company (in 1989) with negligible debt: breathtaking. The following 1990 moves were related to expansion:

UPS acquired Seabourne Express Parcels, a division of United Kingdom- and Belgium-based Seabourne Express Ltd. It bought an interest in Bermuda Delivery Services Ltd. and in July agreed to acquire Prost Transport of France to round out its European presence. It also agreed to buy as much as 17.4 percent of San Diego, Calif.-based Mail Boxes Etc. and started a joint venture, called Unistar Air Cargo, with Japanese partner Yamato Transport.

UPS began building a $53-million hub center in Ontario, Calif. It announced it would begin construction in the fall of 1991 on a $21-million handling facility at Dallas-Fort Worth Airport. It completed a new maintenance hangar, the bulk of a $25-million expansion that brought the total cost of the Louisville air operations facility to $183.5 million.

It ordered 25 Boeing 757 package freighters for a price of $1.7 billion. A $90-million cockpit modernization program began on its McDonnell Douglas DC-8s and Boeing 727s. It completed construction of a $2.5-million Phase III simulator center at Louisville, Ky., and installed the first of three simulators ordered from Britain's Rediffusion Simulation ($34 million total price for all three).

Credit goes to Memphis-based Federal Express for rousing the package giant into action. UPS, lulled into complacency with competition limited to the postal service, stepped up marketing efforts and matched Federal Express' services: same-day pickup and guaranteed 10 a.m. delivery of overnight packages. It started a $1.4-billion, five-year investment program to develop computer technology for its worldwide delivery network to outstrip Federal Express in service. That technology included UPSCODE which allowed UPS to put twice as much information on its labels as conventional bar code labels hold.

Meanwhile, UPS dealt with three forms of culture shock to its work force in 1990: a near-strike by the Teamsters union, difficulty in assimilating small international companies it acquired and a dispute with its pilots' union over pay and flying time. Historically, the Teamsters union represented UPS pilots from the time the company assumed control of its airline in 1988. The IPX pilots elected to join the Teamsters when they first came to UPS. However, UPS pilots became dissatisfied with their Teamsters representatives and voted overwhelmingly—94.4 percent of the 98.8 percent who voted—in the fall of 1989 to form their own breakaway union, the Independent Pilots Association (IPA). UPS averted the feared Teamsters strike, a near-by-product of a leadership tussle within the Teamsters, in August when 65,463 union members voted for the company's proposed contract and 53,091 voted against it.

The world's largest package-delivery company, although a Johnny-come-lately in overnight delivery and international expansion, UPS threw down the gauntlet to upstart Federal Express which seized a flying head start in both arenas before UPS management decided enough market erosion was enough. UPS was in far better financial position for a protracted overnight delivery market-share battle than its chief competitor; UPS' $847.9 million in long-term debt represented only 10.3 percent of assets at year's end 1990, while Federal Express' $2 billion in long-term debt came to almost 36 percent of assets.

UPS expanded its international market share to slightly more than 6 percent; Federal Express in late 1990 had a 7-percent share of the international market. UPS flew to 72 domestic and eight international destinations, including Mexico, the Pacific Rim and Cologne, Germany. Its 99-plane fleet included six B-747s, eight B-727-200s, 15 B-757PFs, 30 B-727-100s and 40 DC-8s. Despite its international losses, UPS finished 1990 with $13.6 billion in corporate revenues—up a healthy 10 percent from 1989—and $596.7 million in net income.

The company entered 1991 still expanding, still repositioning to be even more efficient and competitive than in the past. UPS went on a buying spree overseas, gobbling up 11 package-delivery services in Europe alone and forging partnerships with others. The company also expanded its charter work and flew weekly charters to Europe, several to the Soviet Union and ferried relief supplies to Turkey and Bangladesh. UPS flew its 49 DC-8s and eight B-747s on those long-haul routes.

United Parcel Service

Aircraft fleet: 1987-1992

Aircraft	1987	1988	1989	1990	1991	1992
B-727	36	36	41	47	47	52
B-747	6	6	6	10	11	11
B-757	15	15	15	20	30	30
DC-8	42	42	42	49	49	49
Total	99	99	104	126	137	142

UPS flew to 73 cities in the U.S. and seven outside the country by early 1991. It announced plans to deliver overnight packages on Saturdays in March 1991, a move designed to erase the last deficit between its own service and that of Federal Express in the $8 billion-a-year overnight delivery market. UPS also matched Federal Express in on-demand pickups, computerized package tracking and discount prices for high-volume accounts.

On the labor front, UPS settled its pay-and-work-rules dispute with its pilots in December 1991 after 19 months of negotiations, including several months of federally mediated talks. The IPA pushed the company for more flexibility in scheduling and better wages. The new contract changed schedule bid periods to 56 days from three months and improved pay dramatically; top pay for captains went from $83,000 to $123,700.

UPS stayed true to its bottom-line consciousness by announcing in May 1991 plans to move its 1,000-employee headquarters operation to Atlanta, Ga., from Greenwich, Conn., in 1992. Reasons for the move were twofold: to decrease cost-of-living expenses for employees and to lower the company's overhead expenses. Louisville, Ky., however, would remain UPS' main air hub.

Higher delivery prices, cheaper fuel prices and rate increases helped UPS report revenues of $15.019 billion in calendar year 1991 and a consolidated net income of $700 million, up $103.4 million from 1990.

Federal Express had a 43-percent to 24.5-percent lead over UPS in domestic air shipment market share in 1992, according to analysts. Airborne Express followed with 14 percent and the U.S. Postal Service's Express Mail with 7.4 percent. UPS' international losses continued because of the weak economy in Europe and tough competition from better-known DHL Worldwide, among others. UPS, however, continued to build its own network of brown operations in Europe despite Fed Ex's abrupt withdrawal from the intra-Europe market in May 1992.

UPS rolled out the first of its re-engined B-727-100s modified with Rolls Royce Tay 651-54 engines in the summer of 1992. Its goal: to bring 95 percent of its fleet to Stage Three standards by 1995. Other developments that year included opening its new $96-million West Coast regional air hub in Ontario, Calif.; ordering 30 B-767 freighter aircraft with options to buy 30 more; and beginning a new delivery service, 3-Day Select, that combined both air and ground shipment.

The company finished 1992 with 1,307 pilots and 137 airplanes. Revenues reached a record $16.5 billion in 1992 with net income of $765.07 million before FAS 106, a one-time accounting charge. UPS had domestic regional hubs in Dallas; Ontario, Calif.; and Philadelphia. Cologne and Bonn, Germany; Hong Kong; and Singapore were its international hubs, and Miami served as its regional hub for South America. The UPS Air Group served 349 domestic and 209 international airports.

The UPS officers responsible for operations, maintenance and decision-making at the time of publication are Kent C. Nelson, chairman and chief executive officer; James P. Kelly, chief operating officer; Edwin A. Jacoby, chief financial officer; and Richard O. Oehme, senior vice president of air operations.

United Parcel Service Financial Statistics

(In thousands)	1989	1990	1991	1992
Sales	12,357,918	13,606,344	15,019,830	16,518,621
Net Income (loss)	693,424	596,776	700,170	756,072[1]
Assets	7,888,127	8,176,056	8,858,561	9,037,817
Liabilities	4,299,392	4,569,113	4,985,409	5,317,385
Net Worth	3,588,735	3,606,943	3,873,152	3,720,432

[1] Before FAS 106 charge.

United Parcel Service Statistics

1992 Total Sales
Global/Major Airlines

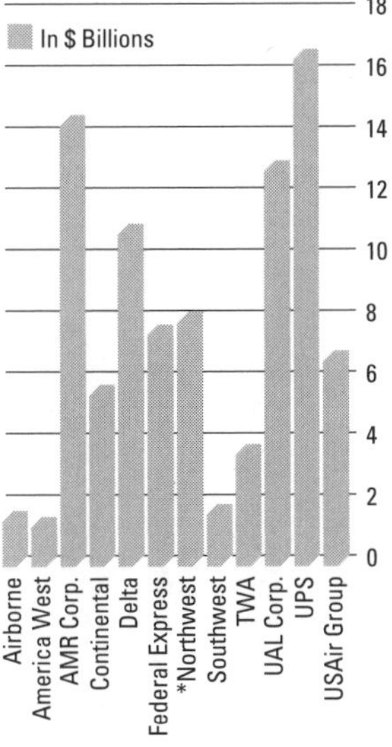

• Information is for Northwest Airlines only and not for parent company NWA Inc.

UPS led the industry with 1992 total revenues of $16.52 billion, $2.1 billion more than second-place AMR Corp.

UPS' revenue growth hovered about 10 percent for each of the past three years, increasing from $12.36 billion in 1989 to $16.52 billion in 1992.

UPS
Total Sales 1989-1992

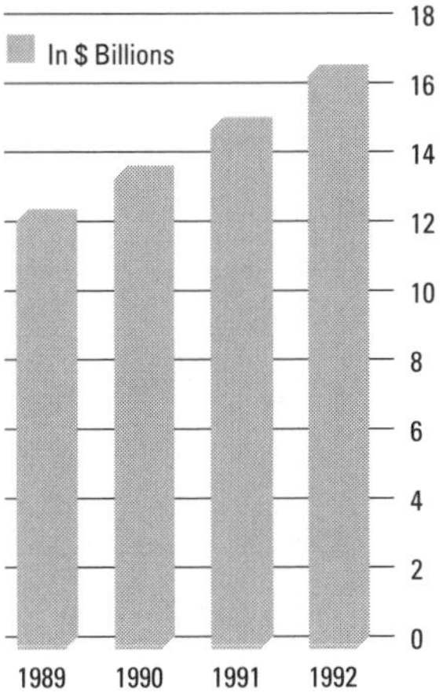

1992 Net Income
Global/Major Airlines

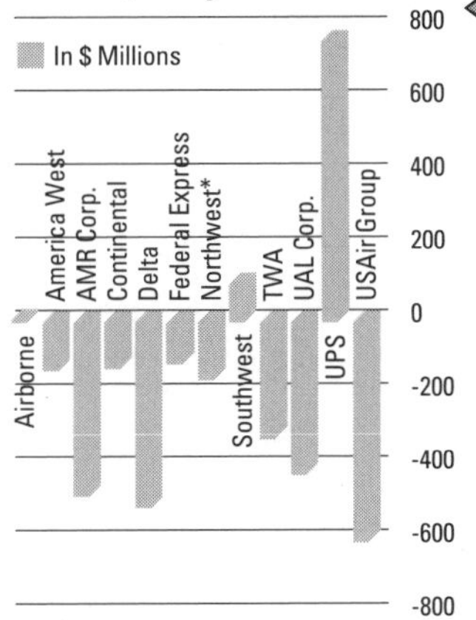

• Information is for Northwest Airlines only and not for parent company NWA Inc.

UPS paced the industry in 1992 with a net profit of $765.1 million before a charge related to FAS 106. Southwest was a distant second with a net profit of $103.6 million.

UPS' net income for 1992 was an all-time high (before FAS 106 charges), as were its revenues. UPS earned $2.755 billion in profits from 1989 through 1992, an average annual profit of $688.86 million over that period.

UPS
Net Income 1989-1992

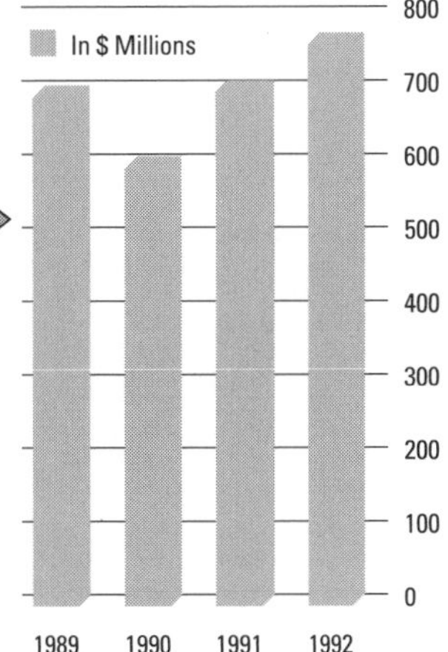

1992 Total Assets & Liabilities

Global/Major Airlines

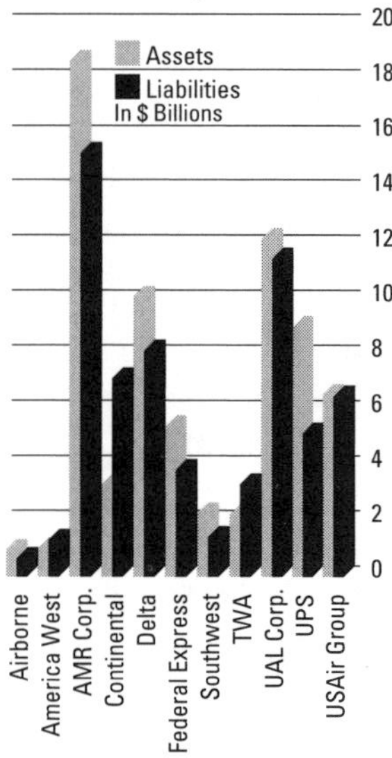

NWA Inc. is a privately held company and would not release 1990-1992 figures.

UPS' assets, valued at $9.038 billion, placed fourth behind AMR, Delta and UAL. Not counting Northwest, whose liabilities for 1992 are unknown, UPS has fewer liabilities than USAir, AMR, Continental, Delta and UAL.

UPS' assets increased 10.5 percent from 1990 to 1992, but jumped only 2 percent in 1992 to $9.038 billion. UPS' liabilities increased 16.4 percent from 1990 to 1992, including a 6.7-percent hike in 1992 to $5.317 billion.

UPS

Assets & Liabilities 1989-1992

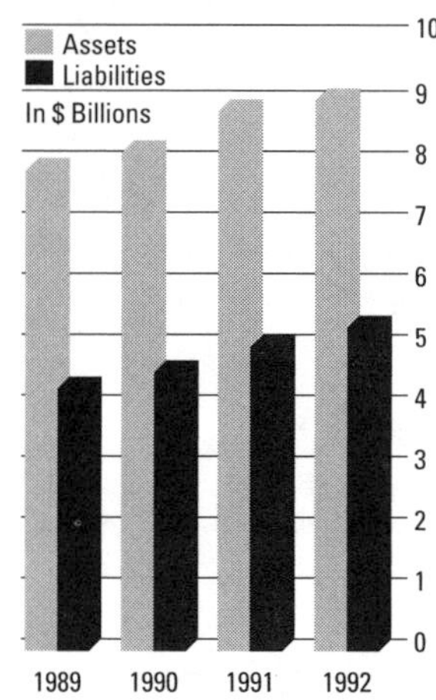

1992 Net Worth

Global/Major Airlines

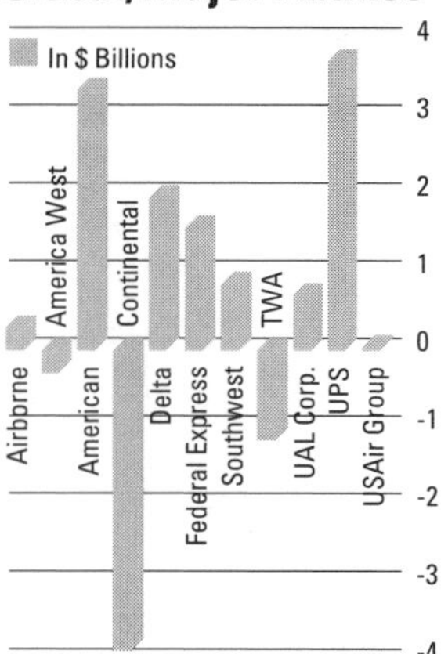

NWA Inc. is a privately held company and would not release 1990-1992 figures.

UPS placed first in the industry for 1992 with a net worth of $3.72 billion. AMR Corp. was second, finishing 1992 with a net worth of $3.349 billion.

Since its liabilities increased at a higher rate than its assets, UPS' net worth actually decreased in 1992. For the period 1990 to 1992, however, UPS' net worth increased 3.1 percent.

UPS

Net Worth 1989-1992

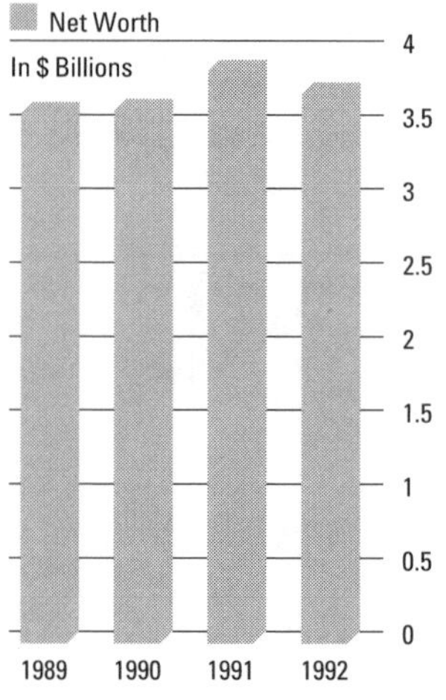

Statistics Related Terms

Assets — A resource having commercial or trade value that is owned (or which the company owns rights to) by a business. Typical examples for an airline include: Cash, securities, property, equipment, capital leases, landing slots and routes.

Available seat miles (ASMs) — Represent the number of seats available for passengers multiplied by the number of scheduled miles those seats are flown.

Cost per available seat mile — Represents operating and interest expense divided by available seat miles.

Financial accounting standard (FAS) 106 — A federally-mandated accounting change made to the way U.S. companies handle post-retirement benefits (other than pensions) to employees. FAS 106, for several U.S. global and major airlines, meant large, one-time, non-cash charges to earnings, further damaging their balance-sheet performance for 1992.

Leveraged buyout (LBO) — Takeover of a company using borrowed funds. Company assets often serve as security for the loans, although investors' assets also may be used.

Liabilities — The total amount the company owes to all creditors.

Net worth or stockholders' equity — The net assets (total assets minus total liabilities) of a company. For companies with more liabilities than assets, the result is a negative net worth or stockholders' deficit.

Passenger load factor — Revenue passenger miles divided by available seat miles over a set period of time.

Revenue passenger miles (RPMs) — The number of miles flown by revenue-producing passengers.

Yield — The average revenue received for each mile a revenue passenger is carried. Determined by dividing total operating revenue by total revenue passenger miles.

United Parcel Service News Abstracts

"A Game of Chicken Between the Teamsters and UPS." *Business Week*, 6 Aug. 1990, p. 32.

". . . And United Parcel Finds Another." *Business Week*, 8 Oct. 1990, p. 48.

"At Presstime. . ." *Air Transport* World, August 1990, p. 4.

"Federal Express Posts 3rd-Period Loss, Cites Charges, Wider Overseas Deficits." *Wall Street Journal*, 19 March 1991, sec. A, p. 6, col. 1.

"First EFIS-Fitted DC-8 Tested as Part of UPS Modernization." *Flight International*, 21-27 Nov. 1990, p. 17.

"Hello, I Must Be Going: On the Road With UPS." *Business Week*, 4 June 1990, p. 82.

"News Briefs, Cargo." *Air Transport World*, August 1990, p. 15.

"Overnight Success." *Flight International*, 27 June-3 July 1990, p. 35.

"Postal Service Expects Delays if UPS Strikes." *Wall Street Journal*, 25 July 1990, sec. B, p. 1, col. 6.

"Stable, Growing UPS Hires More Flightcrews." *Aviation International News*, 1 Jan. 1991, p. 73.

"Teamsters Ratify New Contract With UPS." *Aviation Daily*, 15 Aug. 1990, p. 296.

"Teamsters Vote New UPS Pact by Solid Margin." *Wall Street Journal*, 14 Aug. 1990, sec. A, p. 4, col. 1.

"U.S. Judge Orders Teamsters to Disclose Full Details of Labor Contract With UPS." *Wall Street Journal*, 16 July 1990, sec. C, p. 2, col. 5.

"United Parcel Gives $2.4 Billion Order to Boeing, Dealing Blow to McDonnell." *Wall Street Journal*, 18 Jan. 1993.

"UPS Acquires Seabourne European Express Parcels." *Aviation Daily*, 18 July 1990, p. 110.

"UPS Agrees to Pay Boeing $1.7 Billion for 25 Cargo Planes." *Wall Street Journal*, 7 Nov. 1990, sec. B, p. 4, col. 3.

"UPS Begins Construction of Ontario Facility." *Aviation Daily*, 20 Sept. 1990, p. 530.

"UPS Challenges Leaders in Air Express: Improved Service and Discounts Are Emphasized." *Wall Street Journal*, 20 Dec. 1990, sec. A, p. 5, col. 1.

"UPS, Delta Announce Japan Service Launches." *Aviation Daily*, 6 Feb. 1991, p. 240.

"UPS Heats Up the Race for Fast Deliveries." *The Atlanta Journal-Constitution*, 24 Oct. 1990, sec. D, p. 3, col. 1.

"UPS Orders More 757 Freighters." *Flight International*, 14-20 Nov. 1990, p. 11.

"UPS Pilots Calling for Federally Mandated Contract Talks." *Aviation Daily*, 26 March 1991, p. 558.

"UPS Stability an Attractive Package." *Career Pilot*, July 1990, p. 11.

"UPS, Teamsters to Continue Talks Toward Accord." *Wall Street Journal*, 13 Aug. 1990, sec. B, p. 2, col. 4.

"UPS to Acquire Mail Boxes Etc. Stake of 17.4%." *Wall Street Journal*, 10 July 1990, sec. C, p. 8, col. 3.

"UPS to Acquire 'Quiet' Engines of Rolls-Royce." *Wall Street Journal*, 9 May 1990, sec. C, p. 13, col. 2.

"UPS to Buy Dutch Company." *The Atlanta Journal-Constitution*, 10 Jan. 1992.

"UPS to Make Up Pay Difference to Desert Storm Employees." *Aviation Daily*, 21 March 1991, p. 530.

"UPS to Receive Rediffusion Simulators." *Flight International*, 6-13 June 1990.

"UPS to Start 3-Day Delivery Service." *The Atlanta Journal-Constitution*, 8 Jan. 1993, sec. H, p. 7.

"UPS Wins Contract From JC Penney." *The Atlanta Journal-Constitution*, 31 Dec. 1992.

12

USAir

All American Airways left mail service behind to provide feeder service to small communities. Successor Allegheny Airlines thrived after deregulation, and USAir was born in 1979. Now USAir looks globally as it enters an alliance with British Airways.

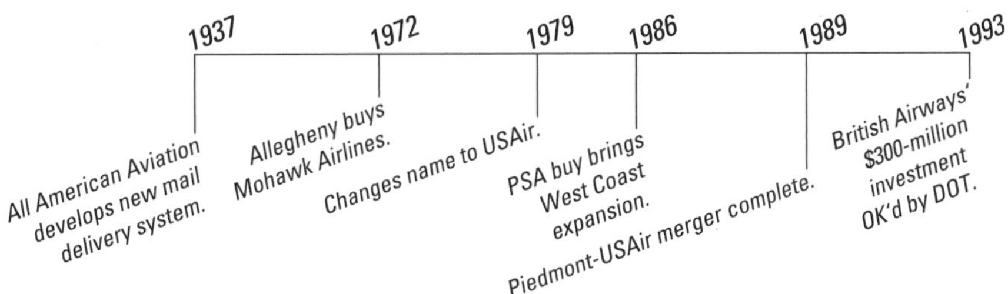

The history of USAir began with an experiment. Delaware businessman Richard C. du Pont incorporated with an inventor's genius his vision for a radical new method of collecting and delivering airmail. The plan called for a Stinson SR-9 "Reliant" to drop mail containers and, without landing, pluck outgoing mail that dangled from tall poles. His idea was communities without airfields could enjoy the benefits of the new airmail service through this means. The fruit of du Pont's labor, All American Aviation, was born in 1939.

All American for one year provided experimental airmail service to small communities in Pennsylvania, Delaware, Maryland, West Virginia and Ohio. The Civil Aeronautics Board (CAB) deemed the experiment a success and awarded All American Aviation a permanent mail route in July 1940. The company began scheduled mail operations on Aug. 12 of that year, servicing routes in Pennsylvania, New York, West Virginia, the District of Columbia and Ohio. All American also helped the Army establish a glider program during World War II. The company's engineers designed pickup devices enabling gliders to transport troops.

Soon after the war, All American's management foresaw the end of airmail pickup. The CAB initially denied All American's request to operate combined passenger/mail pickup service. However, the agency in 1948 ensured the future of the carrier when it sanctioned All American as the conventional feeder line to carry passengers throughout the mid-Atlantic region. The airline flew its inaugural passenger flight in March 1949 as All American Airways, and that year moved its corporate headquarters from Wilmington, Del., to Washington National Airport.

USAir Group
Aircraft fleet and Purchase Commitments
As of May 1993

Aircraft Type	Current Fleet	Firm Orders	Options
B-727	8	0	0
B-737	236	40	118
B-757	15	31	15
B-767	12	1	3
DC-9	73	0	0
F-28	29	0	0
F-100	40	0	0
MD-80	31	0	0
Total	444	72	136

All American changed its name to Allegheny Airlines and had 13 DC-3s and its first president, Leslie O. Barnes, by 1953. Soon it expanded enough to add the Martin Executive 202 to its fleet. Then entered Edwin Colodny, a former lawyer at the CAB, in 1957.

Colodny's background at the CAB gave Allegheny an edge as it sought new routes. Allegheny added flights to several New England cities in 1959 and picked up a Washington-Boston route in 1960. Four years later, the CAB approved a route transfer agreement between TWA and Allegheny that enabled Allegheny to fly from Pittsburgh to Boston. Allegheny, in support of its expanding service, was the first airline to bring the Convair 540 turboprop plane into service. The fleet reached 38 aircraft by 1963.

Barnes' and Colodny's strategy was to service communities that had nonexistent or insufficient air travel by using smaller aircraft that were better suited for short-haul, high-frequency flying. When the CAB approved their plan, Barnes and Colodny sought the services of an existing commuter airline rather than purchase small equipment. They found—and made a deal with—Henson Aviation.

Henson Airlines/Lake Central Airlines/ Mohawk Airlines

R. A. Henson began Hagerstown Commuter on Oct. 1, 1964, as a division of his mom-and-pop FBO, Henson Aviation. Henson entered into an associate agreement with Allegheny in August 1967 to provide commuter service to Washington, D.C., from Hagerstown, Md. This was the quiet beginning of the Allegheny Commuter service (renamed USAir Express).

Allegheny introduced its first all-jet aircraft (as opposed to turboprops) with the delivery of the DC-9 in 1966. It reached an agreement to merge with Lake Central Airlines the following year.

Lake Central Airlines began as Turner Aeronautical Corporation in 1947. The carrier changed its name to Lake Central in 1950 and, like other local service carriers, Lake Central received federal subsidies to provide air service to small communities. Lake Central grew steadily, and in 1965 it was the first U.S. carrier to operate the Nord 262 turboprop.

Mohawk Airlines, another carrier that merged with Allegheny, began in 1945 as Robinson Airlines, an intrastate carrier with flights between Ithaca, N.Y., and New York City. Mohawk, an innovative local service carrier, first coined the term "regional," later adopted by many airlines with similar operations. Mohawk also was the first regional carrier to enter the Jet Age with its purchase of the BAC 1-11 in 1962.

Mohawk was the third largest local service carrier when it merged with Allegheny in 1972. This merger increased Allegheny's fleet to 108 aircraft, brought the BAC 1-11 to the fleet and gave the company additional routes in the Northeast. The combined Lake Central/Mohawk mergers made Allegheny the nation's sixth-largest carrier in terms of passengers boarded.

Allegheny's expansion in the years 1968-1972 was little short of spectacular. The company's revenue passenger miles increased 181 percent from 983.7 million RPMs in 1968 to 2.76 billion RPMs in 1972. Total revenues rose 178 percent from $95.3 million in 1968 to $264.9 million in 1972. The company made consistent profits except when the Lake Central merger proved briefly disruptive in 1968. Colodny replaced Barnes as president when Barnes left Allegheny in 1975 to become chairman of Ryder Systems Inc.

Nineteen seventy-eight was the year of deregulation, of Allegheny's purge of the last non-turbofan aircraft from its fleet and of the company's listing on the New York Stock Exchange. By now Allegheny was established at its Pittsburgh hub. The carrier took advantage of deregulation with several months of controlled growth from Pittsburgh by adding flights to Florida, Texas and Arizona. Allegheny flew to more than 110 cities across the nation, yet the company's marketing research indicated consumers still saw Allegheny as a small, local-service airline. The company changed its name to shatter this image, and on Oct. 28, 1979, USAir was born.

USAir expanded as Allegheny had: a little at a time. It started Pittsburgh-Los Angeles flights in 1983; it added the B-737-300 to its fleet in 1984 and became the first U.S. carrier to order the Fokker 100 in 1985.

USAir's management saw the airline world consolidating around them by 1986. The fear of being small and vulnerable seized them, and they decided the quickest way to achieve the much-bruited "critical mass" was to acquire other airlines. The first product of the new strategy was the purchase of Pacific Southwest Airlines.

USAir Group
Aircraft fleet: 1983-1992

Aircraft	1983	1984	1985	1986	1987	1988	1989	1990	1991	1992
B-757	—	—	—	—	—	—	—	—	2	11
B-767	—	—	—	—	—	6	6	9	11	11
B-727	14	14	14	13	10	44	44	24	17	8
MD-80	—	—	—	—	—	31	31	31	31	31
B-737	18	27	38	46	62	189	212	211	230	234
DC-9	71	71	71	70	70	74	74	74	73	73
BAe-146	—	—	—	—	—	21	21	18	—	—
BAC-111	24	21	20	20	20	11	—	—	—	—
F-28	—	—	—	—	—	45	45	45	42	29
F-100	—	—	—	—	—	—	8	20	35	40
Total	127	133	143	149	162	421	441	432	441	437

Pacific Southwest Airlines

Pacific Southwest Airlines, affectionately known by its West Coast ridership as PSA, began operations in San Diego, Calif., and flew the first flight from its home city to San Francisco in 1949. California's traffic-rich population combined with PSA's low-fare structure allowed the airline to grow rapidly, and by the mid-1970s PSA was one of the largest, truly short-haul carriers in the world.

Deregulation in 1978 allowed PSA to venture out of the intrastate California market. The carrier's brightly-painted aircraft with its trademark smile flew to 15 cities in four states by the end of the decade. PSA also became the dominant carrier along the highly-traveled San Francisco Bay-Los Angeles Basin corridor.

Meanwhile, a succession of mergers in the mid-1980s—including American's acquisition of Air California in 1986, foretold PSA's future. USAir purchased PSA in May 1987 with the merger complete in April 1988.

The PSA merger gave USAir routes in the important intrastate California market. Then the company agreed to absorb Piedmont Airlines in 1988. USAir gradually assimilated the Piedmont organization and culture until the final stage of the merger was complete on Aug. 5, 1989.

Piedmont Airlines

Piedmont Aviation Inc. incorporated in July 1940 as a holding company to manage general aviation and affiliated businesses. Not until after World War II was its airline division, Piedmont Airlines, created. Piedmont Aviation devoted most of its resources during the war to train pilots who later flew for the Air Transport Command or who served as instructors for Army flight schools. The airline received its temporary operating certificate from the CAB in 1947 and made its first flight on Feb. 20, 1948.

The CAB in 1951 acknowledged Piedmont's sterling record under founder and first president Thomas H. Davis by extending its certification an additional seven years beyond the three-year extension received by other newly-authorized local service carriers. This was the longest such renewal awarded by the board to that point.

Piedmont arrived at the year 1978 with a full

understanding of the advantages of the hub-and-spoke system. Piedmont's basic strategy was to build its own hubs away from those of its competitors. Management called its rapid hub buildup at Charlotte, N.C., its "Atlanta bypass strategy." Piedmont went to Dayton, Ohio when it was ready to open a second hub, not to a major metropolis like Chicago or New York. The wisdom of Piedmont's strategy appeared in several ways. For example, while the Professional Air Traffic Control Officers (PATCO) strike of 1981 paralyzed most of the nation's air carriers, it affected Piedmont minimally. Piedmont became a major carrier with annual revenues in excess of $1 billion by the end of 1984.

William R. Howard replaced Davis as president when Davis retired in 1983. Howard led Piedmont through three airline acquisitions from 1983 through 1986: Henson Aviation, Empire Airlines (a New York carrier that flew the Fokker F-28 jet, as did Piedmont) and Jetstream International Airlines Inc. (Henson and Jetstream continued separate operations as part of Piedmont's commuter program. Empire's operations merged into Piedmont.) Then USAir purchased Piedmont.

USAir got one of the most consistently profitable companies in the industry with that acquisition. Piedmont hadn't lost money since 1970; its 1986 profit of $72.4 million (from revenues of $1.87 billion) was greater than its total income of $72.2 million in 1970. But USAir also was one of the industry's consistently profitable carriers. Its 1986 profit was better than Piedmont's: $98 million from revenues of $1.84 billion.

USAir and its affiliates carrying the USAir Express identity served nearly 300 cities in 36 states, two Canadian provinces, Bermuda, the Bahamas and Great Britain by mid-1990. USAir seemed poised to enter the exclusive company of the megacarriers with its highly professional work force, experienced management and large fleet of relatively young aircraft. Its lack of international routes was one drawback that airline experts said could hurt the carrier, especially in a recession.

Recession and soaring fuel costs riddled USAir in 1990 as if on cue. The Pittsburgh-based carrier reported a 1990 loss of $454.4 million on revenues of $6.56 billion. This followed a loss of $63.2 million on sales of $6.25 billion in 1989. Colodny, who remained chairman, retired as CEO on June 1, 1990, replaced by Seth Schofield.

USAir responded to its crisis and laid off more than 7,000 employees by mid-1991; it reduced service at Cleveland and Baltimore; it parked 18 BAe-146-200s when it eliminated nearly one-third of its intra-California flights after Southwest entered the market with $19 one-way fares; it closed flight crew bases at Miami, Syracuse, N.Y., San Diego and Greensboro, N.C.; it delayed delivery of 16 aircraft; and it sought overseas capital. The carrier attributed these actions to its poor financial performance in a recessionary economy. Others believed the growth binge resulting from the Piedmont and PSA mergers caused financial problems and left USAir badly overstaffed and awash in integration problems.

On the positive side, starting in late 1991, USAir in less than three months spent $61 million to acquire Continental Airlines' facilities at New York's

USAir Financial Statistics

(In millions)	1983	1984	1985	1986	1987	1988	1989	1990	1991	1992
Sales	1,432	1,630	1,765	1,835	3,001	5,707	6,252	6,559	6,514	6,686
Net Income (loss)	81	122	117	98	195	165	(63.2)	(454.4)	(305.3)	(600.8)
Assets	1,318	1,621	1,951	2,147	5,257	5,349	6,069	6,574	6,454	6,595
Liabilities	703	884	995	1,089	3,362	3,279	4,176	5,140	5,136	6,551
Net Worth	615	737	956	1,058	1,895	2,070	1,893	1,434	1,318	44
ASMs	12,235	14,098	16,433	18,254	20,014	52,107	55,609	59.484	58,261	59,667
RPMs	7,245	8,191	9,732	11,155	13,072	31,282	33,697	35,551	34,120	35,097
Load Factors	59.2%	58.1%	59.2%	61.1%	65.3%	60%	60.6%	59.8%	58.6%	58.8%

La Guardia Airport (108 takeoff and landing slots and the new East End Terminal); $16 million to obtain a management agreement and option to buy the Trump Shuttle; and $50 million to buy Trans World Airlines' routes to London from Philadelphia and Baltimore. It added flights to Pittsburgh as it prepared to complete and occupy a cavernous new terminal there. USAir also closed the gap on its losses, cutting its 1991 operating loss to $173.5 million and net loss to $305 million on revenues of $6.5 billion.

The year 1992 brought with it many changes. USAir continued to restructure and refine its domestic operations by eliminating its unprofitable Dayton hub and strengthening its Florida and Northeast service. The USAir Shuttle (formerly the Trump Shuttle) began hourly service along the Boston-New York-Washington corridor, and USAir's first B-757s joined its fleet. USAir also expanded its international reach with new service between Philadelphia and Paris, Philadelphia-London and Baltimore-London.

Meanwhile, management focused on wrangling concessions from its unions in a plan to reduce labor costs by $400 million. A pivotal step was forging a contract agreement with its pilots in May 1992 that gave management $100 million in concessions and triggered wage reductions for non-contract employees. (USAir said it would not cut pay of non-contract workers until at least one major union signed a concessionary contract.) The Machinists' union agreed to a new contract that included one-year salary give backs, medical care contributions and work rule changes, but not until a five-day walkout in October by union members created havoc for the carrier. The flight attendants' union reached a tentative contract agreement with the company in February 1993.

USAir continued to post massive losses despite the cost cutting. The airline reported a net loss in 1992 of $1.2 billion—though the figure included $982 million in one-time, pre-tax charges. The year's loss was $600.8 million before FAS-106, a $56-million improvement over 1991 before charges for that year.

Good news came when the DOT approved a $300-million investment in USAir by British Airways in March 1993. The new proposal came one month after British Airways pulled out of a previous deal hours before the DOT was set to reject the bid. British Airways' original offer involved a $750-million investment for a 44-percent ownership stake in USAir, including 21 percent of the voting stock and veto power over decisions by the USAir board. Competing airlines—United, American and Delta—vigorously opposed the alliance and rallied the DOT to deny the transaction unless Britain agreed to open more air routes to U.S. carriers. The new proposal, however, was within the 25-percent limit on foreign ownership of U.S. carriers and did not contain the provision allowing the British carrier veto power over USAir board decisions. British Airways maintained the option to invest a total of $750 million in five years if the U.S. eases restrictions on foreign ownership.

The officers responsible for USAir's operations, maintenance and decision-making at the time of publication are Seth E. Schofield, chairman, president and chief executive officer; W. Thomas Lagow, executive vice president of marketing; Michael R. Schwab, executive vice president of operations; Frederick L. Kocher, senior vice president of maintenance operations; and Gene F. Sharp, vice president of flight operations.

USAir Statistics

1992 Total Sales
Global/Major Airlines

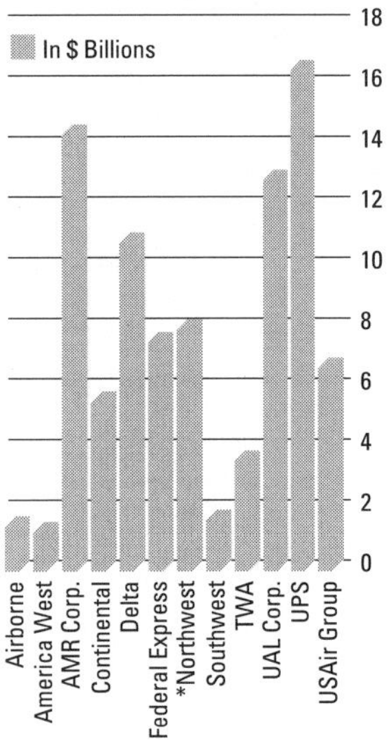

• Information is for Northwest Airlines only and not for parent company NWA Inc.

USAir Group Inc.'s total sales of $6.69 billion was the industry's seventh-highest total in 1992.

USAir's total sales increased 367 percent between 1983 and 1992. This increase is due primarily to expansion, including the PSA and Piedmont acquisitions in the late 1980s.

USAir Group Inc.
Total Sales 1983-1992

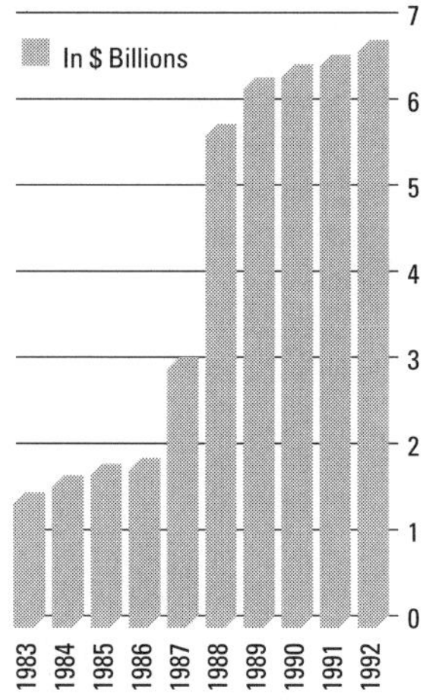

1992 Net Income
Global/Major Airlines

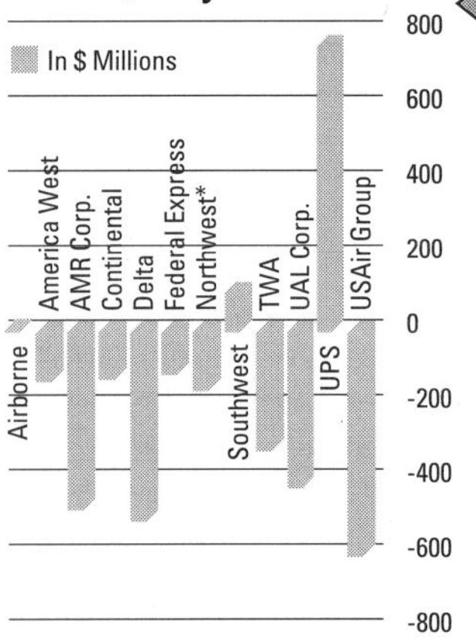

• Information is for Northwest Airlines only and not for parent company NWA Inc.

USAir experienced a $600.8-million net loss in 1992. The net loss, which was before non-cash charges due to FAS 106, was the industry's largest for 1992.

USAir Group Inc. suffered a $63.2-million net loss in 1989 after many years of profitability. The losses continued into the 1990s as USAir lost $1.36 billion from 1990-1992.

USAir Group Inc.
Net Income 1983-1992

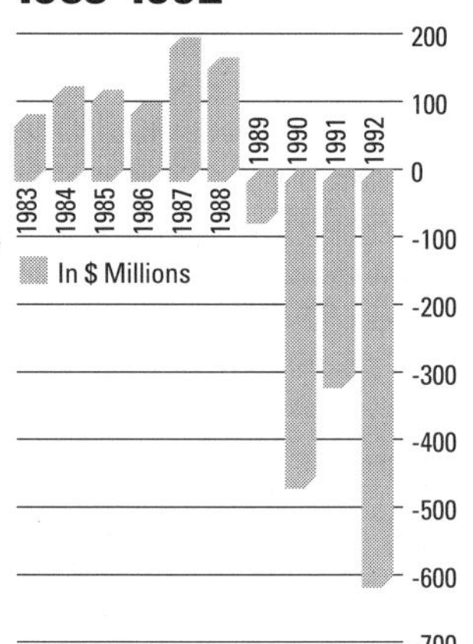

1992 Total Assets & Liabilities

Global/Major Airlines

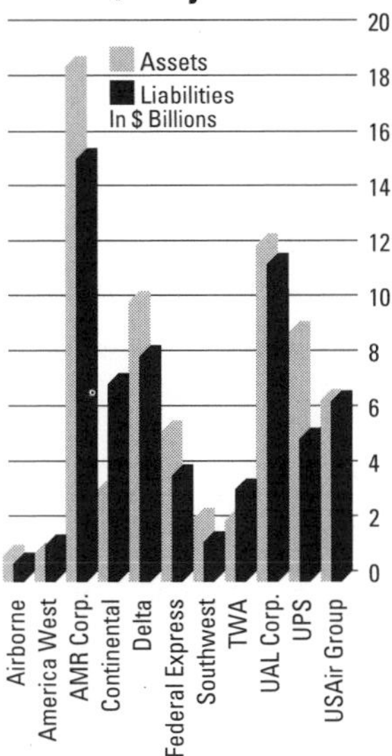

NWA Inc. is a privately held company and would not release 1990-1992 figures.

USAir's assets were valued at $6.6 billion in 1992.

USAir's assets increased in value 400 percent from 1983 to 1992, from $1.32 billion in 1983 to $6.6 billion in 1992.

Its liabilities increased 832 percent during the same period, from $703 million in 1983 to $6.65 billion in 1992, partially because of its mergers with PSA and Piedmont in the late 1980s.

USAir Group Inc.

Assets & Liabilities 1983-1992

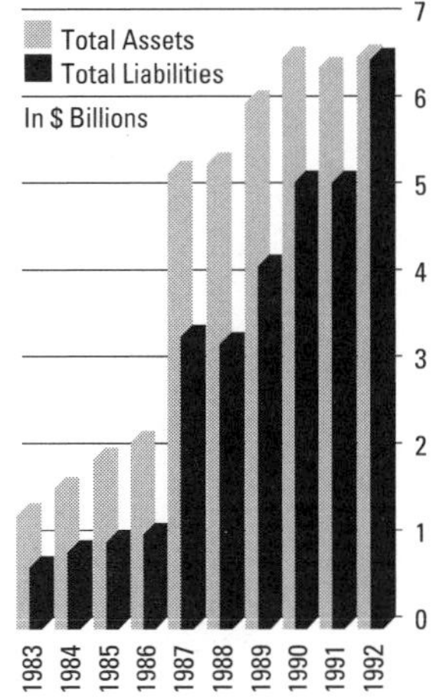

1992 ASMs & RPMs

Global/Major Airlines

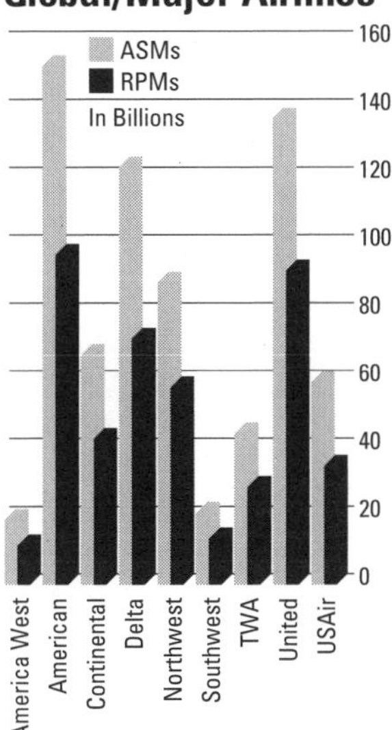

USAir finished 1992 as the industry's sixth-largest carrier in terms of capacity as measured by available seat miles (ASMs).

As a result of USAir's mergers in the 1980s, its capacity soared 388 percent between 1983 and 1992, although its ASMs leveled off in the 1990s.

Its revenue passenger miles (RPMs) increased 384 percent during the same period. USAir registered a 1992 load factor of 58.8 percent.

USAir

ASMs & RPMs 1983-1992

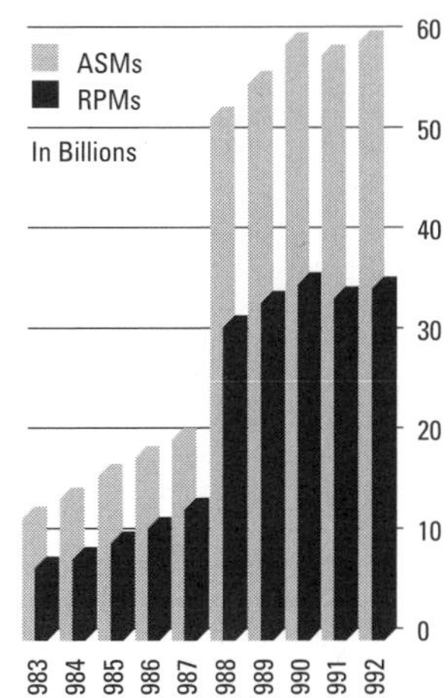

1992 Net Worth
Global/Major Airlines

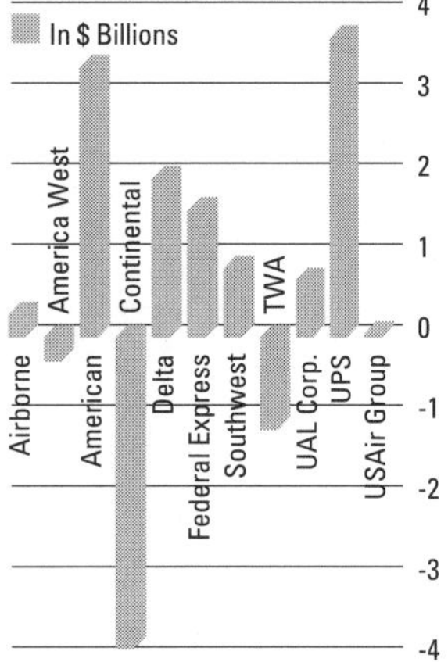

NWA Inc. is a privately held company and would not release 1990-1992 figures.

USAir's net worth at the close of 1992 was $44 million.

USAir experienced tremendous growth in total assets between 1983 and 1988 partially because of its mergers in the late 1980s. Its assets leveled off in the 1990s. Its assets increased in value 400 percent between 1983 and 1992, from $1.32 billion to $6.6 billion. Its liabilities increased 832 percent during this same period—from $703 million in 1983 to $6.55 billion in 1992. Its net worth decreased from $615 million in 1983 to $44 million in 1992, a 92.8-percent decline.

USAir Group Inc.
Net Worth 1983-1992

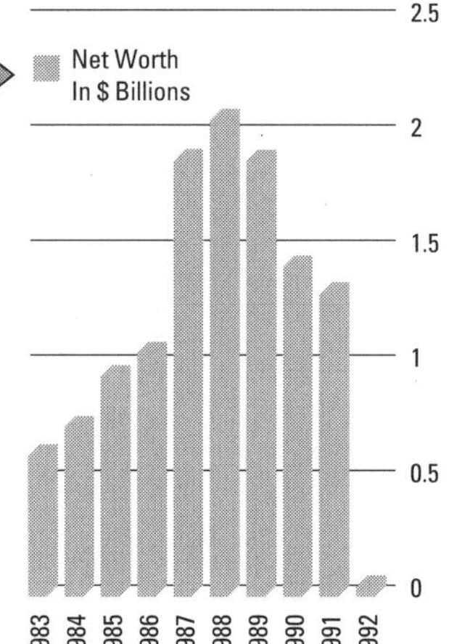

Statistics Related Terms

Assets — A resource having commercial or trade value that is owned (or which the company owns rights to) by a business. Typical examples for an airline include: Cash, securities, property, equipment, capital leases, landing slots and routes.

Available seat miles (ASMs) — Represent the number of seats available for passengers multiplied by the number of scheduled miles those seats are flown.

Cost per available seat mile — Represents operating and interest expense divided by available seat miles.

Financial accounting standard (FAS) 106 — A federally-mandated accounting change made to the way U.S. companies handle post-retirement benefits (other than pensions) to employees. FAS 106, for several U.S. global and major airlines, meant large, one-time, non-cash charges to earnings, further damaging their balance-sheet performance for 1992.

Leveraged buyout (LBO) — Takeover of a company using borrowed funds. Company assets often serve as security for the loans, although investors' assets also may be used.

Liabilities — The total amount the company owes to all creditors.

Net worth or stockholders' equity — The net assets (total assets minus total liabilities) of a company. For companies with more liabilities than assets, the result is a negative net worth or stockholders' deficit.

Passenger load factor — Revenue passenger miles divided by available seat miles over a set period of time.

Revenue passenger miles (RPMs) — The number of miles flown by revenue-producing passengers.

Yield — The average revenue received for each mile a revenue passenger is carried. Determined by dividing total operating revenue by total revenue passenger miles.

USAir News Abstracts

"A Spark for the Shuttle." *Air Transport World*, Oct. 1992, pp. 29-34.

"Aiming for a Global Carrier." *Air Transport World*, Sep. 1992, p. 45.

"Airlines Dueling Over Fares on Trans-Atlantic Routes." *Wall Street Journal*, 12 Feb. 1991, sec. B, p. 1, col. 3.

"American Air, Delta Beat Out USAir for Right to Fly to Manchester, England." *Wall Street Journal*, 25 April 1991, sec. A, p. 5, col. 1.

"British Air, USAir: Purchase Will Fly." *USA Today*, 1 Dec. 1992, p. 1.

"Delta Air, USAir are Poised to Grab TWA's Remaining Routes to London." *Wall Street Journal*, 18 March 1991, sec. A, p. 3, col. 1.

"Delta Main Buyer of Eastern Assets." *The Atlanta Journal-Constitution*, 6 Feb. 1991, sec. C, p. 1, col. 2.

"Delta, USAir Post Big Losses for the Quarter." *Wall Street Journal*, 24 July 1992, sec. A, p. 3.

"Investment Firms Cite Fare Wars, Recession in Downgrading USAir." *Aviation Week & Space Technology*, 8 April 1991, p. 27.

"Lufthansa Eyes USAir in Effort to Find Partner." *Wall Street Journal*, 7 Nov. 1991.

"Machinists' Strike Hits USAir at Tough Time." *The Atlanta Journal-Constitution*, 6 Oct. 1992, sec. F, p. 1.

"Schofield: USAir Looks to Expand." *USA Today*, 23 Aug. 1991, sec. B, p. 2.

"USAir Control Issue Rages." *The Atlanta Journal-Constitution*, 4 Dec. 1992.

"USAir Cost-Control Program Targets Salaries and Benefits to Reverse Losses." *Aviation Week & Space Technology*, 21 Oct. 1991, p. 28.

"USAir Cuts Service as Machinists Strike." *The Atlanta Journal-Constitution*, 6 Oct. 1992, sec. F, p. 3.

"USAir Cutting 142 Flights, Parking 146-200s to Stem Losses." *Aviation Week & Space Technology*, 4 Feb. 1991, p. 33.

"USAir Given 'Whole New Life'." *USA Today*, 22 July 1992, p. 1.

"USAir Group Inc.; Company Posts Wider Loss, Higher Revenue in Quarter." *Wall Street Journal*, 24 April 1991, sec. A, p. 2, col. 3.

"USAir is Said to Mull Buying Assets of TWA." *Wall Street Journal*, 29 June 1992.

"USAir is Struck by Machinists, Creating Chaos." *Wall Street Journal*, 6 Oct. 1992, sec. B, p. 1.

"USAir May Have Trouble Getting Unions to Agree to Other Workers' Concessions." *Wall Street Journal*, 7 Oct. 1991.

"USAir Plan to Run Trump Shuttle Gets Approval from U.S." *Wall Street Journal*, 30 March 1992, sec. A, p. 4.

"USAir Reaches Tentative Pact with Machinists." *Wall Street Journal*, 9 Oct. 1992.

"USAir Regaining Balance After Damaging Mergers." *The Atlanta Journal-Constitution*, 19 Jan. 1992, sec. G, p. 7.

"USAir Settles Suit by Black Pilots Over Hiring Bias." *Wall Street Journal*, 13 June 1991.

"USAir to Reduce Service; Wider Loss Posted for Quarter." *Wall Street Journal,* 28 Jan. 1991, sec. A, p. 12, col. 5.

"USAir Union Recommends Vote to Strike." *Wall Street Journal,* 29 Sep. 1992, sec. A, p. 3.

"USAir Vows to Survive in Shrinking Airline Industry." *Wall Street Journal,* 7 May 1992.

"USAir Will Get $750 Million from British Air." *Wall Street Journal,* 22 July 1992.

"USAir's Vice Chairman Malin Ousted, Apparently Blamed for Carrier's Woes." *Wall Street Journal,* 5 Feb. 1992.

13

Epitaph

Eastern Air Lines
1928-1991

Pitcairn Aviation, a small carrier begun on May 1, 1928, was the germ of Eastern Air Lines. Harold F. Pitcairn started the operation with eight PA-5 Pitcairn Mailwings flying a single route between New Brunswick, N.J., and Atlanta. North American Aviation Inc. bought the company from Pitcairn in 1929, renamed it Eastern Air Transport Inc., and on Aug. 18, 1930, began passenger service with 10-passenger Ford TriMotors.

Eastern, like other aviation pioneers, had trouble making a go of it and soon North American Aviation hired former racing driver and World War I pilot Edward V. "Eddie" Rickenbacker as a vice president to help Eastern fly out of the red. Rickenbacker became general manager on Jan. 1, 1935, inheriting the wheel of a company that posted a loss of $700,000 in 1934. Rickenbacker moved the airline's operations and maintenance headquarters from Atlanta to Miami; replaced the fleet of Mailwings, Condors, Kingbirds and Stinsons with the new Douglas DC-2; and tightened fiscal and operational controls. The turnaround was dramatic: Eastern generated a profit of $90,000 in 1935.

Eastern never lost a single dime in the years between 1934 and 1960. Rickenbacker turned Eastern into one of the giants of the industry and the dominant carrier along the north-south routes of the Eastern Seaboard. Rickenbacker, with the help of several associates, bought Eastern from North American Aviation for $3.5 million and became president and general manager in 1938.

Eastern expanded rapidly after World War II, extending its service to Central and South America during the 1950s. Its purchase of Colonial Airlines in 1956 gave it access to Bermuda and Canada. It entered the Jet Age in 1959 with the Lockheed Electra turboprop; Eastern's first pure jet, the DC-8, entered service in 1960.

Rickenbacker's retirement in 1960 coincided with Eastern's first fiscal year loss since 1934. The carrier, however, was hailed in 1961 when it introduced the concept of shuttle service with hourly flights linking Boston, New York and Washington, D.C. Despite this innovation, Eastern was in serious trouble by 1963. The company had lost $30.5 million since 1960; its market share eroded, its fleet needed modernizing and employee morale was at an all-time low. Eastern reached outside for new leadership, hiring Floyd D. Hall from TWA as president.

Hall initiated a new marketing strategy, reorganized the maintenance division and modernized the fleet. He revamped flight scheduling and created a more streamlined, efficient operation. These measures generated a record $29.7-million profit in 1965 and a $15-million profit in 1966.

Recovery complete, Hall turned his attention to further fleet upgrades and expansion of the route system. Eastern in 1963 was the first airline to operate the B-727; the DC-9 joined its fleet in 1966. Eastern ordered 37 Lockheed L-1011s in 1968 and later became the first airline to put these aircraft into service.

But, Hall's fleet modernization plan began the massive debt load that handicapped Eastern in a deregulated environment. The carrier's financial situation continued deteriorating through 1975 when, in the throes of a major national recession, Eastern lost $49.7 million.

Fresh blood arrived in 1975. Former astronaut Frank Borman became president and CEO. He convinced both union and non-union employees to take part in a wage freeze, he eliminated some top management positions and he instituted rigid cost controls. With these measures and with the help of a reviving national economy, Eastern reported a 1976 profit of $39.1 million—its best ever. Eastern continued to report profits in 1977 and 1978.

Eastern reported a profit of $57.6 million in 1979, though the year is remembered as a watershed year for Eastern. With the exception of a $6.3-million profit in 1985, succeeding years brought a sea of red ink. Those years also brought the failure of the Borman era which was caught between Eastern's unions and the banks to which it owed so much money.

Eastern was the third-largest domestic carrier (behind United and American) based on revenue passenger miles by the end of 1982. The downside to its stature: about 78 percent of all passengers flying in the United States by 1982 traveled on discounted fares. Eastern particularly was hard hit by virtue of its extensive north-south route system, the most competitive extended corridor in the nation. Meanwhile, Eastern continued to expand, notably westward and into South America.

As Eastern expanded, it accumulated losses. The $183.7-million loss in 1983 was a milestone: It told management it had to do something about Eastern's staggering debt load. Yet, a 1984 attempt to refinance the debt failed.

Eastern lost $6.3 million in 1985 and Borman entered another round of bargaining with employees for wage concessions. The International Association of Machinists and Aerospace Workers (IAM) refused to concede anything and Borman sold the airline and its 87-percent debt-to-equity ratio to Frank Lorenzo's Texas Air Corp. for $640 million.

Phil Bakes moved from Continental and became president of Eastern. Eastern's unions almost immediately charged Texas Air with "upstreaming" assets to Continental at Eastern's expense as Lorenzo sold Eastern assets—including its System One computer reservations system—one-by-one to Texas Air and transferred routes to Continental. Lorenzo & Co. also sold 11 of Eastern's Newark gates to Continental. A union lawsuit blocked Texas Air's attempt to purchase Eastern's shuttle.

Infighting between labor and management, bad publicity about Eastern's maintenance practices and erosion of market share resulted in a 1988 loss of $335.4 million. The machinists went on strike on March 4, 1989, and Eastern's pilots and flight attendants joined the machinists in a sympathy strike that surprised industry analysts and Lorenzo. Eastern, with its fleet virtually grounded, sought protection from its creditors under Chapter 11 of the bankruptcy laws five days after the strike began.

Eastern drastically downsized after its Chapter 11 filing, selling off about $1.8 billion in assets. The carrier got back in the air with replacement workers, but continued to have crippling problems that caused it to lose $852 million in 1989. The bankruptcy court removed Eastern's management in April 1990 in the face of mounting evidence that Texas Air abused Eastern, and chose Martin Shugrue, a former president of Continental Airlines, as Eastern's trustee.

Shugrue for nine months proclaimed the beginning of a "new Eastern." Television ads boasted of revamped service as Eastern doubled the number of first-class seats in its planes, selling them to business fliers at coach prices. Shugrue denied persistent rumors he would sell the carrier to another airline that then would liquidate it. However, the Persian Gulf crisis and its impact on fuel prices and passenger traffic took its toll. Eastern failed in a last ditch effort to find a buyer for the carrier and at midnight, Jan. 18, 1991, Eastern ceased operations, ending 62 years in the air.

Pan American World Airways 1927-1991

Juan T. Trippe, a former naval aviator, formed Aviation Corp. of America in the mid-1920s with the assistance of two former Yale classmates. Trippe's immediate objective was to acquire the Key West-to-Havana mail route. As luck would have it, another company bidding on the Havana-Key West route, Pan American Airways, decided the best way to ensure success was to merge with Trippe's company. The merger made Pan American Airways (Pan Am) a subsidiary of Aviation Corp. of America and put Trippe at the helm of Pan Am as president and general manager.

Pan Am received the first international airmail contract in 1927. Pan Am inaugurated scheduled passenger service to Havana within three months of the first airmail flight, and followed up with passenger service to other Caribbean islands, to Mexico and to Central and South American destinations. The company provided air service to 23 Latin American nations along a route structure that stretched over 12,000 miles by the end of 1929.

Pan Am next turned its attention to the Pacific. The first Martin M-130, dubbed the China Clipper, left San Francisco on Nov. 22, 1935, and landed six days later at its destination, Manila. The world's first trans-Pacific flight was completed. Pan Am next set out to establish service across the Atlantic. Pan Am accepted the first Boeing B-314 in January 1939, and four months later launched its Yankee Clipper on the world's first scheduled trans-Atlantic flight.

Pan Am was the world's premier international air carrier after 12 years in business, providing service around the globe. And it established a formidable reputation inside and outside the airline industry. Trippe's airline during those early years, according to ALPA historian George E. Hopkins, "self-consciously projected an 'aristocratic' image modeled on the military's, and its pilot corps was practically a naval aviation auxiliary." The image carried over to Pan Am's in-flight service and stewardess corps.

Pan Am was the sole U.S. airline flying international routes before World War II. Pan Am, like all the other U.S. airlines of any size, was called on to support the United States and, directly or indirectly, Pan Am allocated virtually all its resources to the war effort. Yet, in the years immediately after World War II, the regulators at the Civil Aeronautics Board allowed ever-tougher competition in international arenas while refusing Pan Am any domestic routes. This arbitrary behavior set the stage for the decline of Pan Am through erosion of its market share and its inability not only to earn profits but to make the required capital expenditures.

Pan American Airways changed its name to Pan American World Airways in 1950 to reflect its global route structure. Pan Am then led the United States into the Jet Age when, on Oct. 26, 1958, it introduced the first B-707 into service. The Pan Am Clipper America's flight from New York to Paris with 11 passengers aboard marked the first commercial flight by an American-built jet transport, the first commercial jet flight by a U.S. airline and the beginning of daily trans-Atlantic jet service.

Meanwhile, Juan Trippe retired in 1968 and Harold E. Gray, the pilot who flew Pan Am's Yankee Clipper on its first trans-Atlantic flight in 1939, took over as chairman of the board. Hajeeb E. Halaby, the former head of the Federal Aviation Administration, became the company's new president. Trippe receded to the background, remaining as an honorary director until his death in 1981.

The historical significance of Pan Am's being the

first airline to fly the B-747 jumbo jet in 1970 was overshadowed by the added burden the aircraft placed on a company already in financial crisis. Unfortunately, the capacity and efficiencies of the B-747 were of no avail in the recession that hit the United States and much of the rest of the world in the 1970s.

William T. Seawall, retired brigadier general, graduate of West Point and Harvard School of Law, became Pan Am's chairman and CEO in 1972. He tried the seldom-successful tactic of retrenchment, trimming the work force and eliminating unprofitable routes. The wall crumbled, the sea came in: Pan Am lost $149.4 million between 1973 and 1975.

With thinking room provided by the respite of a $99.9-million 1976 profit earned off an improving economy and a paralyzing strike against Northwest Airlines, Pan Am in 1977 cast about for a growth strategy and made a $400-million mistake. Pan Am decided to purchase National Airlines to gain a domestic route structure even as deregulation waited just around the next bend in time.

National Airlines

National, formed in 1934 by George T. ("Ted") Baker, from the beginning was one of the most strife-torn airlines in the history of aviation. National grew into a major airline and in 1964 achieved the distinction of becoming the first all-jet carrier in the United States despite a devil's plenty of labor/management strife. A strike by the International Association of Machinists and Aerospace Workers in 1974 appeared to signal the end of National unless it could find a merger partner. National found Pan Am, and in 1978 the Carter administration approved Pan Am's purchase of National.

Integrating the Pan Am and National work forces proved more than management could handle, and employee morale plummeted. The mood was not lost on Pan Am's customers, who looked elsewhere for service. Pan Am began losing money again in 1981, and in September Edward Acker became Pan Am's chairman and CEO.

In 1985 under Acker, Pan Am made the sale that changed the kind of airline it was: It surrendered its Pacific division, including personnel, aircraft and facilities, to United Airlines for $750 million. Pan Am's $341-million gain from this sale gave it a $51.7-million 1985 profit, but Pan Am never again would be the preeminent international airline that Juan Trippe founded.

Pan Am Corp. formed in 1984 as a holding company for two subsidiaries, Pan Am World Airways Inc. and Pan Am World Services Inc. Pan Am Corp. picked up a third subsidiary in 1986, the Pan Am Shuttle, the assets of which it acquired from Texas Air Corp. for $65 million. Also in 1986, Pan Am Corp. acquired Ransome Airlines, a well-run regional/commuter carrier that fed Pan Am from a dozen cities in the northeastern U.S. and southeastern Canada under the name Pan Am Express Inc.

Reorganizing and refocusing Pan Am failed to make the carrier profitable. Thomas Plaskett, former president of Continental Airlines, took over when Acker left Pan Am in 1987, but profits remained elusive. Pan Am reported a loss of $72.7 million in 1988 before once again selling off assets to service debt and stay aloft.

Then a miracle almost happened: Plaskett, a tough cookie, appeared to have Pan Am on course toward a profit in 1989 until the tragic bombing of Flight 103 over Lockerbie, Scotland, in December 1988 destroyed the carrier's momentum. Pan Am's traffic to Europe dropped off steeply. Competitors swooped down on Pan Am in all markets, international and domestic. Management saw that 1989 would be a disaster for Pan Am.

Pan Am led the way in transoceanic flying, pioneered the Jet Age and carried the U.S. flag to all quarters of the globe. That heritage was motivation enough for everyone at Pan Am, from Plaskett on down, to give their all in trying to keep the nation's eighth-largest carrier flying. So the company fought back, adding Pan Am Express service to a dozen central European cities to beef up Pan Am's load factors and trying to find a merger partner. Pan Am, however, was not healthy. Its long-term debt at the end of 1989, counting $585 million owed to its pension funds, stood around $1.455 billion. The better part of Pan Am's fleet was old, and its primary assets were its attractive gate positions at airports around the world and its European and South American route systems.

"Pan Am is a wasting asset," a Wall Street analyst said in May 1991 as the airline that Juan Trippe started continued to shrivel and suffer narrow escapes from liquidation after its Jan. 8 Chapter 11 filing. The Chapter 11 filing came after high fuel costs drained Pan American World Airways Inc.'s cash reserves to $30 million (and the airline lost $268.8 million in the first nine months of 1990). The bankruptcy court approved a $150-million loan on Jan. 11 to keep Pan Am flying. United Airlines provided $50 million; Bankers Trust Co. provided $100 million. The purpose of the loan was to tide Pan Am over until completion of a $400-million deal for United to buy Pan Am's lucrative London routes. Pan Am's London routes accounted for about 12 percent of its business. The U.S. and Britain reached an accord in March that finally permitted Pan Am to transfer its London route authority to United.

By late May, however, Pan Am Corp., parent of Pan American World Airways, said it could not assure that Pan Am would continue operating through the end of 1991. New York-based Pan Am's only hope appeared to rest in its purchase by another airline. However, Pan Am's pension plans were underfunded by $800 million and its many unions and union difficulties made other airlines reluctant to buy Pan Am whole, as Plaskett insisted it must. The only airline interested in acquiring all of Pan Am's problems in one fell swoop was Delta.

Delta seemed the savior when in July the Atlanta-based carrier bought Pan Am's European routes, planes, Frankfurt hub and Northeast shuttle for $416 million. Delta, as part of the deal, also agreed to bankroll a smaller Pan Am that would continue to operate as a Miami-based carrier serving Latin America. Delta initially gave the reorganized Pan Am $115 million in loans but withheld additional financing after Pan Am continued to post large losses. Delta ultimately withdrew from a proposed reorganization plan and Pan Am failed to find a new backer. The 64-year-old "Clipper" ceased operations on Dec. 4, 1991.

Braniff International Airways 1928-1992

Brothers Tom and Paul Braniff founded Braniff in 1928. Insurance-business owner Tom Braniff bankrolled Paul's idea for "The Braniff Airline," and Paul piloted Braniff's first scheduled flight between Oklahoma City and Tulsa on June 20, 1928, in a Stinson "Detroiter." The airline's first schedule consisted of three daily Tulsa-Oklahoma City round trips.

The venture lost money from the beginning. The brothers then launched Braniff Airways in November 1930.

Braniff, surviving the depression of the 1930s, moved its headquarters from Oklahoma City to Dallas-Love Field in 1942, but turned over half its fleet to the U.S. government for World War II service. A period of growth, albeit slow, ensued after the war, but the founding Braniff brothers never lived to see the airline prosper into a world class international company. Both died in 1954.

The 1960s and 1970s were years of explosive growth. Dallas-based Great America Corp. purchased the 37-year-old company in 1965. Braniff bought Pan American-Grace Airways (Panagra) a year later to become a major presence in Latin America. Nonstop B-747 service from Dallas-Love Field to Honolulu began in 1969, and in 1978 the airline ran a daily B-747 nonstop flight from Dallas/Fort Worth International to London-Gatwick Airport.

Yet, a company that seemed to be on a never-ending roll was about to hit very turbulent weather. Braniff president Harding Lawrence threw caution to the winds with the passage of the Airline Deregulation Act in 1978 and applied for more than 700 new routes. Unfortunately, most of the routes were long-dormant ones abandoned by other airlines as money-losing services. Lawrence could do no better, and what he saw as the critical mass that would propel the airline to greater success instead caused its undoing.

The crumbling began by 1980. Management asked employees to make salary concessions and things got so bad that Lawrence resigned in 1981. Howard Putnam, former president of Southwest Airlines, replaced Lawrence in September 1981, but Putnam's administration could not halt Braniff's nose dive into insolvency. The airline's great international network fell apart. American Airlines picked up the Dallas-London route and Eastern leased the old Panagra routes to South America for five years. An attempt to refocus the airline to the discount travel market could not stop the slide. Braniff filed for bankruptcy and ceased operations in the spring of 1982. Most of the airline community figured the once proud carrier, noted for its fleet of colorfully-painted B-727s, B-747s and DC-8s, never would fly again.

Braniff proved the experts wrong. The airline took to the skies again on March 1, 1984, very much downsized and under new ownership. Jay Pritzker, board chairman of the Hyatt Corp. hotel chain, established Dalfort Corp. as the holding company that purchased Braniff. The company redefined its marketing niche, offering long-haul flights at low, unrestricted fares. The new approach resulted in a retrenchment in the fleet and number of cities served.

The company then went through a period of profits and losses with more changes at the top. Patrick Foley, chairman of Hyatt Hotels Corp., became president in May 1987. Braniff in the fall of that year began negotiations to acquire Orlando-based Florida Express which formally merged into the company in April 1988.

With on-again/off-again profitability, the Pritzker family seriously considered selling the company. Two East Coast real estate magnates, Jeffrey R. Chodorow and Arthur G. Cohen, came forward and set up BIA-COR Holdings to initiate a leveraged buyout of Braniff. Chodorow and Cohen each put up $5 million of the total purchase price of about $117 million. They borrowed the rest: $20 million from European American Bank with the balance of funds coming from PaineWebber ($33 million), American Airlines ($21 million) and asset sales. When the smoke cleared, BIA-COR Holdings purchased 80 percent of the airline's stock from Dalfort Corp. Stockholders of Braniff Inc. approved the merger of the airline with BIA-COR Holdings on October 24, 1988, and Braniff's long-term debt rose from $22 million before the buyout to $53.5 million afterwards.

With Piedmont merging into the USAir Group, BIA-COR Holdings lured the top management of Piedmont Airlines into the Braniff fold. William G. McGee, Piedmont's former president and CEO, took command of Braniff and brought several Piedmont top executives with him. Then, on Aug. 31, 1988, Eastern Air Lines greatly reduced its service from its Kansas City International Airport hub. With the Eastern pullback, Braniff's new management saw an opportunity to enhance the airline's operations at Kansas City and become the dominant carrier at that airport. Chodorow and McGee launched a major expansion, adding routes and signing agreements to lease or buy nearly $2 billion in new planes—including 50 A-320s originally intended for cash-strapped Pan Am. According to McGee and Co., fleet expansion would allow them to achieve their ultimate goal: "to build Braniff into one of the major airlines operating in the U.S." As part of the expansion Braniff moved its corporate headquarters from Dallas to Orlando.

The expansion plan went awry. Braniff lost $21 million in the last half of the fiscal year ended Jan. 31, 1989, and another $43 million through the first six months of fiscal year 1990. McGee attributed Braniff's financial turmoil to the competitive advantage enjoyed by major carriers and their sophisticated computer reservations systems, frequent flyer programs and other services. Analysts say Braniff's problems came to a head after it financially overextended itself, buying Florida Express and attempting a major expansion in a stagnant domestic airline market. Braniff grounded its fleet on Sept. 27, 1989 and filed for Chapter 11 bankruptcy protection for the second time in seven years the following morning. Braniff had about $10 million in cash at the time of its filing, and the airline continued operating under Chapter 11 protection until calling it quits just after midnight Nov. 9, 1989.

The carrier then resurfaced for a third time. BN Air, a company created by former Braniff executive Jeffrey Chodorow, purchased the rights to the Braniff name in April 1990 and bought failed carrier Emerald Air's operating certificate. The new carrier's strategy: set up shop in markets ignored by other carriers and lure with cheap fares price-conscious flyers willing to forego major carrier amenities such as frequent flyer mileage and numerous flights. Braniff International Airlines began operations in July 1991 with 5 B-727s, 3 DC-9s and 12 daily flights out of Islip, N.Y.; Orlando; Dallas; and Los Angeles. The airline filed for bankruptcy protection five weeks later, becoming the third carrier flying under the Braniff name to go of business in 10 years. The airline ceased operations altogether on July 3, 1992.

Bibliography

A History of TWA Aircraft. New York: TWA Corporate Communications, 1985.

"A New Kind of Flight Plan for Small Freight." *Business Week,* 3 Nov. 1973, pp. 66-67.

"Airborne Freight Charges Teamsters With Slowdown." *Wall Street Journal,* 23 Aug. 1991.

"Airline of the Year. Southwest Airlines." *Air Transport World,* Feb. 1992, p. 51.

Altman, Henry. "A Business Visionary Who Really Delivered." *Nations Business,* Nov. 1981, pp. 50-55.

America West Airlines Chronological History. Phoenix: America West Airlines Corporate Communications, 1990.

America West Airlines Fact Sheet. Phoenix: America West Airlines Corporate Communications, 1990.

America West Airlines Inc. 1983 Annual Report. Phoenix: America West Airlines Inc., 1984.

America West Airlines Inc. 1984 Annual Report. Phoenix: America West Airlines Inc., 1985.

America West Airlines Inc. 1985 Annual Report. Phoenix: America West Airlines Inc., 1986.

America West Airlines Inc. 1986 Annual Report. Phoenix: America West Airlines Inc., 1987.

America West Airlines Inc. 1987 Annual Report. Phoenix: America West Airlines Inc., 1988.

America West Airlines Inc. 1988 Annual Report. Phoenix: America West Airlines Inc., 1989.

America West Airlines Inc. 1989 Annual Report. Phoenix: America West Airlines Inc., 1990.

"America West Gets Tentative Approval for $53 Million Loan." *Wall Street Journal,* 28 Aug. 1992.

"America West Names Franke as Chairman, Six Others to Board." *Wall Street Journal,* 18 Sep. 1992.

"America West to Acquire 737-200s From Ansett Airlines of Australia." *Aviation Week & Space Technology,* 16 Sep. 1985, p. 49.

"American Air Posts '82 Loss, Indicates Small 4th-Period Net." *Wall Street Journal,* 20 Jan. 1983, p. 4.

"American Airlines Boss Blasts U.S. Policy." *USA Today,* 21 Sep. 1992, sec. B, p. 6.

"American Airlines is Trimming 576 Managers' Jobs." *The Atlanta Journal-Constitution,* 1 Dec. 1992.

"American to Buy TWA's O'Hare Assets." *The Atlanta Journal-Constitution,* 10 July 1992, sec. H, p. 8.

"American, TWA Bid for Pan Am." *The Atlanta Journal-Constitution,* 22 July 1991, sec. C, p. 1.

AMR Corp. 1986 Annual Report. Dallas: AMR Corp., 1987.

AMR Corp. 1987 Annual Report. Dallas: AMR Corp., 1988.

AMR Corp. 1988 Annual Report. Dallas: AMR Corp., 1989.

AMR Corp. 1989 Annual Report. Dallas: AMR Corp., 1990.

AMR Corp. 1990 Annual Report. Dallas: AMR Corp., 1991

AMR Corp. 1991 Annual Report. Dallas: AMR Corp., 1992.

AMR Corp. 1992 Annual Report. Dallas: AMR Corp., 1993.

Anders, George. "Icahn is Set to Walk Away From TWA Sadder and at Least $111 Million Poorer." *Wall Street Journal*, 8 Dec. 1992, sec. A, p. 5, col. 1.

"Ansett's Stock Purchase Will Place Foreign Stake in America West at 20 Percent." *Aviation Week & Space Technology*, 20 July 1987, p. 41.

Bancroft, Bill. *Southwest Airlines Celebrates 15 Years of Love*. Dallas: Southwest Airlines Corporate Communications, 1986.

Berss, Marcia. "How Do You Put a Lien on an Elephant?" *Forbes*, 30 Oct. 1989, pp. 114-116.

Blood, Katharine. "Fasten Your Seat Belts." *Forbes*, 8 April 1985, pp. 154-155.

Bovier, Connie. "Southwest Airlines: The Rah-Rah's for Real." *Career Pilot*, Nov. 1991, pp. 20-28.

Bovier, Connie. "An American Tale: Aggression and Success." *Career Pilot*, Aug. 1991, pp. 18-27.

Bovier, Connie. "Cautious Optimism Prevails at Continental." *Career Pilot*, May 1993, pp. 18-24.

Bovier, Connie. "Southwest Airlines Charts its Own Course." *Career Pilot*, Feb. 1993, pp. 18-24.

Bovier, Connie. "The American Way: Procedures, Professionalism." *Career Pilot*, Aug. 1992, p. 30.

Bradsher, Keith. "NWA Profit Up Sharply in 2nd Quarter." *New York Times*, 25 July 1989, sec. D, p. 17, col. 2.

Bremer, Karl. "Northwest: Planning for Long-Term Survival." *Career Pilot*, April 1992, pp. 18-28.

Bremer, Karl. "The New Northwest Awaits Economic Upturn." *Career Pilot*, Jan. 1991, pp. 18-27.

Brown, David A. "Boeing 737 Shortage Slowing Southwest Plans for Midway Airport Base." *Aviation Week & Space Technology*, 25 Nov. 1991, p. 42.

Brown, David A. "Shrewd Capital Planning Allows Southwest to Outperform Competition." *Aviation Week & Space Technology*, 25 May 1992, pp. 56-57.

Bulban, Erwin J. "Falcons Used in Cargo Service." *Aviation Week & Space Technology*, 24 July 1972, pp. 44-45.

Carroll, Doug. "Airline Has no Shortage of Suitors." *USA Today*, 7 Oct. 1992, p. 1.

Carroll, Doug. "Continental CEO Harris Quits." *USA Today*, 22 Aug. 1991.

Carroll, Doug. "Delta Chief Adds Titles, Quashing Talk of Ouster." *USA Today*, 29 Jan. 1993, sec. B, p. 2.

Carroll, Doug. "Icahn Has Much to Lose if TWA Goes Down." *USA Today*, 3 Feb. 1992.

Carroll, Doug. "Once a Highflier, it Fights to Cut Costs." *USA Today*, 28 Jan. 1993, sec. B, p. 6.

Carroll, Doug. "Turnaround on Horizon for USAir." *USA Today*, 9 May 1991. sec. B, p. 3.

Carroll, Doug. "USAir Agrees to Take Over Trump Shuttle." *USA Today*, 20 Dec. 1991, sec. B, p. 6.

"Checchi Pressures Eastern to Sell Valuable Assets." *Aviation Week & Space Technology*, 30 July 1990, p. 86.

"Chest Expansion of an Airline." *Fortune*, April 1945, p. 132.

Chipello, Christopher J. and Robert Tomsho. "Air Canada and Investment Group Join the Bidding for Continental Airlines." *Wall Street Journal*, 28 Aug. 1992.

Cole, Jeff and James Hirsch. "Delta to Cut Spending Plan by $5 Billion." *Wall Street Journal*, 30 April 1992, sec. A, p. 3.

Colvin, Geoffrey. "Federal Express Dives Into Air Mail." *Fortune*, 15 June 1981, pp. 106-108.

"Continental Air Elects a President." *New York Times*, 19 April 1984, sec. D, p. 2, cols. 5-6.

Continental Airlines Corp. 1983 Annual Report. Houston: Continental Airlines Corp., 1983.

"Continental Finds Chief at American." *New York Times*, 29 Oct. 1986, sec. D, p. 2, cols. 5-6.

Continental: The First 50 Years. Houston: Continental Airlines Corporate Communications, 1984.

Davis, R.E.G. *A History of the World's Airlines*. London: Oxford University Press, 1964.

Davis, Thomas H. *The History of Piedmont: Setting a Special Pace*. New York: The Newcomen Society in North America, 1982.

Delta - Highlights of Our History. Atlanta: Delta Air Lines Inc., Public Relations Department, 1987.

Delta Air Lines Inc. Annual Report 1987. Atlanta: Delta Air Lines Inc., 1987.

Delta Air Lines Inc. Annual Report 1988. Atlanta: Delta Air Lines Inc., 1988.

Delta Air Lines Inc. Annual Report 1989. Atlanta: Delta Air Lines Inc., 1989.

Delta Air Lines Inc. Annual Report 1990. Atlanta: Delta Air Lines Inc., 1990.

Delta Air Lines Inc. Annual Report 1991. Atlanta: Delta Air Lines Inc., 1991.

Delta Air Lines Inc. Annual Report 1992. Atlanta: Delta Air Lines Inc., 1992.

"Delta Air Posts 4th Period Loss of $25.5 Million." *Wall Street Journal*, 29 July 1983, p. 4, col. 1.

"Delta Air Profit Fell in Fiscal 4th Quarter." *Wall Street Journal*, 23 July 1982, p. 24, col. 2.

Donlan, Thomas G. "Turbulent Trip: Texas Air's Acquisition Binge Runs Into Heavy Going." *Barron's*, 8 June 1987, p. 8.

Dorfman, Dan. "Overnight Highflier." *Esquire*, 15 Aug. 1978, pp. 10-11.

Dornheim, Michael A. "America West Cuts Route Capacity in Response to $46-Million Loss." *Aviation Week & Space Technology*, 25 April 1988, pp. 102-103.

Dubin, Reggi Ann. "The Pan Am-United Deal: Truly a Win-Win Situation." *Business Week*, 6 May 1985, p. 45.

Eblen, Tom and Andy Miller. "Delta Cancels Plan to Furlough Pilots." *The Atlanta Journal-Constitution*, 20 Nov. 1992.

Ellis, James E. "Allegis: Is a Name Change Enough for UAL?" *Business Week*, 2 March 1987. pp. 54-56.

Ellis, James E. "Heeding a Gospel of Measured Growth." *Business Week*, 21 Sep. 1987, p. 62.

Ellis, James E. "UAL's Pilots May Put the Airline Into Play." *Business Week*, 20 April 1987, p. 25.

Ellis, James E. "United's Pilots Are Inching Closer to a Coup." *Business Week*, 31 Aug. 1987, pp. 32-33.

Ennis, Michael. "Sky King." *Business Month*, Sep. 1988, p. 27.

Fairlie, Henry. "Air Sickness: The Unfriendly Skies of Frank Lorenzo." *The New Republic*, 5 June 1989, pp. 14-18.

"Federal Express Buys 727s From United." *Aviation Week & Space Technology*, 1 May 1978, p. 30.

Federal Express Corp. 1989 Annual Report. Memphis, Tenn.: Federal Express Corp., 1989.

Federal Express Corp. 1990 Annual Report. Memphis, Tenn.: Federal Express Corp., 1990.

Federal Express Corp. 1991 Annual Report. Memphis, Tenn.: Federal Express Corp., 1991.

Federal Express Corp. 1992 Annual Report. Memphis, Tenn.: Federal Express Corp., 1992.

"Federal Express Drops Option on More Continental DC-10s." *Aviation Week & Space Technology*, 10 Nov. 1980, p. 27.

"Federal Express Gambles on Electronic Mail." *Business Week*, 9 July 1984, p. 82.

"Federal Express Plans to Increase Satellite Transmission Service." *Aviation Week & Space Technology*, 4 March 1985, pp. 40-41.

"Federal Express Rides the Small-Package Boom." *Business Week*, 31 March 1980, pp. 108-112.

"Federal Express Seeking Four Continental DC-10s." *Aviation Week & Space Technology*, 17 Dec. 1979, p. 28.

"Federal Express Takes a Nosedive." *Business Week*, 15 June 1974, p. 114.

"Federal Express to Acquire Launcher Rights." *Aviation Week & Space Technology*, 23 May 1983, p. 24.

Fetterman, Mindy. "Southwest Lands Punchlines, Profits." *USA Today*, 2 March 1992.

Field, Alan M. "Revenge is Sour." *Forbes*, 24 Feb. 1986, p. 36.

Flaherty, Robert J. "Breathing Under Water." *Forbes*, 1 March 1977, pp. 36-38.

Flint, Perry. "What Does Icahn Want?" *Air Transport World*, Oct. 1991, pp. 93-95.

Fotos, Christopher P. "Delta Pilots Face First Cuts in 35 Years." *Aviation Week and Space Technology*, 26 Oct. 1992, p. 20.

Fotos, Christopher P. "USAir and Pilots Reach Agreement, Attendants and Machinists Await Pacts." *Aviation Week & Space Technology*, 11 May 1992, p. 26.

Foust, Dean, and Ron W. King. "Why Federal Express Has Overnight Anxiety." *Business Week*, 9 Nov. 1987, pp. 62-63.

Fradenburg, Leo G. *United States Airlines: Trunk and Regional Carriers, Their Operations and Management*. Dubuque, Iowa: Kendall/Hunt Publishing Co., 1980.

"Frank Lorenzo Lures a Copilot to Continental." *Business Week*, 6 Dec. 1982, pp. 42-44.

"Fuel Delays Passenger Service Plans." *Aviation Week & Space Technology*, 6 Aug. 1979, p. 34.

Gaffney, Timothy R. "Airborne Assets—Quick Upgrades, Stable Careers." *Career Pilot*, July 1991, pp. 18-27.

Gaffney, Timothy R. "Hard-Charging Airborne Wrings Out Profits." *Career Pilot*, July 1992, pp. 18-27.

Gaffney, Timothy R. "Persistence Gives UPS an Inside Track." *Career Pilot*, Jan. 1993, pp. 18-27.

"Good Ideas and Big Money Aren't All You Need." *Forbes*, 15 Nov. 1975, pp. 30-31.

Goss, William. "Where is Delta Headed?" *Agency Management*, Jan. 1989, p. 54.

Grossman, Laurie M. "Federal Express Pilots Vote to Unionize, But Firm Moves to Contest the Election." *Wall Street Journal*, 15 Jan. 1993.

Grover, Ron, Russell Mitchell and Michael Oneal. "Dealmakers in the Cockpit." *Business Week*, 5 March 1990, pp. 54-62.

Grover, Ronald, et al. "Landing Northwest: Now Al Checchi Has to Run His New Airline." *Business Week*, 3 July 1989, pp. 24-25.

Harbrecht, Douglas, and Dean Foust. "How to Win Friends and Influence Lawmakers." *Business Week*, 7 Nov. 1988, p. 36.

Hayes, Thomas C. "Continental's Chief Yields to Lorenzo." *New York Times*, 22 July 1987, sec. D, p. 1, cols 2-5.

Henderson, Danna. "America West's Risks and Rewards." *Career Pilot*, March 1991, p. 20.

Hirsch, James S. "Debt-Burdened America West Seeks a Safe Landing." *Wall Street Journal*, 22 April 1992.

"Hitching a Ride." *Forbes*, 7 Jan. 1991, p. 189.

Houston, Patrick, and Seth Payne. "Northwest and Republic: A Wedding But No Honeymoon." *Business Week*, 18 Aug. 1986, pp. 56-57.

Houston, Patrick. "Steve Rothmeier's Northwest Looks Great—On Paper." *Business Week*, 28 Sep. 1987, pp. 58-59.

Johnson, Robert. "Continental Air Receives Second Offer, $385 Million From Mexican Investor." *Wall Street Journal*, 10 Aug. 1992.

Jones, Del. "Southwest Flies High With Cut-Rate Niche." *USA Today*, 7 May 1992, sec. B, pp. 1-2.

Karr, Albert R. "Uncharacteristic Solidarity Keeps Pilots From Crossing Picket Lines." *Wall Street Journal*, 6 March 1989, sec. A, p. 4, col. 3.

Kelleher, Herbert D. "Southwest Airlines: Past, Present, and Future." *Executive Speeches*, Dec. 1988, pp. 16-21.

Kim, James. "Delta Cleared to Buy Most of Pan Am." *USA Today*, 13 Aug. 1991, sec. B, p. 1.

King, Jim. "Delta Halts Plans for 35 Planes." *The Atlanta Journal-Constitution*, 20 Feb. 1993.

Kohn, Bernie. "USAir's Road to Recovery." *Career Pilot*, Dec. 1992, pp. 18-24.

Labich, Kenneth. "Winners in the Air Wars." *Fortune*, 11 May 1987, pp. 68-79.

Louis, Arthur M. "The Great Electronic Mail Shootout." *Fortune*, 20 Aug. 1984, pp. 167-172.

Manning, Ric. "UPS: Timing Growth to the Letter." *Career Pilot*, Sep. 1991, pp. 18-28.

Mark, Robert. "United Declares War on Market Woes." *Career Pilot*, April 1993, pp. 18-24.

McKenna, James T. "Northwest Wins Approval to Buy All Midway Airlines Assets." *Aviation Week & Space Technology*, 14 Oct. 1991, pp. 30-31.

Merwin, John. "Anticipating the Evolution." *Forbes*, 4 Nov. 1985, pp. 163-166.

Miller, James P. "Pilots Counter Northwest Air Concession Plan." *Wall Street Journal*, 21 Sep. 1992.

Murphy, Michael E. *The Airline That Pride Almost Bought*. New York: Franklin Watts, 1986.

Nomani, Asra Q. and Randall Smith. "Trump Shuttle Banks to Talk With Airlines." *Wall Street Journal*, 16 Sep. 1991.

Nomani, Asra Q. and Brett Pulley. "United Air Raises its Offer to Pan Am to $235 Million." *Wall Street Journal*, 24 July 1991.

Nomani, Asra Q. and Bridget O'Brian. "AMR to Buy 3 TWA Routes to London for Price it Had Agreed to Pay for Six." *Wall Street Journal*, 3 May 1991.

Nomani, Asra Q. "Northwest Air 3rd-Period Net Fell 32%; Carrier Says it Expects 4th-Quarter Loss." *Wall Street Journal*, 13 Nov. 1990.

Nomani, Asra Q. "Northwest Air to Acquire 25% of Hawaiian Air." *Wall Street Journal*, 11 Dec. 1990.

Nomani, Asra Q. "NWA Unit May Give Midway Air a Loan as First Step in Possible Acquisition Bid." *Wall Street Journal*, 23 Sep. 1991.

Nomani, Asra Q. "TWA's Emergence From Chapter 11 Hinges on Icahn's Ability to Slash Debt." *Wall Street Journal*, 3 Feb. 1992, sec, A, p. 3.

Nomani, Asra Q. "UAL's Net Fell 76% in Third Quarter; Chairman Assails Chapter 11 Airlines." *Wall Street Journal*, 1 Nov. 1991, sec. A, p. 7.

Nomani, Asra, Q. "Midway Faces Shutdown as Northwest Withdraws From Pact to Purchase Assets." *Wall Street Journal*, 14 Nov. 1991.

"Northwest Air to Buy Some Eastern Assets in $23.2 Million Deal." *Wall Street Journal*, 23 Jan. 1991.

"Northwest Airlines Claims Vindication in Report on Midway." *Wall Street Journal*, 25 Feb. 1992.

Northwest Airlines Inc., The Birth of an Airline. Eagan, Minn.: NWA Inc. Corporate Communications, 1986.

"NWA Back in the Black." *New York Times*, 21 April 1989, sec. D, p. 17, col. 5.

NWA Inc. 1984 Annual Report. Eagan, Minn.: NWA Inc., 1985.

NWA Inc. 1985 Annual Report. Eagan, Minn.: NWA Inc., 1986.

NWA Inc. 1986 Annual Report. Eagan, Minn.: NWA Inc., 1987.

NWA Inc. 1987 Annual Report. Eagan, Minn.: NWA Inc., 1988.

NWA Inc. 1988 Annual Report. Eagan, Minn.: NWA Inc., 1989.

NWA Inc. 1989 Annual Report. Eagan, Minn.: NWA Inc., 1990.

O'Brian, Bridget, and Brett Pulley. "Delta, UAL and Continental Report Losses." *Wall Street Journal,* 29 Jan. 1993, sec. A, p. 3.

O'Brian, Bridget, and Brett Pulley. "Airline Stocks Nosedive as Wall Street Responds Negatively to New Fare Cuts." *Wall Street Journal,* 29 May 1992.

O'Brian, Bridget. "America West Airlines to Keep Flying in Chapter 11 Despite Cash Shortage." *Wall Street Journal,* 1 July 1991.

O'Brian, Bridget. "America West Freezes Wages, Plans a Pay Cut." *Wall Street Journal,* 3 July 1991.

O'Brian, Bridget. "American Air Sets Layoffs of Managers." *Wall Street Journal,* 16 Oct. 1992, sec. A, p. 3.

O'Brian, Bridget. "American Air to Ground 11% of Its Flights." *Wall Street Journal,* 7 Jan. 1991, sec. A, p. 3.

O'Brian, Bridget. "AMR's Bid for Simpler Fares Takes Off." *Wall Street Journal,* 12 April 1992, sec. B.

O'Brian, Bridget. "AMR, in a Sharp Reversal, Curbs Outlays, Jet Options." *Wall Street Journal,* 12 Sep. 1991, sec. A, p. 3.

O'Brian, Bridget. "Continental Air Creditors Oppose Move; America West to Dismiss 10% of Staff." *Wall Street Journal,* 8 Aug. 1991.

O'Brian, Bridget. "Continental Air Ends Attempts to Sell Itself." *Wall Street Journal,* 1 April 1991.

O'Brian, Bridget. "Continental Air Reorganization Plan Erases Stock, Makes Creditors Owners." *Wall Street Journal,* 7 Feb. 1992, sec. A, p. 7.

O'Brian, Bridget. "Continental Air Will Offer Plan to Court Today." *Wall Street Journal,* 16 Nov. 1992, sec. A, p. 4, col. 1.

O'Brian, Bridget. "Continental Pilots Agree to Measures to Conserve Cash." *Wall Street Journal,* 15 Jan. 1991, sec. C, p. 20, col. 6.

O'Brian, Bridget. "Delta Air Lines Steps Up Drive to Slash Costs." *Wall Street Journal,* 18 Dec. 1992, sec. A, p. 3, col. 1.

O'Brian, Bridget. "Delta Air Makes Painful Cuts in Effort to Stem Red Ink." *Wall Street Journal,* 10 Sep. 1992.

O'Brian, Bridget. "Feud Between Bryan, Lorenzo Explains Much, But Not All." *Wall Street Journal,* 6 March 1989, sec. A, p. 4, col. 1.

O'Brian, Bridget. "Group Including Air Canada Wins Continental Air." *Wall Street Journal,* 10 Nov. 1992, Sec. A, p. 3.

O'Brian, Bridget. "Southwest Air Orders 34 737s For $1.2 Billion." *Wall Street Journal,* 7 Aug. 1992.

O'Hanlon, Thomas. "The Mess That Made Beggars of Pan Am and TWA." *Fortune,* Oct. 1974, p. 123.

"Once-Little Firms That Made it Big." *U.S. News & World Report,* 24 Dec. 1979, p. 76.

Ott, James. "Federal Express Plans New Hub, Buys McDonnell Douglas Freighters." *Aviation Week & Space Technology,* 26 Jan. 1987, pp. 45-46.

Ott, James. "Midway Halts Operations as Northwest Drops Buyout." *Aviation Week & Space Technology,* 18 Nov. 1991, pp. 22-23.

Ott, James. "USAir to Close Struggling Dayton Hub in Restructuring of Midwest Operations." *Aviation Week & Space Technology,* 2 Sep. 1991, p. 34.

"Overnight Wonder." *Time,* 15 Feb. 1982, p. 42.

"Pan Am: TWA-American Bid Likely to Boost Price." *The Atlanta Journal-Constitution,* 23 July 1991, sec. C, p. 1.

Payne, Seth. "The Heat is on Airline Deals." *Business Week,* 2 Oct. 1989, p. 32.

Pearl, Daniel. "Airborne Express Rushes to Keep Pace With its Rivals." *Wall Street Journal,* 13 July 1992.

Pearl, Daniel. "Federal Express Finds its Pioneering Formula Falls Flat Overseas." *Wall Street Journal,* 15 April 1991, sec. A, p. 1.

Pearl, Daniel. "Federal Express Pins Hopes on New Strategy in Europe." *Wall Street Journal,* 18 March 1992, sec. B, p. 4.

Pearl, Daniel. "Federal Express Plans to Trim Assets in Europe." *Wall Street Journal,* 17 March 1992, sec. A, p. 3.

Pearl, Daniel. "Federal Express Says Barkdale Quit 2 Top Posts." *Wall Street Journal,* 23 Oct. 1991, sec. B, p. 10.

Pearl, Daniel. "Federal Express's Pilots Again Reject Unionism in Vote." *Wall Street Journal,* 23 Aug. 1991.

Pearl, Daniel. "Pilots Union Seeks to Hold Election at Federal Express." *Wall Street Journal,* 31 May 1991.

"People in the News." *Wall Street Journal,* 9 Jan. 1989, sec. B, p. 5, col. 3.

"People in the News." *Wall Street Journal*, 13 Feb. 1989, sec. B, p. 9, col. 3.

Petzinger, Thomas Jr. and Paulette Thomas. "House of Mirrors: Lorenzo's Texas Air Keeps Collecting Fees From Its Ailing Units." *Wall Street Journal*, 7 April 1988, sec. A, p. 1, col. 6.

Phillips, Carolyn. "America West Air Sets Agreements for $55 Million." *Wall Street Journal*, 19 Aug. 1991.

Piedmont Aviation Inc. 1982 Annual Report. Winston-Salem, N.C.: Piedmont Aviation Inc., 1983.

Piedmont Aviation Inc. 1984 Annual Report. Winston-Salem, N.C.: Piedmont Aviation Inc., 1985.

Piedmont Aviation Inc. 1986 Annual Report. Winston-Salem, N.C.: Piedmont Aviation Inc., 1987.

Poole, Sheila M. and Scott Thurston. "Atlanta to be New UPS Home." *The Atlanta Journal-Constitution*, 9 May 1991, sec. E, p. 1.

Power, Christopher. "A Squeeze Play at Northwest." *Business Week*, 1 May 1989, p. 30.

Powers, Marie. "Delta: Dealing With Bold Growth, Fiscal Loss." *Career Pilot*, Nov. 1992, pp. 22-32.

Preble, Cecilia. "America West Airlines Plans to Slow Its Growth Rate in 1985." *Aviation Week & Space Technology*, 28 Jan. 1985, pp. 43-44.

Pulley, Brett, and Bridget O'Brian. "UAL and Delta Post Big Losses for Quarter." *Wall Street Journal*, 26 April 1991.

Pulley, Brett, and Robert L. Rose. "United Air Cuts 10 Executive Positions; Unions Resist Bid for Labor Concessions." *Wall Street Journal*, 27 Jan. 1993.

Pulley, Brett, and Bruce Ingersoll. "U.S. Gives Tentative Clearance to KLM, Northwest to Start Integrating Service." *Wall Street Journal*, 17 Nov. 1992.

Pulley, Brett. "British Airways to Acquire 25% Share of USAir." *Wall Street Journal*, 21 July 1992, sec. A, p. 3.

Pulley, Brett. "Northwest Airlines Asks Pilots' Union For Big Concessions." *Wall Street Journal*, 15 July 1992.

Pulley, Brett. "TWA Seeking to Reorganize in Smaller Form." *Wall Street Journal*, 9 Sep. 1992.

Pulley, Brett. "TWA to End Meals on More Flights; Hiring Freeze Set." *Wall Street Journal*, 12 June 1992.

Pulley, Brett. "TWA's Icahn is Preparing to Step Down." *Wall Street Journal*, 3 Aug. 1992.

Pulley, Brett. "UAL's United Reaches Accord With its Pilots." *Wall Street Journal*, 5 April 1991.

Pulley, Brett. "United Air Joins Bidding for Assets of TWA at O'Hare." *Wall Street Journal*, 15 June 1992.

Pulley, Brett. "USAir Group Plans Cost Cutting Steps; Move Likely to Involve Wage Concessions." *Wall Street Journal*, 30 Sep. 1991.

Republic Airlines Inc. 1984 Annual Report. Minneapolis: Republic Airlines Inc., 1985.

Republic Airlines Inc. 1985 Annual Report. Minneapolis: Republic Airlines Inc., 1986.

Rose, Robert L. and Brian Coleman. "British Airways Buys Stake in USAir, Drawing Protests From Other Carriers." *Wall Street Journal*, 22 Jan. 1993.

Rose, Robert L. "United Airlines Plans Layoffs to Trim Costs." *Wall Street Journal*, 7 Jan. 1993, sec. A, p. 3.

Rose, Robert L. and Jonathan Dahl. "Aborted Takeoffs: Skies Are Deregulated, But Just Try Starting a Sizable New Airline." *Wall Street Journal*, 19 July 1989, sec. A, p. 1, col. 6.

Rose, Robert L., Bruce Ingersoll and Tony Horwitz. "British Air Drops $750 Million Bid for USAir Stake." *Wall Street Journal*, 23 Dec. 1992.

Salpukas, Agis. "Ex-Pan Am Executive Gets Continental Post." *New York Times*, 3 Feb. 1988, sec. D, p. 8, cols. 5-6.

Salpukas, Agis. "KLM Commits Funds to Aid Northwest's Credit Bid." *The Atlanta Journal-Constitution*, 20 Nov. 1992.

Schmit, Julie. "Northwest, KLM Plan Gets Clearance." *USA Today*, 12 Nov. 1993.

Schneider, Charles E. "Carrier Seeks Small Air Package Control." *Aviation Week & Space Technology*, 21 July 1975, pp. 36-38.

Schonbak, Judith. "Delta Digs in for Long-Term Prosperity." *Career Pilot*, May 1991, pp. 18-28.

Schwartz, John, and Erik Calonius. "A Boss They Love to Hate." *Newsweek*, 20 March 1989, pp. 20-24.

Schwartz, John, and Randy Collier. "Deregulation's Latest Darling: America West Grows Up." *Newsweek*, 7 Dec. 1987, p. 68.

Seago, Les. "Fed Ex Meets Challenge of Industry Slowdown." *Career Pilot*, May 1992, pp. 18-27.

Seago, Les. "Fed Ex: A Big Thing From Small Packages." *Career Pilot*, April 1991, pp. 20-29.

Sigafoos, Robert A. *Absolutely Positively Overnight: The Unofficial Corporate History of Federal Express.* Memphis, Tenn.: St. Lukes Press, 1988.

Significant Dates in TWA History. New York: TWA Corporate Communications, 1985.

Smith, Bruce A. "America West Continues Expansion With Transcontinental 757 Service." *Aviation Week & Space Technology,* 2 March 1987, pp. 42-43.

Smith, Bruce A. "America West Expands Routes Served." *Aviation Week & Space Technology,* 19 Dec. 1983, pp. 42-43.

Smith, Bruce A. "America West to Upgrade Fleet, Facilities, Employee Salaries." *Aviation Week & Space Technology,* 25 Aug. 1986, pp. 45-46.

Smith, Myron J., Jr. *The Airline Bibliography: The Salem College Guide to Sources on Commercial Aviation, Volume I: The United States.* West Cornwall, Conn.: Locust Hill Press, 1986.

Solberg, Carl. *Conquest of the Skies: A History of Commercial Aviation in America.* Boston: Little, Brown, and Co., 1979.

Solomon, Caleb. "American Air Cuts Spending By $8 Billion." *Wall Street Journal,* 18 Nov. 1991, sec. A, p. 6.

Solomon, Caleb. "Continental Air to Ground 22 Planes, Cut Flights 6%, Defer Debt Payments." *Wall Street Journal,* 21 Aug. 1991.

Southwest Airlines Co. 1982 Annual Report. Dallas: Southwest Airlines Co., 1983.

Southwest Airlines Co. 1983 Annual Report. Dallas: Southwest Airlines Co., 1984.

Southwest Airlines Co. 1984 Annual Report. Dallas: Southwest Airlines Co., 1985.

Southwest Airlines Co. 1985 Annual Report. Dallas: Southwest Airlines Co., 1986.

Southwest Airlines Co. 1986 Annual Report. Dallas: Southwest Airlines Co., 1987.

Southwest Airlines Co. 1987 Annual Report. Dallas: Southwest Airlines Co., 1988.

Southwest Airlines Co. 1988 Annual Report. Dallas: Southwest Airlines Co., 1989.

Southwest Airlines Co. 1989 Annual Report. Dallas: Southwest Airlines Co., 1990.

Southwest Airlines Co. 1990 Annual Report. Dallas: Southwest Airlines., 1991.

Southwest Airlines Co. 1991 Annual Report. Dallas: Southwest Airlines Co., 1992.

Southwest Airlines Co. 1992 Annual Report. Dallas: Southwest Airlines Co., 1993.

Spence, Charlie. "Northwest Meets With Unions to Cut Costs." *Flight International,* 10 Oct. 1990, p. 12.

"Taking On an Airline Giant." *Newsweek,* 25 April 1988, pp. 12-14.

Taylor, John H. "Risk Taker." *Forbes,* 14 Nov. 1988, p. 108.

Texas Air Corp. 1988 Annual Report. Houston: Texas Air Corp., 1989.

Texas Air Corp. 1989 Annual Report. Houston: Texas Air Corp., 1990.

"Texas Air Corp. to Protest Merger of Muse, Southwest." *Aviation Week & Space Technology,* 18 March 1985, p. 296.

"The Great Globalists." *Forbes,* 1 Nov. 1954, pp. 17-21.

The History of USAir. Arlington, Va.: USAir Corp. Communications.

"The Man in the Pilot's Seat." *Fortune,* 17 Aug. 1987, p. 35.

"The Pilot Behind TWA's Success." *Business Week,* 23 April 1966, p. 103.

Thomas, Paulette. "Texas Air Had Record Losses in Quarter, Year." *Wall Street Journal,* 8 Feb. 1988, p. 2, col. 2.

Thurston, Scott. "'Economic Conditions' Prompt Delta to Put Latin American Flights on Hold." *The Atlanta Journal-Constitution,* 12 Dec. 1992.

Thurston, Scott. "Cuts May Accompany Delta Loss for Quarter." *The Atlanta Journal-Constitution,* 23 July 1992.

Thurston, Scott. "Delta Pilots Reject Delay in Pay Hike." *The Atlanta Journal-Constitution,* 15 Aug. 1992, sec. B.

Thurston, Scott. "Delta Plans to Furlough 103 Pilots to Cut Costs." *The Atlanta Journal-Constitution,* 21 Oct. 1992.

Thurston, Scott. "Delta to Ax Part-Time Jobs, Cut Benefits." *The Atlanta Journal-Constitution,* 24 July 1992, sec. G, p. 1.

Thurston, Scott. "Harris is Striving for Goals That Proved Elusive at Delta." *The Atlanta Journal-Constitution,* 7 April 1991.

Thurston, Scott. "Northwest to Halt D.C. Flights From Hartsfield." *The Atlanta Journal-Constitution,* 10 March 1992.

Thurston, Scott. "UPS Marches to Nonsense Drummer." *The Atlanta Journal-Constitution,* 27 April 1992, sec. H.

Thurston, Scott. "UPS to Start 3-Day Delivery Service." *The Atlanta Journal-Constitution,* 8 Jan. 1993, sec. H., p. 7.

Thurston, Scott. "Workers Told Northwest May Seek Merger." *The Atlanta Journal-Constitution,* 12 Feb. 1991, sec. D, p. 3.

Ticer, Scott, et al. "Why Zapmail Finally Got Zapped." *Business Week,* 13 Oct. 1986, pp. 48-49.

"Time for Shrinking." *Forbes,* 11 Nov. 1978, pp. 53-54.

Toy, Stewart. "The Last of the Upstarts May Be Falling." *Business Week,* 14 March 1988, p. 35.

Toy, Stewart. "This Upstart Could Be Flying a Bit Too High." *Business Week,* 15 June 1987, p. 76.

Trans World Airlines Inc. 1983 10-K Report. Mt. Kisco, N.Y.: Trans World Airlines Inc., 1984.

Trans World Airlines Inc. 1984 10-K Report. Mt. Kisco, N.Y.: Trans World Airlines Inc., 1985.

Trans World Airlines Inc. 1985 10-K Report. Mt. Kisco, N.Y.: Trans World Airlines Inc., 1986.

Trans World Airlines Inc. 1986 10-K Report. Mt. Kisco, N.Y.: Trans World Airlines Inc., 1987.

Trans World Airlines Inc. 1987 10-K Report. Mt. Kisco, N.Y.: Trans World Airlines Inc., 1988.

Trans World Airlines Inc. 1988 10-K Report. Mt. Kisco, N.Y.: Trans World Airlines Inc., 1989.

Trans World Airlines Inc. 1989 10-K Report. Mt. Kisco, N.Y.: Trans World Airlines Inc., 1990.

Troxell, Thomas N., Jr. "Deregulation in Stride: Only Bad Weather, it Seems, Can Faze Southwest Airlines." *Barron's,* 23 Jan. 1984, p. 54.

Troxell, Thomas N., Jr. "With the Muse: Merger With Rival Promises Big Gains for Southwest Airlines." *Barron's,* 29 April 1985, pp. 43-44.

"TWA Chief Threatened With Suit." *The Atlanta Journal-Constitution,* 26 Oct. 1992.

"TWA Pilots Vote Wage Concessions For 45% Equity Stake." *The Atlanta Journal-Constitution,* 1 Oct 1992.

"TWA's Past—and Its Future." *Business Week,* 16 July 1949, pp. 74-78.

"TWA: A Time for Growth, a Time for Shrinking." *Forbes,* 11 Nov. 1978, pp. 53-54.

"TWA: New Hands at the Helm." *Forbes,* 1 July 1961, pp. 11-14.

"UAL Chief is Nation's Best-Paid CEO at $18.3 Million." *The Atlanta Journal-Constitution,* 26 April 1991.

UAL Corp. 1982 Annual Report. Chicago: UAL Corp., 1983.

UAL Corp. 1983 Annual Report. Chicago: UAL Corp., 1984.

UAL Corp. 1984 Annual Report. Chicago: UAL Corp., 1985.

UAL Corp. 1985 Annual Report. Chicago: UAL Corp., 1986.

UAL Corp. 1986 Annual Report. Chicago: UAL Corp., 1987.

UAL Corp. 1987 Annual Report. Chicago: UAL Corp., 1988.

UAL Corp. 1988 Annual Report. Chicago: UAL Corp., 1989.

UAL Corp. 1989 Annual Report. Chicago: UAL Corp., 1990.

UAL Corp. 1990 Annual Report. Chicago: UAL Corp., 1991.

UAL Corp. 1991 Annual Report. Chicago: UAL Corp., 1992.

UAL Corp. 1992 Annual Report. Chicago: UAL Corp., 1993.

USAir Group Inc. 1985 Annual Report. Arlington, Va.: USAir Group Inc., 1986.

USAir Group Inc. 1986 Annual Report. Arlington, Va.: USAir Group Inc., 1987.

USAir Group Inc. 1987 Annual Report. Arlington, Va.: USAir Group Inc., 1988.

USAir Group Inc. 1988 10-K Report. Arlington, Va.: USAir Group Inc., 1989.

USAir Group Inc. 1989 Annual Report. Arlington, Va.: USAir Group Inc., 1990.

USAir Group Inc. 1990 Annual Report. Arlington, Va.: USAir Group Inc., 1991.

USAir Group Inc. 1991 Annual Report. Arlington, Va.: USAir Group Inc., 1992.

USAir Group Inc. 1992 Annual Report. Arlington, Va.: USAir Group Inc., 1993.

Valente, Judith. "NWA, Northwest Air's Parent, Taps Dasburg for Chief." *Wall Street Journal,* 13 Nov. 1990.

Velocci, Anthony Jr. "Icahn Struggles to Keep TWA Flying in Hard Times." *Aviation Week & Space Technology,* 20 Jan. 1992, pp. 44-46.

Vogel, Todd. "Can UPS Deliver the Goods in a New World?" *Business Week,* 4 June 1990, pp. 80-82.

Vogel, Todd. "Texas Air: Empire in Jeopardy." *Business Week,* 27 March 1989, pp. 28-30.

Waldman, Peter. "Federal Express Faces Problems Overseas." *Wall Street Journal,* 20 July 1990, sec. A, p. 4.

Waldman, Peter. "Federal Express Faces Test of Pilots' Loyalty Since Purchasing Tiger." *Wall Street Journal,* 23 Oct. 1989, sec. A, p. 1.

Waldman, Peter. "Federal Express Gets Clearance to Merge Its Pilot Seniority List With That of Tiger." *Wall Street Journal,* 30 May 1990.

Weber, Joseph. "Where 'Frill' is a Four-Letter Word." *Business Week,* 21 Sep. 1987, p. 58.

Weiner, Steven B. "A Profitable Survivor." *Forbes*, 9 March 1987, p. 106.

Western Air Lines Inc. 1981 Annual Report. Salt Lake City: Western Air Lines Inc., 1982.

Western Air Lines Inc. 1982 Annual Report. Salt Lake City: Western Air Lines Inc., 1983.

Western Air Lines Inc. 1983 Annual Report. Salt Lake City: Western Air Lines Inc., 1984.

"Why TWA's Board Wanted a New President." *Business Week*, 7 July 1975, pp. 52-53.

Woolsey, James P. "United: What Big Can Do." *Air Transport World*, Feb. 1992, pp. 24-29.

Ziemba, Stanley. "United on Track in Megacarrier Race." *Career Pilot*, Dec. 1991, pp. 18-28.

Index

A

B

C

D

E

F

G

KNACK®

MAKE IT EASY

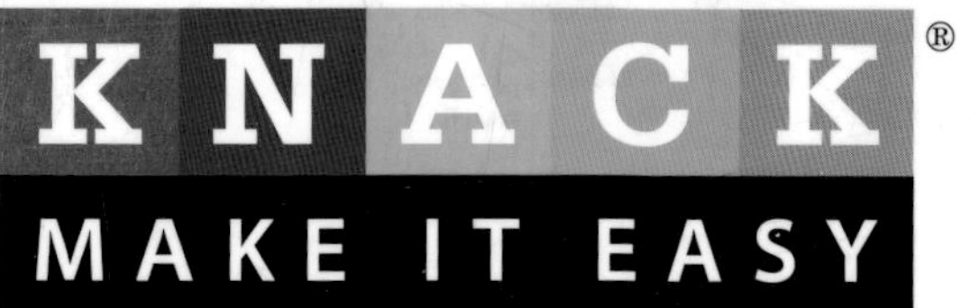

FIRST AID

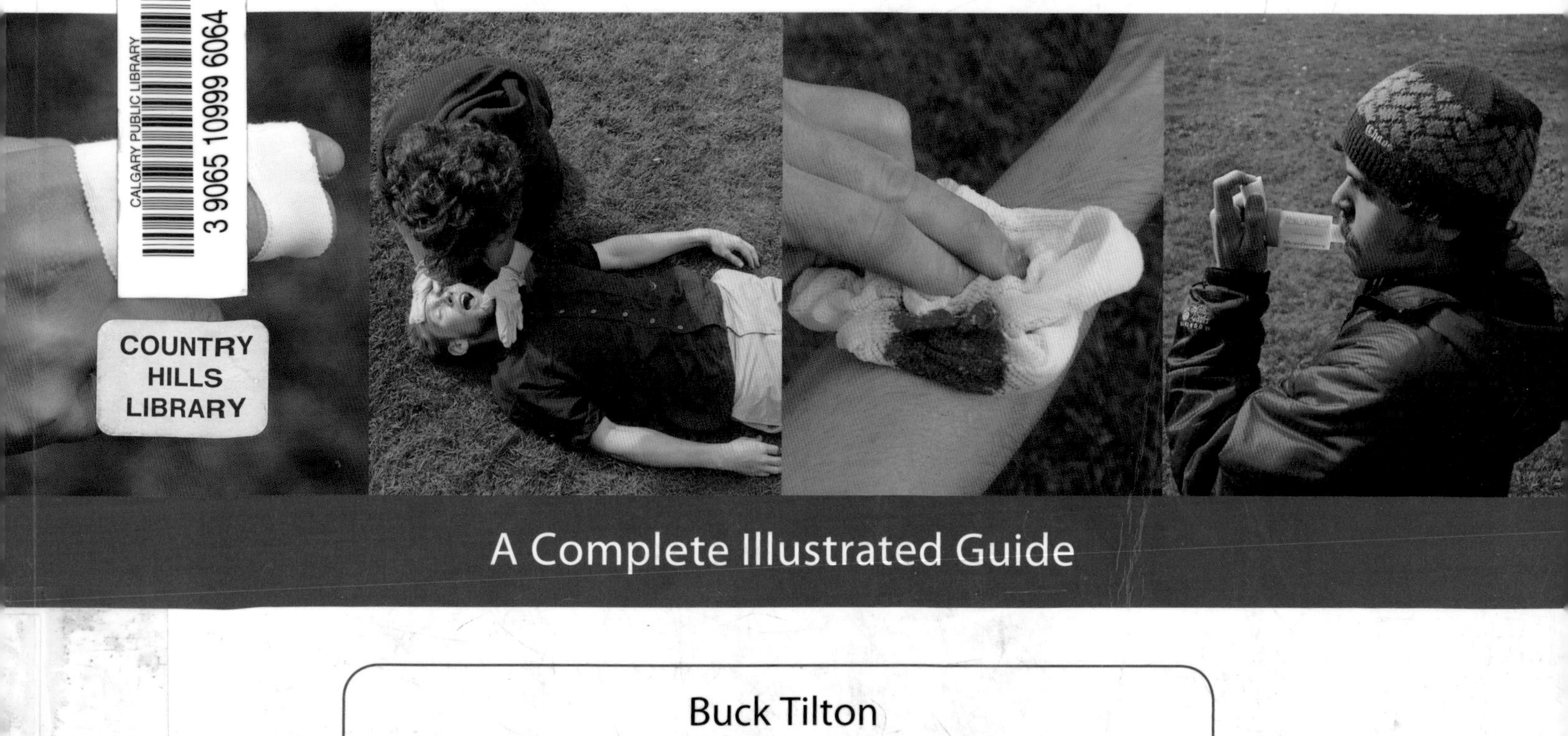

A Complete Illustrated Guide

Buck Tilton

Photographs by Stephen Gorman and Eli Burakian

Make It Easy!

and get information *fast!*

Welcome to **Knack®!** This innovative series represents a new era in do-it-yourself guides. Packed with color photographs and designed for visual learners, these books make it easy to get information fast. You'll love the quick-reading, picture-driven organization. Our expert authors use detailed photography to show you all the options—whether you need to get a job done **step-by-step,** make the perfect decision, or gain new knowledge and skills.

Look for handwritten notes throughout that give you practical advice, tips, and shortcuts. There are other great features, too: green light, yellow light, **red light,** and zoom sidebars.

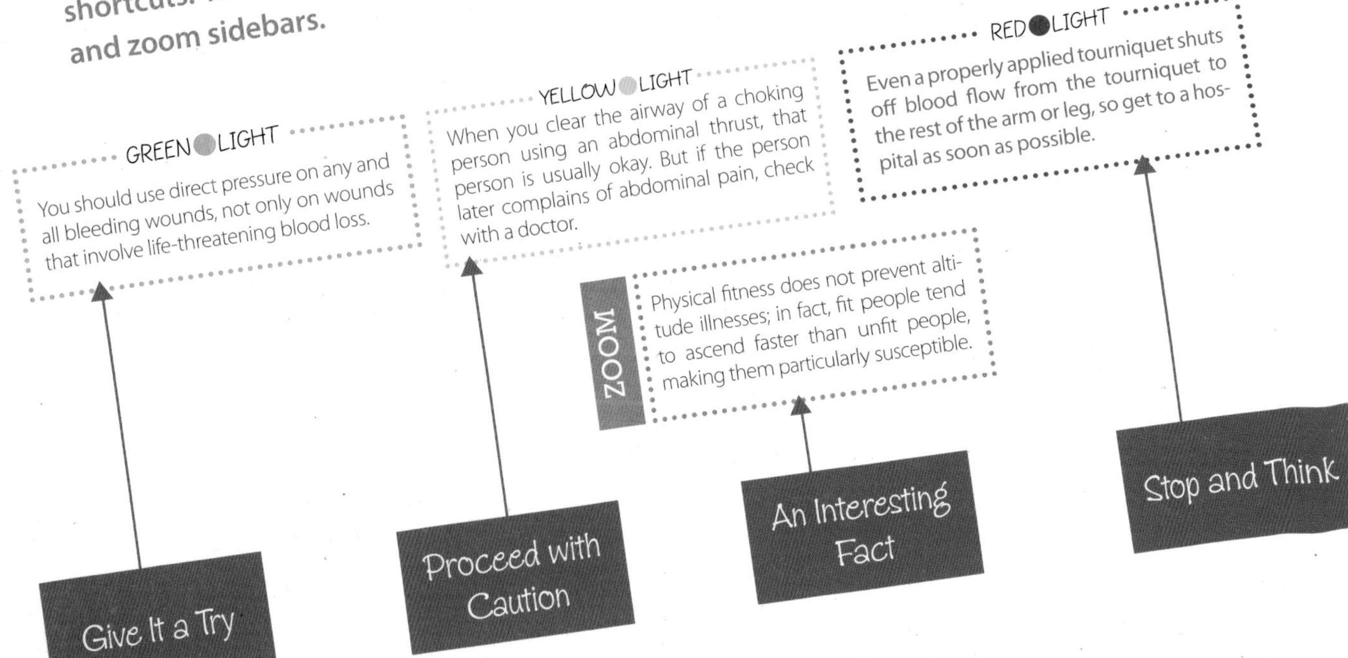